PENGUIN BOOKS

The Child Care Crisis

Raised in Saskatchewan and Manitoba, Fredelle Maynard
studied at the University of Manitoba and the University
of Toronto before taking her Ph.D. at Radcliffe. She has
taught at Radcliffe, Wellesley and elsewhere, and her articles have been published in *Woman's Day, Chatelaine,* the
New Republic and many other journals. Her books include
Guiding Your Child to a More Creative Life and *Raisins and
Almonds*, a volume of memoirs. The mother of two grown
daughters, both of whom also write, Ms Maynard now lives
in Toronto.

Burton L. White, author of *The First Three Years of Life,* is
Director of the Center for Parent Education in Newton,
Massachusetts.

The
Child
Care
Crisis

The thinking parent's guide to day care

Fredelle Maynard
with a foreword by Burton L. White

Contemporary Family Issues

Penguin Books

Penguin Books Canada Limited, 2801 John Street, Markham, Ontario, Canada L3R 1B4
Penguin Books Ltd., Harmondsworth, Middlesex, England
Penguin Books, 40 West 23rd Street, New York, New York 10010 U.S.A.
Penguin Books Australia Ltd., Ringwood, Victoria, Australia
Penguin Books (N.Z.) Ltd., Private Bag, Takapuna, Auckland 9, New Zealand

First published by Penguin Books Canada Limited, 1985

Published in this edition by Penguin Books, 1986

Copyright © Fredelle Maynard, 1985
Foreword copyright © Burton L. White, 1985

All rights reserved.

Manufactured in Canada by Gagne Printing Ltd.

Canadian Cataloguing in Publication Data

Maynard, Fredelle Bruser.
  The child care crisis

Bibliography: p.
ISBN 0-14-007080-X

1. Day care centres — Canada.   I. Title.

HV861.C36M39 1986   362.7'12'0971   C83-098794-0

Except in the United States of America,
this book is sold subject to the condition
that it shall not, by way of trade or otherwise,
be lent, re-sold, hired out, or otherwise circulated
without the publisher's prior consent in any form
of binding or cover other than that in which it
is published and without a similar condition
including this condition being
imposed on the subsequent purchaser.

Acknowledgements

This book owes its existence to Penelope Leach, whose book *Who Cares?* first stimulated my interest in day care problems, and Elliott Barker, head of the Canadian Society for the Prevention of Cruelty to Children, who encouraged me to think about those problems. My conclusions do not always agree with theirs — but we share a common concern with the best interests of the child.

For time, thought and generous assistance I thank Rob Dales, Renee Edwards, Elena Hannah, Alice S. Honig, Marna Ramsden, Annette Silbert, Elaine and Rubin Todres, Eleanor Ward, Ilona and Anya Weber, Otto Weininger.

To the memory of my mother, who sent me out into the world with confidence, joy and a sense of infinite possibility.

Contents

Foreword

I believe that the subject of this book, child care, is of extra-ordinary importance, not just to parents but to society at large. For almost thirty years now I have pursued only one professional goal — understanding where well developed people come from. My research career has led me to the conclusion that the experiences of the first few years of life play a surprisingly important role in determining what kind of human beings we become.

The last twenty years have seen the emergence of two trends which affect the experiences of young children and, unfortunately, conflict with each other. On the one hand we have the accumulation of much new useful information about how to help a child to the best start in life; on the other hand we have also seen a development which threatens to result in poorer outcomes for large numbers of our children — the extensive use of full-time substitute care for infants and toddlers. The first trend had its origins in the U.S. government's Head Start Project. That revolutionary program began in 1965 with the primary purpose of helping three- and four-year-old children from low income families get a better foundation for conventional education. The Head Start Project in turn led to a dramatic increase in serious study of the details of development during the first six years of life. Surprisingly, although parents and many professionals have long had a very deep interest in the topic, it was not approached in a systematic way much before the mid-1960s. Today, however, as a result of recent unprecedented research on the topic, we know far more about the initial stages of intellectual, linguistic and social skill development than has ever been known before. This knowledge has convinced many of us that the experiences of the first years of life, especially the first three, are of profound significance.

Shortly after this substantial research effort got underway a new societal trend of striking importance surfaced — the rise of feminism. The early 1970s saw powerful arguments advanced for expanding the potential roles of young women to include considerably more than the traditional role of child-rearing. As more and more women began to adopt these ideas, the use of substitute child care for infants and toddlers began to expand dramatically. Today, many young families assume that placing children as young as one or two months of age into a substitute care situation for eight or nine hours a day, five days a week, is a perfectly reasonable practice. In effect, what that means is that the primary responsibility for raising very young babies is often being transferred from the nuclear family to others. Unfortunately, substitute child care, while occasionally of very high quality, is more often than not of questionable quality and, indeed, fairly often of remarkably poor quality. The result for those of us seriously concerned with the well-being of young children is a conflict of major proportions.

In my view, many of us are currently engaged in a struggle for the thoughts of parents, providers and policy makers in respect to this issue. Thirty years ago the general assumption about child-rearing was that it was best done at home by parents along with others closely related to the child. Today many people take it for granted that soon after a new child is born it is perfectly all right for the child-rearing responsibility to be assumed by other members of society paid for the task. This point of view alarms me — and not only me but also a fair number of other people who have taken a hard look at the situation. *The Child Care Crisis* is one of a small number of superb treatments of this subject that have surfaced only within the last five years.

This book should be of tremendous value to expectant and new parents. It should also be read by day care providers, policy makers and anyone concerned with young children and the shape of society. People who have already arranged full-time substitute child care for their own infants and toddlers have more often than not carried with them ambivalent feelings about doing so. In most such circumstances, it would appear that feelings of guilt lie just beneath the surface. Anyone, professional or layman, who raises a voice questioning the wisdom of such practices is likely to rub nerve endings the wrong way and, indeed, produce an inflamed response. Given this situation, it takes a certain amount of courage and a first-rate, clear mind to deal fairly with the issues. It is my judgment that Fredelle Maynard is just such a person. Yet another reason to read this book is that at the moment, there simply is not enough active, intelligent debate taking place on this very important issue, and Ms Maynard not only adds a thoughtful voice to the discussion but also offers sensible, constructive advice to parents faced with the dilemma of choosing surrogate care for their children.

I hope that *The Child Care Crisis* will be read and discussed seriously, in the spirit in which it was written. It is intended not to shock or arouse guilt in parents but to help them choose what they want for their children.

One final word: I urge expectant or new parents not to forget that babies grow up very quickly, and the joys they can give you are as wonderful as any you'll ever experience in life.

Burton L. White, Ph.D.
Center for Parent Education
Newton, Massachusetts
January, 1985

Preface

"I hear you're writing a book against day care," a friend said.
Let me set the record straight. This is not a book "against day
care." How could any reasonable, aware individual oppose
all kinds of surrogate care in a world where so many women
— and men — cannot manage without it? I should like to see
the best possible day care provided for those children whose
parents *must* work outside the home. In that category I include not only single parents, couples in desperate financial
straits, teenagers completing their education, but also women
whose temperament unfits them for child care. Not every
mother is a tender madonna. If a woman is truly made so
frantic by being left alone with young children that she
becomes hostile, abusive or depressed, then those children
are better off in a kindly stranger's care. Fortunately most
women, persisting in spite of frequent weariness, irritation,
boredom and frustration, discover that a small child enlarges
and enriches their world — that ultimately rewards outweigh
costs. My hope is to persuade parents that, if they have a
choice, one parent should be chief caretaker for the first three
years of a child's life. Everything we know about child
development, everything research reveals about the effects of
substitute care, suggests that those three years — at very least
two — are vitally important to the child's, the whole family's,
flourishing. For parents who make this commitment, this
book suggests ways to alleviate boredom and isolation. For
those without the luxury of choice, the later chapters provide
guidance in selecting the kind of care best for a particular
child.

What about the complaint — I hear it often — that criticism of early day care lays a heavy guilt trip on working

mothers (who feel guilty enough already, thank you, without having experts castigate them)? I sympathize deeply with women who *must* work — many of whom would prefer to stay home with their children. I also sympathize with women who, staying home with children, feel guilty because they're *not* out in the world earning and achieving. But surely what's important here are the feelings, the *life*, of children. If the best available evidence indicates that infants and toddlers need their parents, then it is irresponsible to pretend otherwise. To say that a substitute mother can be just the same as the real mother is at best double-think, at worst nonsense. Three decades of exciting, tumultuous social progress have established women's right to move into the work world on a basis of full equality with men. Perhaps it's time to reaffirm their right, as young mothers, to stay home with children, and to recognize child care as one of the most valuable kinds of work a man or woman can do.

In preparation for this book I have read dozens of books on day care and hundreds of journal articles reporting day care research in Canada, the United States, Britain, Sweden, Cuba, China and Israel. I have visited every type of day care arrangement, talked to psychologists, educators, day care providers, parents and children. Though I have tried to be objective and dispassionate, I write inevitably out of my own convictions and from my own distinctive point of view.

As a new ambassador's first task is to present his credentials, let me, a new arrival in embattled territory, present mine. My academic training is not in psychology or social work but in the humanities. After graduate study at Harvard University (where I received a Ph.D. in Renaissance literature), I became enormously interested, as teacher and as parent, in child development. For the past twenty-five years my reading and writing have focused chiefly on the world of children. I have had no personal experience with day care. My own mother, a working woman, stayed home until I started school. Maybe I missed experiences good group care might have offered. I don't know. My childhood memories, after half a century, are memories of Mother — the fragrance of yeast dough rising under a fresh linen towel, the light tuneless hum that accompanied her dusting or sweeping, the clean bright swiftness and briskness of her movement through the house, her laughter. So it seemed natural that, after my children were born, I should stay home for five years.

I know all about the conflicts engendered by such a choice. I remember the restlessness, the impatience, the sheer drudgery, the frequent feelings of defeat. I also remember the ecstasy of the first smile, the first tooth, the first step, the first finger-painting, the first word, the first real sentence (my 2½-year-old at dusk, wide-eyed at the window: "Oh, I see night is navy blue!"). I am convinced, despite all the ills that parenthood is heir to, that I gave my children in those years of rocking, walking, trips to the library, sand castles and cookie baking and doll clothes and ring-around-a-rosy, strength for the road ahead. Certainly they gave me my life's most profound experience of joy.

A word about pronouns. Obviously I am equally concerned, in this examination of day care, with boys and girls. For the sake of clarity, however, I reserve she/her for the mother and use he/him for the child.

Fredelle Maynard
Toronto, January 1985

Part 1

The Issues

Chapter I

The Working Parent's Dilemma:
Is Day Care the Answer?

The subject of day care is embattled territory. On one side are ranged conscientious, dedicated, passionate advocates (mostly women) whose demand is that high quality care be universally accessible, publicly funded and available twenty-four hours a day. ("The question has become not only whether the family can cope with childbearing on its own, but whether it is reasonable or even desirable to expect it to do so.")[1] On the other side, lances and research reports at the ready, stand conscientious, dedicated, passionate opponents (women *and* men) insisting that day-long child care centres are "inventions of the Devil, conceived as a second-class and expedient solution to a deeply rooted societal problem."[2] The first group marches towards a promised land in which happy working mothers achieve fulfilment while their babes cavort in safe, clean, stimulating, friendly, well-organized environments tended by loving day care workers. The second cherishes the image of children at home with a mother who reads, sings, rocks, plays and instructs as she performs the routine duties of her well-managed household.

Real life, alas, seldom matches either dream. The day care centre is often overcrowded and understaffed, providing a service merely custodial; the mother at home is often bored, exhausted, frantic. It is only recently, however, that the choice between mother care and surrogate care has become a matter of urgent public debate. Day care at its inception, and for more than a century after, was designed not as a substitute for traditional mothering, but as an emergency measure for the children of the poor.[3] In both Canada and the

United States, centralized child care arrangements emerged in response to the triple pressures of urbanization, industrialization and immigration. Obliged to leave home for work, the first day care mothers, often foreign born and always poor, were frankly dependent on the charity of church groups and volunteer organizations. The Boston Infant School, established in 1838, defined its goal as freeing indigent women for employment while, at the same time, removing their children "from the unhappy association of want and vice" and subjecting them to "better influences."[4] Not stated, but a motive in many such philanthropic enterprises, was the convenience of employers. Before centre care, many women brought their children to the workplace — a practice which offended employer sensibilities. A 1900 newspaper article observes: "These nurslings of poverty cannot be expected to behave like little ladies and gentlemen, and we cannot blame private families for objecting to their washerwoman or seamstress bringing their offspring along."[5] Programs for the nurslings of poverty emphasized "cleanliness, obedience, good manners, religion and habits of thrift."[6] Stimulation, enrichment, emotional support — such notions played no part in the planning of a system which was seen as an alternative to the orphanage or outright abandonment.

A major shift in attitudes towards day care came with World War II, as labour shortages compelled government support for the large numbers of women with children entering the work force. No longer a humble suppliant suitably grateful for the charity bestowed upon her, the day care mother was transformed into Rosie the Riveter, a national heroine leaving her hearth for the public good. Though war's end brought with it a curtailment in day care services and a generally less hospitable attitude (time now for the mothers to go back home), the child care landscape was permanently altered by the 1940s experience. For the first time day care policies had been shaped by a serious concern for physical and emotional health, nutrition, intellectual growth and normal developmental needs. For the first time also, accordingly, it became possible to view day care as not a low-status, inferior substitute for home care but possibly, under ideal circumstances, an acceptable, positive alternative.

Today's push for universal publicly funded day care is the result of complex social forces. Most notable, overwhelming in its impact, has been what economist Eli Ginzberg calls "the single most outstanding phenomenon of the twentieth century,"[7] the movement of women into the labour force. The phenomenon is world-wide. Of course women have always worked. Before the Industrial Revolution, however, they generally worked at home or in home-based cottage industries. Fifty years ago only one married woman in ten held a job outside the home. By 1950 the ratio was roughly three in ten[8] — with the working women likely to be childless or mothers of grown children. Today one out of every two married women goes out to work, the fastest-growing sector of the work force consisting of mothers of infants.[9] The traditional pattern of women "retiring" with a first pregnancy has given way to a life rhythm in which the pregnant woman works until the last possible moment and returns to her job after maternity leave, sometimes as early as six weeks after the birth. This trend shows every sign of strengthening. It is estimated that by 1990, three out of every four mothers will be employed outside the home — forty-five percent of all women with children under six.[10]

In the United States, between 1960 and 1975, the proportion of employed married women increased by twenty-eight percent, and of employed mothers with pre-schoolers by fifty-seven percent. This accelerating movement into the work force has produced, in the course of three decades, a dramatic change in popular attitudes. Ann Landers, that reliable barometer of social trends, mirrors the change. An early column described with scornful disapproval the working mother who, oblivious of her children's needs, "wriggles into a girdle and beats it out of the house." Commenting recently on "The New Rules of the Marriage Game," Landers comes down firmly on the side of the (ungirdled) working wife. "Her husband has an obligation to get off his duff and help with the housework, cooking, marketing, laundry and the children." Twenty years ago the job-holding mother was considered selfishly derelict in her maternal responsibilities, her husband either a poor provider or a Milquetoast who "permitted" his wife to work. Today the working mother is widely praised for her enterprise and congratulated on freeing children from the burdens of maternal obsession.

Unquestionably the world has changed, and women with it. For women coming of age in the 1980s, the feminine mystique (woman as devoted mother, perfect wife) has largely been replaced by the feminist mystique (woman dressed for success, with a fifty-fifty marriage, an upwardly mobile career and a superkid in day care). The notion of realizing herself through a man is anathema to the liberated woman; through her children, only slightly less so. "Motherhood as recent generations have known it is tottering," a feminist announced at the dawn of the brave new world. "Traditional child rearing has been strictly tête-à-tête; one mother totally engrossed in and at the service of one child, one child totally involved with one mother. . . . Going off to work and abdicating to a mother-surrogate was inexcusable. Those women who did so were always subtly, or not so subtly, tainted. The *best* mothers didn't."[11]

The women's movement, with its push for equal educational and work opportunities, has legitimized the ambitions of job- and career-oriented women, regardless of maternal status. Did the movement create new ideals or free women for a life they had always wanted? Whatever the answer, it is clear that for many women today, self-esteem and confidence are firmly linked to outside employment. (This is particularly true for the well educated. The likelihood of paid employment increases as a woman moves up the educational ladder. In 1976, when just over forty percent of all Canadian women were in the labour force, seventy percent of women holding a university degree were employed.)[12] In one recent survey seventy-five percent of employed women said they would work whether they needed the money or not. But of course, money is always a factor, increasing a woman's sense of independence and (with divorce so common) security. The fact that families are now smaller and formed later means that women are likelier to think in terms of whole-life employment. A woman who has her first child at thirty-five rather than at twenty is used to having a job and the income it provides. She values her work experience, protects her seniority. Motherhood, then, becomes the occasion for maternity leave rather than withdrawal from the work force.

The new scarlet letter, a badge of shame, is H — for Homemaker, Housewife. Day care expert Alison Clarke-Stewart observes that the U.S. Department of Labor Dictionary of Occupational Titles, which ranks occupations according to skill levels, places homemaker at the bottom, along with restroom attendant, parking-lot attendant and poultry offal shoveler.[13] It's the stay-at-home mothers, now, who feel guilty. Why are they spending the best years of their lives talking baby talk, wiping small noses and small bottoms? Why are they not out in the world making waves, achieving? Historian Edward Shorter argues persuasively that the trend in family life from the nineteenth to the twentieth century has been from "community obligations" to "self-fulfilment," from "allegiance" to "sanctioned egoism."[14] Certainly women, traditionally the nurturant and self-sacrificing sex, more often now subscribe to that aggressively male motto: "Look out for number one." But since old habits die hard, ardent feminists claim that what's good for number one is also good for number two (husband) and three (children) — in other words, mothers who reject "the drudgery involved in raising kids privately"[15] free their children for the superior joys of surrogate care. An early manifesto, "Child Care and Women's Liberation," soars far beyond any modest claims for day care as equal to mother care. "What has to be admitted," Elizabeth Hagen wrote, "is the poverty of the individual family setting compared with the richness of a good day care centre in terms of the stimulus, skill and dedication of the staff."[16]

The message of the women's movement — "Don't just sit there; *do* something" — is powerfully reinforced by the conditions of modern urban life. It is doubtful whether most mothers a generation ago saw themselves as "stuck at home with their children." They weren't. Families were larger, more sociable units; neighbours were closer in every sense; the world was a safer world. When I was a young mother living on a small income, we had a yard and garden. My children played hopscotch and Red Rover outdoors unsupervised; they walked or biked to friends' houses. I went visiting a lot, pushing a baby carriage or stroller (in those days when there was no need for collapsible put-it-in-the-car strollers). And lots of people, besides friends, came to my door: the milk man, the bread man, the vegetable man, the Fuller Brush man, the magazine salesman. . . Contrast this with the situation of a young woman marooned with an infant on the twenty-second floor of a high-rise building. She may have recently moved to this city. She may not know another soul on her floor, in her building. She almost certainly does not own that vanishing artifact, a baby carriage. Except for the child's father (if he's in residence), she may not see another adult for days at a time. Unless she makes a special effort to move into the community with her child, she easily feels bored, isolated, depressed. She is also likely to feel irritated and frustrated by the child. According to an intriguing research study of city and country families, urban mothers see their children as less independent, less self-reliant and less helpful than do country or village mothers.[17] Is it any wonder that such women see the work world as a welcome escape — with day care as its necessary concomitant?

The lure of the work world would count for little if that

world were closed. In actual fact, however, though discrimi-
natory practices remain, opportunities for women have
expanded enormously. Service occupations — in banks,
government offices, restaurants, hospitals, schools — have
been traditionally a female province and have increased; prejudices concerning "male" jobs (policeman, engineer,
plumber, surgeon) have decreased; technical advances have
diminished or eliminated the importance of physical strength.
The woman who wants a *real* job in preference to child care
and housework may be deluding herself; the child and the
housework will be waiting for her at day's end. But her
chances of finding a job are about as good as a man's. And
when she does find one, she'll need day care.

That day care now generally means professional care is a
fact of social change. Time was when most young couples
enjoyed the support of an extended family network, his and
hers — a reserve force of grandparents, uncles and aunts and
cousins happy to take on an extra child or two. Time was
when households commonly included members of three
generations, live-in baby-sitters, and when, in the large
family, older siblings could be counted on to help with the little ones. That time is long gone. A high rate of mobility —
the average North American family moves once every three
or four years — means that most young parents don't live
near Grandma (and in any case, Grandma probably has a
job). Shrinking family size makes it unlikely that an infant
can be handed over to a sister or brother in the third grade or
a third-grader put in the care of a teenager. Few indeed are
the couples who share their home with a parent. The tradition of a family caring for its own survives largely in new-
immigrant groups. This is probably the last generation which
can hope to rely, for child care, on the generation that went
before.

And then there is the fact that today's nuclear family is
often a very small nucleus — not mother, father and one or
two children but one parent, one child. Only seven percent of

families now conform to the traditional pattern of working husband, children and wife at home.[18] This trend is not simply an urban phenomenon; it's true for all regions. Two out of five marriages now end in divorce, most of them in the early years; that means a staggering number of households where the resident parent, as sole provider, must arrange for child care while he or she is out providing. Add to this figure the number of households which have single parents from the start: teenage girls who become pregnant out of ignorance, negligence, innocent romanticism or desperation and who mostly keep their babies; single women who (perhaps in equal ignorance of realities) undertake to have and raise a child without benefit of partner. By 1974 one out of every eight children under three was living in a single-parent household; eighty percent of these household heads were employed full-time and in need of supplementary child care. Census bureau projections suggest that the demand for day care will increase still further as the children of the baby boom era (1946–1964) become parents. The number of pre-schoolers in the United States, for example, is expected to rise from a low of 17.1 million in 1977 to a high of 23.3 million in 1990. An estimated half of the mothers of these pre-schoolers will enter the work force. Unless a single parent is prepared to live on welfare, he or she *must* find some form of day care.[19]

From *must* to *needs* is, in the current economic climate, a short step. "In modern America," says Yale University's Edward Zigler, "mothers work for the same reasons fathers do — economic necessity." By 1976 only forty percent of jobs paid enough to support a family.[20] So it's not surprising to find that in 1976 sixty-four percent of men earning between $5,000 and $10,000 had a working wife.[21] Many two-parent families have no real choice; they need two jobs just to keep afloat. An unskilled labourer with four children, say, will sink wretchedly below the poverty line unless his wife too finds employment (in all probability also unskilled and low-paid). Other families might stay afloat but are committed to sailing with a certain style (a second car, a home of their own). Inflation, high interest rates, rising costs and constantly rising expectations have made the two-income family the shape of the future.

Finally, by no means inconsiderable as a source of pressure for more and better day care, one consequence of burgeoning psychological research has been an altered view of early childhood needs — intellectual, social and emotional. Because the first three years are now seen as crucial for intellectual stimulation and growth, high quality professional day care is recommended for children from "disadvantaged" homes; the U.S. Head Start program for pre-schoolers is probably the most visible and dramatic response to this conviction. Some form of other-than-mother care is also urged for children from any home, however advantaged, as a valuable social experience. Long before school age, experts say, children should get used to being with, getting along with, other children. As Harvard's Jerome Bruner observes, in the anonymous urban society "where the isolated nuclear family has succeeded the more connected extended one, what before happened naturally must now be arranged."[22] Nuclear isolation has also popularized the relatively new notion that, for at least part of the time, children profit from being free of "adult pressures" and parents from the continuous stress of child presences. Mental health professionals frequently propose day care as a response (if not actually a solution) to critical situations: emotionally disturbed children, emotionally disturbed mothers, handicapped children, children from homes so conflicted or so paralysed that the child's welfare is truly at risk.

The mounting pressure for day care, combined with the generally acknowledged shortage of high-quality day care facilities, constitutes a true crisis. What are working parents to do? Can they hold fulltime paying jobs and still ensure the healthy development of young children? The answer hinges, obviously, on what's available, affordable, in the way of child care. And this is a matter on which opinions differ.

To take one dramatic example: a 1984 report on Quebec day care centres[23] — "Les garderies, jardins ou jungles?" — presents the appalling spectacle of thirty or forty children crowded into quarters designed for a single family, large noisy groups with a ratio of twenty charges per caretaker, poorly supervised children glassy-eyed at the TV, two-year-olds marching single file and obliged to maintain strict silence during meals, three-year-olds kneeling in a corner as punishment, five-year-olds forced to take naps . . . and the cumulative horror, a four-month-old infant found dead, suffocated by her pillowcase. This report, published in *L'Actualité*, produced a storm of indignant protest from both satisfied parents and day care officials. Mme Stella Guy, head of the province's day care services, denounced the article as largely false and totally sensational; her inspection tours throughout the province had shown the situation to be nothing like as grim as depicted. ("The quality of our services is steadily improving. . . .") What is the reality, the truth? How is a parent to know?

One would hope that the literature on day care might provide answers. Certainly there exists now a tremendous amount of research. Thanks to the efforts of psychologists and educators around the world, we know a lot about "Effects of Maternal Employment on the Child," about "Anxious Attachment and Defensive Reactions Associated with Day Care" and about "Affective and Cognitive Consequences of Polymatric Infant Care in the East African Highlands." (For those who really want to get into it, there's "Induced Mental and Social Deficits in Rhesus Monkeys.") Whether as general information or as intellectual exercise, much of this material is fascinating. It is not particularly helpful to anxious parents faced with an awesome decision: shall we put this child, this unique person with unique qualities and needs, in some form of other-than-mother care? If we do, can we be sure of his continuing safety, health, happiness and all-round development? Is day care good for children?

The first problem is terminology. "Day care," so confidently defended or attacked, is actually an umbrella label for a whole spectrum of caretaking arrangements: in-home care by a relative, friend or nanny; care in the home of a relative, friend or friendly stranger; family day care (in the home of a "provider" who takes in a number of children and cares for them along with her own); parent co-ops, small centres run and partly staffed by parents; day care centres caring for preschool children of different ages, with some professional staff and generally a formal program of activities. Centres may be commercial, part of a national chain; they may be non-profit and run by a church, hospital, university or service organization; they may be corporate, owned and run by a large company for its employees; they may be publicly supported by federal or local government. Obviously, these are very different kinds of arrangements, each with its characteristic advantages and disadvantages. "Day care" for a child who goes to Mini-Skools is an experience bearing no relation to that of a child who goes down the street to Aunt Gertrude. Generalizations are more than usually treacherous here. It is not possible to talk helpfully about day care without knowing what kind.

Now, about that research. Standard research techniques are clearly not well suited to assessing the virtues of Aunt Gertrude. They're not terribly useful in the world of family day care, where everything depends on the caretaker (her temperament, intelligence, skills, feeling for children) and the atmosphere of her home. There's no laboratory instrument, no super-Geiger counter, to pick up good humour, intuition, patience — or hostility and resentment. In Britain's Oxford Pre-school Research Project (1975-78) research teams under the direction of Harvard's Jerome Bruner did indeed complete a model study of family day care (in Britain called "minding") using personal interviews with minders and mothers and repeated close, sensitive observations of minded children in different settings.[24] But even with such a study, when all possible conclusions have been drawn, one is thrown back on the fact that here is information about *these* particular caretakers, *these* children.

It's not surprising, then, that most research concentrates on group centre care, which lends itself to categories. But centre care happens to be the form of day care least used. In Canada, the United States and Great Britain the majority of working mothers' children are cared for by family members or friends, generally in the child's own home. The next most common arrangement is care in someone else's home, perhaps in the company of other children. The least common arrangement is formal centre care (in Canada about fifteen percent of all day care children, in the United States eighteen percent, in Britain eleven percent).[25] To put this another way: the largest body of day care knowledge concerns a situation not relevant for roughly eighty to ninety percent of day care users.

A further, damaging qualification. What we know about centre care is not based on brave, struggling centres run by the church or the local women's club. Research on group care has been conducted almost exclusively at large, well-equipped, professionally staffed, well-run and handsomely funded centres. Some have expenses of $10,000 per child per year — more than three times the average expenditure for a non-profit centre. Often these facilities are attached to a major university and maintained specifically for research or demonstration purposes. For example: *The Challenge of Daycare*, jointly written by a professor of pediatrics, a professor of social work and a professor of child development, reports the truly inspiring work done at Yale University's Children's House, a day care centre supported by a grant from the U.S. Children's Bureau.[26] The ratio of staff to children was unusually generous: one caretaker for every two children under three and one for every three or four children between the ages of three and five. Staff members were professionally trained in teaching, nursing and child care; physicians and psychologists stood ready for consultation and help. Since this is not ordinary day care, available for $60 a week, the project's accomplishments tell us little about ordinary care.

Or take Harvard professor Jerome Kagan's experimental day care centre in Boston, established for the express purpose of comparing a matched group of day care and home care children.[27] Like Yale's Children's House, the Tremont Street Infant Centre had everything: intelligent direction and almost unlimited resources, a staff so well paid that turnover, a perennial day care problem, was minimal. Before he embarked on this project, Kagan had expressed some anxiety about the effects of group care on vulnerable pre-schoolers. He concluded, at project's end, that "day care and home-reared children developed similarly with respect to cognitive, social and affective qualities during the first three years of life" — provided that staff to child ratio was low and the caretaker nurturant and capable, sharing the values of the child's family; provided that the centre was not too large or too crowded and that child language and child autonomy were appropriately stimulated. . . A lot of *provideds*.

The Utopian nature of Kagan's centre can be suggested by a few salient comparisons. His centre accommodated thirty-three young children; in Canada provincial regulations set centre maximum at sixty to eighty. Kagan's caretaker-child ratio was one to three for infants, one to five for toddlers; in Quebec the legal ratio for ages two to ten is one caretaker for every eleven children (New Brunswick and Prince Edward Island have similarly relaxed standards of supervision).[28] During the five years of Kagan's project, only two staff members left; in an average centre (average = low pay, long hours, poor working conditions) turnover is constant and disruptive. (For a far-worse-than-average record consider this from a 1981 study: in one English centre, staff turnover was 438% a year, with each member absent an average of fifty-three days annually.)[29]

Do these melancholy comparisons mean that Kagan's study — and similar model research designs — have no validity? Not at all. They point the way. They demonstrate what first rate day care can be and can do. But they tell us nothing about the effects of average, poor or terrible day care, and the reality of day care in our society at this time is that much of it is substandard. Howard Clifford, day care consultant for the Canadian Department of Health and Welfare, says "too many centres now have standards so low that no knowledge-able day care person could, in good conscience, recommend that parents use them."[30] "My most reasonable guess," he told a 1980 seminar, "is that fifty percent of all day care centres licensed in Canada shouldn't be, and the doors should be closed now."[31] Clifford's guess approximates closely one of the few American studies attempting to assess the quality of centre care: it found fifty-one percent of non-profit centres "fair" and fifty percent of commercial centres decidedly "poor."[32]

Give or take a few percentage points, it is clear that day care research has little bearing on the choices available to most working parents.

The next problem has to do with the structure and goals of most day care research. Neil Postman, author of *The Disappearance of Childhood*, tells a story which illustrates the crucial importance of the question asked. Once upon a time in Transylvania, the story goes, an unusual problem arose. The inhabitants of a small village succumbed frequently to a curious disease, mostly but not always fatal, whose onset was signalled by a deathlike coma. The problem: how to be abso-lutely certain that persons buried were not merely comatose but dead? One faction proposed stocking coffins with water and food, just in case. Another, more practical and cost-conscious, proposed a twelve-inch stake fixed to the coffin lid at heart level. With this design, shutting the coffin ended all doubt.

The point here is that what emerges depends on the question asked. The first solution is a response to "How can we make sure that we don't bury people who are still alive?" and the second to "How can we make sure everyone we bury is dead?" Shifting from Transylvania to the current scene: day care research has for decades asked three central questions inspired by the work of British psychoanalyst John Bowlby.[33] Will children placed very early in day care suffer maternal deprivation? Will they become unable to make normal human attachments? Will they be perilously vulnerable to anxiety at separation from familiar figures? These concerns arise from Bowlby's enormously influential studies of children whose lives were disrupted by World War II. On the basis of work in foster homes and institutions, Bowlby concluded that to become secure, competent adults, infants required a close continuous nurturant relationship with a single caretaker, preferably the mother. Without this early foundation of love and trust, the victims of "maternal deprivation" might be gravely damaged for life, pathologically suspicious and detached. Bowlby's followers extended and supported these investigations. Rene Spitz found that children raised in institutions became listless, apathetic and in some cases retarded.[34] James and Joyce Robertson, filming hospitalized children, recorded a grim progression from rage to despair to indifference.[35] Harry Harlow, experimenting with rhesus monkeys, found that monkeys raised without mother-contact became incompetent adults, unable either to mate normally or to raise their own young.[36]

The implications of these studies, serious and troubling, will be examined later (see Chapter VI). For the moment, it is enough to observe that questions about maternal deprivation are, at least in Bowlby's sense, not strictly relevant to the day care issue. Regular separations and reunions, Monday to Friday, eight to five or whatever, are hardly comparable to institutional care. Hundreds of studies, designed to test Bowlby's hypotheses, have cast their nets into a sea of red herrings and come up empty. Michael Rutter, a professor of child psychiatry at the University of London (England), in an exhaustive review of the evidence, concludes that though "the concept of 'maternal deprivation' has undoubtedly been useful in focusing attention on the sometimes grave consequences of deficient or disturbed care in early life . . . it has served its purpose and should now be abandoned."[37] Nevertheless, a new American paper on maternal deprivation appeared last month — and no doubt there'll be another next month. Old questions die hard.

Meantime, new — or at least different, more appropriate — questions are *not* being asked. Almost no one is asking how day care affects values, surely a central parental concern. If a child spends most of his waking hours, from three months to age six, in the care of strangers (however decent and kind), whose standards will he absorb — caretakers' or parents'? Who will shape his sense of integrity and fairness, his capacity for compassion and responsibility? These are hard questions, and it's easy to see why they are not being asked in psychometric laboratories. How, for instance, do you measure compassion? No one is asking how a mother's feeling for her child and her knowing him are affected by early day care. No one asks about such desirable intangibles as creativity, curiosity, capacity for independent activity and thought. Above all, the big question is framed as "Does day care harm children?" and not "Does day care help children?" Psychologist Elliott Barker, founder of the Canadian Society for the Prevention of Cruelty to Children, says, "The question that ought to be asked that isn't is: What's best for the child? Nobody is setting up day care because they think it's the best thing for infants. They're saying it's the easiest, best compromise. Show me a place where they're saying, 'I now believe that this kind of group care is absolutely the best thing for this infant, in terms of his developing a capacity for trust and for empathy and affection down the line!' Then I'll rush and put my next kid in it. But they're not anywhere saying *that*."[38]

Day care research is at every point limited by the fact that human beings cannot, like rhesus monkeys, be caged and observed under controlled conditions. The day care child is not an isolated subject who can be studied, understood in and by himself. He's part of a family — a family which may include mother, father, siblings, uncles, aunts, cousins and grandparents. That researchers cannot tackle the extended family is understandable. That fathers — their role, involvement, attitudes — play so little part in day care studies is at least surprising. Mothers are more often included, either by direct observation or through interviews to determine the mother's perceptions and experience of surrogate care. The problem with interviews is that few women are totally unambivalent about the decision to place a child in someone else's care. So the tendency is to put a bright face on things. Major child care surveys like the U.S. National Day Care Study (1978-79) and the National Child Care Consumer Study (1976) found that most parents expressed satisfaction with their child care arrangements. A major Canadian study funded by Health and Welfare found that ninety-seven percent of day care users claimed to be satisfied with the choice they'd made.[39] The explanation for this remarkable enthusiasm and unanimity is suggested by an anecdote in Sheila B. Kamerman's *Parenting in an Unresponsive Society*. When Kamerman presented at an open meeting her day care findings — to an overwhelming majority of contented parents — two young women commented that they weren't surprised. "After all," one said, "the sense of guilt could be overwhelming for some women if they had to acknowledge that their child care arrangements were not satisfactory — especially if they thought them unsatisfactory for the child!" The second woman agreed. "And if it's unsatisfactory from the mother's point of view, because it's hard on her, that's also difficult to acknowledge. When I was asked that question, I too answered that the arrangement was 'satisfactory.' I didn't know it could be any different than it was and I thought I had no alternative, so why complain? In retrospect, that particular 'package' was the worst arrangement I had since the baby was born four years ago — yet I said I was satisfied with it."[40]

And what about the prime consumer of day care, the child? How does the young child feel about being wakened early every morning, perhaps rushed through breakfast, bundled into the car by a parent (who hopes, often, that that runny nose doesn't mean anything) and returned after ten hours to parents who may be hepped up for "quality time" but are just as likely to be tired and cross? Does the child believe Mummy *has* to take him to the sitter or centre because she's got a job, or does he fear she doesn't want to be with him? What does he feel about the substitute home, the caretakers? We don't know, probably will never know. Three-year-olds are poor interview subjects and so, often, are ten-year-olds — though one taciturn ten-year-old produced a curiously eloquent comment on his experience. Asked which of his eight or ten day care arrangements he had liked best, the child replied, "None. My best day care is home." Here are other glimmers, child voices from *Good Day Care*. "I don't like everything that happens at my day care. I don't like having a nap because I'm not tired in the afternoon. I don't like it when the teacher puts up a bed so we can't see or talk to each other. That's not fair." "The only thing I don't like about day care is having to go when I'm not feeling well. Sometimes I just want to stay *home!*"[41] Or consider this, from a working mother's passionate defence of day care: "Miles did cry the first week when I left him. Then I told him I felt bad when he cried and he said he wouldn't anymore. He doesn't. He doesn't have time to anyway. As soon as he arrives, the alert and smiling teacher scoops him up into the day's activities." Is little Miles truly delighted with that alert and smiling scoop?

Does the fact of his not crying indicate happiness — or an anxious desire not to grieve and disobey his mother? (If the latter, then his burden is heavy indeed.) To repeat: research can never uncover this vital information, *What about the child?*

Research is also curiously unsatisfactory about long-term effects of day care. The first generation of children raised largely in day care has yet to come of age. Meantime, a "long-term" study is not likely to go beyond the term of the Yale Children's House project: three years. Such studies produce some evidence concerning the difference, at school-starting age, between home-reared and day care children. Will these differences persist over time? Will there emerge, at a later date, what one investigator calls "sleeper effects"? The only existing long-term research did indeed find such effects. In Britain T. Moore followed two groups of London children from age six through fifteen. One group consisted of children who had experienced some form of substitute care for at least a year before age five, the other of children cared for (apart from occasional baby-sitting) exclusively by mothers. Moore discovered that initial differences between the two groups *increased* progressively over a nine-year period, the later effects of substitute care being more marked (and more disturbing) in boys than in girls.[42] In the absence of similar North American studies, parents concerned about possible effects of surrogate care at, say, adolescence are thrown back on that familiar conclusion of day care research: "The data is not yet available. There is still much to be learned about the psychological requirements of the very young child."

In an attempt to determine both psychological requirements and psychological effects, day care research employs a now standard series of instruments. Probably the most common of these tests is Ainsworth's "strange situation," designed to measure the quality of a child's attachment to his mother.[43] In this experiment mother and child are taken to a test room containing three chairs and miscellaneous toys. The child is set down on the floor, free to explore; mother reads a magazine. A stranger enters, sits quietly a moment, "interacts" with mother and then with child. Mother leaves; the stranger remains, responding to or comforting the child as necessary. Mother returns, stranger leaves, mother comforts child if he is distressed and directs his attention to the toys. Mother leaves child alone in room. Stranger enters, does comfort routine again, returns to chair, leaves as mother enters. Mother comforts and brings on the toys. This little scenario takes place over a twenty-minute period. Meantime, through the one-way vision glass, observers note and score *exploratory manipulation* ("banging, turning over or other active involvement with a toy"), *oral behaviour* ("chewing or sucking fingers or toys"), *distance interaction with mother* ("smiling, showing toy to mother, vocalizing") and *crying* . . . (well, we know what crying is). These observations form the basis of judgment as to whether day care children are more or less warmly and trustingly attached to their mothers than home care children.

The first thing to say about the strange situation test is that to the child it must seem strange indeed — new place, new person, new toys and a puzzling sequence of untypical events. Does a child's response to this drama truly indicate real-life feelings and behaviour? (A child who cheerfully accepts an unfamiliar sitter in his own home, waving Mummy goodbye, may panic in a laboratory.) Urie Bronfenbrenner is surely right in arguing that much of contemporary developmental psychology can be described as "the science of the strange behaviour of children in strange situations with strange adults for the briefest possible period of time."[44] Even if we accept the responses as valid, questions of interpretation remain. Say the child passionately embraces the returning mother. Does that demonstrate secure attachment ("I'm glad to see you!") as Ainsworth presumes — or insecure attachment ("Don't leave me again!")? If the child shows neither joy nor relief at mother's return, does that indicate alarming sad detachment or happy absorption in play? Does it perhaps demonstrate autonomy? Is it the normal response of a child accustomed to the comings and goings of a working mother? (The theory is that anger or avoidance shows insecure attachment.) More than most attempts to measure human response, the test is fraught with imponderables. The child may be cranky, coming down with a cold. He may have just acquired a new sister or lost a beloved grandparent. He may simply be a detached kind of child. (Some children from infancy resist cuddling and pull away from any embrace — like the ten-monther whose first words, eluding a hug, are "hot face!" Or the babe-in-arms whose mother says, ruefully, "She treats me like I had bad breath.") With the strange situation experiment, we are back in the familiar *maybe* territory of psychological research. "Accurately measuring children's actions and reactions in day care is a very tricky business. It is likely that the kinds of measures used may not be the right ones to determine if day care has negative effects on later development."[45]

A further tricky-business element in day care research is the population studied. Investigators cannot arbitrarily assign children to home or day care (with rats or monkeys we might create a truly controlled experiment). So day care children are the offspring of parents who have *chosen* day care; home care children have mothers who *chose* to stay home. We may, then, be talking about very different kinds of families, different from the start. This has profound implications for child behaviour and development. There is virtually no research which takes into account pre-existing individual differences in the children studied, or which observes the day care child in his *home* setting. There has been very little investigation of day care children from intact, middle class families. Major projects generally involve "disadvantaged" children and so, not surprisingly, find that their charges make considerable progress in a stimulating day care setting.

A final, obvious limitation: There is simply no way to isolate the effects of day care from all the other elements in a child's life. Is Anthony insecure because he has been in group care from infancy or because his mother is depressed and the family moves constantly? Has Margaret blossomed because of the day care program or because her mother's remarriage has created a more stable home situation?

When all the research is in, all the results tabulated and scored, we are thrown back on the limited, constrained and tentative conclusions of researchers. "The wise citizen who is trying to use facts to make decisions should view most psychological conclusions with great caution."[46] That is Jerome Kagan, one of the most open-minded and cautious investigators. "Day care can be used wisely or unwisely. The same program can benefit one child and not another. Some programs are reasonably good for most children. Some that are beneficial for 4-year-olds would be damaging for infants."[47] That is Sally Provence, a richly experienced and knowledgeable day care expert. From the prestigious Merrill-Palmer Institute, a pioneer in child study, comes this uneasy conclusion: "According to our preliminary findings, day care is not necessarily harmful. But some day care programs might produce harm. How is a parent to know? There are consumer guides for cars, refrigerators, and soaps. The sad fact is that there are no such guides for day care settings, or any other human service institutions."[48]

The bottom line is that parents must decide for themselves what seems absolutely best for their child.

Chapter II

Do You Really Want a Child?

In a book addressed to parents, this chapter's leading question may seem gratuitous or downright rude. It is made relevant, even urgent, by dramatic social changes of the past two decades. This is the first generation in history to have a real choice in the matter of childbearing. Effective contraception, male and female sterilization and legalized abortion have combined to produce a world in which, theoretically, every baby could be a *wanted* child. Of course, accidental and unwanted pregnancies are still common, particularly among teenagers. A quite different and perhaps growing phenomenon is the increase in wanted children, without a corresponding readiness to raise those children in a traditional sense. Consider, for instance, this from a young father expressing appreciation of the centre which has cared for his two boys from the age of four months to school entrance: "How many of the children at the centre would not have been created had the day care centre not existed? There is a whole bunch of our children who owe their existence to the day care centre."[1]

Without in any way questioning this father's pleasure in his offspring, one can still be moved to ask: Is it appropriate, is it *right* to bring children into the world with the confident expectation that someone else will care for them during the entire period which experts agree is critically important, the first five years of life? Evidently this father was fortunate in the care available at a local co-operative centre. But the same volume which contains his testimony presents an appalling picture of the day care worker's situation. Since looking after children is unimportant, unskilled work, we are told, trained and knowledgeable people must work under very poor conditions for very low wages. "Apparently, day care workers are expected to exist on fresh air, sunlight and the fact that they enjoy working with young children."[2] Though details vary from one centre to another, some conditions are common: long hours (eight-hour shifts, five days a week), low staff-child ratios, heavy responsibility (not just child welfare, but often menial housekeeping tasks), little holiday time and sickness as a constant occupational hazard, though "being sick is a luxury that most workers cannot afford." Pay is so poor that single women cannot afford to live alone. Pressure is unremitting; even coffee breaks and lunch tend to be taken up with meetings or watching a sick child. Result? "Workers can do no more than just cope. . . . They are unable to create the enriched experiences they are trained to provide. Work that should be challenging and stimulating is instead frustrating and tiring."[3] So of course, staff turnover is high. A child who has made the difficult transition from home to centre, becoming warmly attached to one caretaker, will very likely in the course of his day care experience be obliged to make other difficult transitions as familiar beloved figures give up and depart.

Obviously, centre workers deserve a better break, and day care activists are lobbying for change. But there is no sign that, any time in the near future, those who care for young children will be paid as well as plumbers or electricians. In the meantime, it is simply unrealistic to expect that a harried individual earning the minimum wage can offer the ten or twelve pre-schoolers in her charge a mother's interest, attention, tenderness, stimulation and sensitive response. "To replace a mother with an employee cannot be done,"[4] says British developmental psychologist Penelope Leach. No hired caretaker, however devoted, can match a mother's feeling for the child; furthermore, the conditions of employment (time off, promotion, resignation) make impossible a continuous close relationship. Another British child care expert, writing in A Fairer Future for Children, is even more emphatic: "To

bring children into the world without one parent being willing to devote at least three years to their full-time care,
should come to be regarded as selfish indulgence."[5]

Now it is surely true that many parents turn to substitute
care not out of selfish indulgence but because they *must*. A
marriage ends, a mother becomes ill, a father loses his job,
drugs or alcohol or mental breakdown diminish a family's
capacity to cope. It is also true that some women have a child
much as they might acquire a Pekinese — a diversion, a
status symbol, an "in" thing as well as a love object. A notable
'80s phenomenon has been what one magazine saluted as
"The Rise of the Middle Class Unwed Mother" — the woman
who, generally over thirty, well-educated, ambitious and independent, deliberately conceives a child she plans to raise
alone, without interrupting her work rhythm. The out-of-
wedlock baby boom is said to be particularly evident in New
York City, where phrases like "elective parent" and "single
mother by choice" are suddenly cropping up in cocktail conversations. "Everybody seems to know somebody who is
doing it or at least talking about doing it."[6] To preserve the
purity, the exclusiveness of the mother-child unit, many elective parents use artificial insemination. This eliminates
troublesome involvement with fathers. Canadian newspapers
and magazines have noted a similar boomlet — with the
difference that Canadian single-by-choice mothers incline to
reproduction the old-fashioned way, with a mate who may
or may not understand his role as sperm-bearer.[7]

How do these enterprising women cope with the conflicting demands of child and job? Day care. A typical reported
routine is up at 6:30 A.M., bottle, breakfast, dress, feed the
cat, smoke a cigarette and off to the centre by 8:00 A.M. Six
o'clock, pick up the baby, home to feed the cat and heat up
the Spaghetti-O's. Play with the baby, drop into bed
exhausted by ten and up at six. . . . One mother, discouraged
by centre experience, has settled for family day care — "ten
kids in this small filthy room. I had to push the junkies out of

the way just to get in the door." If this situation troubles her, she is (like many day care mothers) not saying. She insists it's "much healthier" for her daughter. "As a city kid, she'll have to fend for herself. I grew up in a very sheltered environment and I want it to be different for my children."[8]

That the world will be different for these children goes without saying. John Munden Ross, a clinical psychologist, comments on the narcissism of many single-by-choice mothers. "They're focusing on personal fulfilment rather than thinking about what's best for a child. A woman alone has no real family life. How can she give a baby a sense of security and belonging, especially if he's left in a day care centre forty hours a week?"

Though the single-by-choice mothers in New York are no doubt extreme examples, the *me* decade mentality they represent is not uncommon. "I invested ten years of my life in medical training," a physician mother says. "My work is tremendously gratifying and absorbing. How could I throw all that over to stay home with the kids?" One might respond with another question. Then why did you have kids? On this matter, Penelope Leach speaks for a host of child development experts: "The rearing of babies and young children is, and if it is to be satisfactory for all concerned, should be, a highly involving and creative business. It cannot be well and happily done as an afterthought to a life which is already both practically and emotionally full."[9]

Many people have babies for poor or questionable reasons. The commonest (happily less common than it used to be) is fulfilling imagined social or family expectations. You get married; you buy a house; you're *supposed* to put a baby in the nursery. Some parents still subject their young adult children to not-so-subtle pressure: "When are you going to make me a grandma?" Some young adults are bewitched by thoughts of carrying on a family line. Men are especially prone to the son-and-heir fantasy, even though the son may be heir to nothing more than a name and a thirty-year mortgage. Others, accustomed to the vision of life as competition, want a superkid as entry in the race — a child brighter, better looking, more accomplished than anyone else's. Couples in a troubled relationship often imagine that a child will bring them together (images of happy family gathered around the fireplace or the Christmas tree) — the truth being that the strain of parenthood usually makes a bad marriage worse, drives husband and wife apart. A natural but equally illusory hope is the desire to be loved. Parents *will* be loved generally, in time (and perhaps in complicated, ambivalent fashion), but it takes a long time. Babies do not "love" in the adult sense. They seek out the parent, they cling, they register delight, they depend, they demand . . . most of all demand to be fed, changed, held, entertained, comforted. They attach, but they are not grateful. Teenage mothers, who have babies out of longing for affection not otherwise present in their lives, are notoriously prone to disappointment when the baby doesn't love them back. So are older mothers who haven't come to terms with the facts of human development. With an infant, love and giving is a one-way street.

And then there is the whole host of illusions fostered by television and the baby powder ads: babies are cute, cuddly, comical, softly fragrant, all smiles and gurgles and coos and kicks. So they are, when well cared for. Babies are also whiney, smelly, fretful, messy, noisy and recalcitrant. Furthermore, they are always around. No one invites a baby to visit on his own for a weekend. From the moment of birth and for years afterwards, a child must be provided for; no one should embark on parenthood without that awareness.

Some motives for parenthood verge on the pathological. Men as well as women may want a child to use as a weapon against the mate or as a means of manipulation. They may attempt to counteract feelings of powerlessness by having a small person to dominate and control. Not pathological, but still questionable, is the desire to reproduce as evidence of manliness or womanliness. Dr Mary Howell, a pediatrician and child psychologist, reports the curious pattern of women who do not want a baby at first, but set out to have one after a physician has judged them to be possibly sterile or infertile. Bearing a child, then, becomes a response to a challenge, a refusal to be denied a unique female experience, proof that "the machinery works."[10] The new mystique of birthing (as opposed to old-fashioned delivery) and bonding leads many women to concentrate on nine months culminating in a magic moment. "Childbirth was absolutely incredible," says Linda Lee, author of *Out of Wedlock*. "I was high, stoned on my own hormones." Fine. The ultimate reality, however, is not hormone-highs and ceremonies involving the placenta (planting it under a rose-bush, for instance) but years of care.

Children cost a lot — in time, energy, money. (Estimates of the cost of raising and educating a child are rapidly approaching the $100,000 mark.) They are, as Francis Bacon said centuries ago, "hostages to fortune," limiting personal freedom and enormously increasing responsibility. I think there are ultimately a few good simple reasons for choosing to become a parent. Have a child if you enjoy children and want to be with them. If you are prepared to devote to them most of your time for the first few years. If you feel reasonably confident of being able to provide a nurturing environment. If you feel your life would be enriched, not by your child's love, gratitude or accomplishment, but by your child's *being*. If you have the energy and drive to combine motherhood with a career, it is prudent to choose one which can be interrupted for a few years, which can reasonably be undertaken after children are launched or which lends itself to a period of part-time involvement. Even then, of course, you must be prepared for years of juggling responsibilities. Your school age child will come down with measles just when you're slated to present a report or fly to Rome; parents' night at the school or a music recital will fatally coincide with an important meeting. It is probably not possible to be a Supermother and a Superachiever too; something has to give.

As for the choice between personal achievement and having children, consider this testimony from an unexpected source, singer-composer John Lennon, who seemed in the '60s an exemplar of freedom, personal expression and self-realization. Announcing "yes, I looked after the baby and I made bread and I was a househusband and I am proud of it," Lennon concludes: "When I look at what life is about, I can't quite convince myself that making a record or having a career is more important, or even as important, as my child, or any child."[11] And here are two voices from the past. One is the Roman matron Cornelia who, legend has it, was visited by a proud and wealthy acquaintance. The visitor talked of her servants and her fine house, displayed her gold. "And you, my dear," she inquired. "What have you to show?" Cornelia left the room and returned leading two small children by the hand. "These," she said quietly, "are my jewels."

The last voice is a father's. This is Shakespeare's contemporary, Ben Jonson's, epitaph on the death of his child:

Rest in soft peace, and, asked, say here doth lie
Ben Jonson his best piece of poetry.

Chapter III

What Do You Want for Your Child?

What kind of person do you hope your child will become? That's a large and complicated question. Parents of very young children, mired in the daily realities of bottles and diapers and night-time calls, may feel they cannot spare energy for matters metaphysical. Until you've considered goals, however, it's impossible to deal realistically with the child care question. Bettye Caldwell, a pioneer in day care research, puts a firm finger on the central issue: there is no point talking about "curriculum design," "the Piaget model" or anything else in the childrearing scene until you have decided what you hope for. "Do you want obedient children? Happy children? Militant children? Bright children? Group-oriented children? Individuals?" In a totalitarian society the state defines goals and provides institutions appropriate to their realization. For example: the Soviet day care system, where toilet training begins at six months and the group takes precedence over the individual, is ideally designed to produce Soviet citizens. At drawing time everyone copies the same flower arrangement and no one signs his name to the finished product. Pluralistic societies foster a wide range of both goals and child-rearing systems. The parent who wants a task-oriented child chooses Montessori, the one who values self-expression and spontaneity looks for something along Summerhill lines. Still, there's considerable agreement as to the qualities most desirable for a child growing up in a free democratic society.

SELF ESTEEM is primary. Whatever his natural endowments, the child needs to feel that he is a unique individual, loved and valued for what he is, not for what he does or doesn't do.

He needs to feel that he matters, he's special. Though this priceless conviction can be sustained and nurtured in many different ways — by life successes, by the response of teachers and friends — its powerful origin is parental love. This is not the Cartesian "I think, therefore I am" but "They love me, therefore I am good." How do children know they're loved? Certainly not by verbal assurances alone, however frequent. The baby feels loved when his cry brings comfort; the toddler when he's allowed to venture and fail and try again; the child of any age when parents really listen, pay attention, give their time. Love may be honey and lemon for a cough, being held close during a thunderstorm, a doll's tea party with real tea, piggy-back rides after the bath, an unexpected note in the lunchbox. Its heart is recognition — *I see you* — and acceptance — as TV's Mr Rogers says, *I like you just the way you are.*

The threats to self-esteem are ridicule, humiliation, judgments which can become self-fulfilling prophecies. Ideally the child in the early years is not constrained by adult appraisals like "She's awfully shy, isn't she?" or "He's always so happy, never complains." Both pronouncements put the child in a box, doomed to shyness or obliged, commanded, to be happy.

SELF-RELIANCE. This comes only through competence. Though it has become fashionable to insist *I'm OK, you're OK*, the truth is a child can trust himself only if he knows himself to be capable, capable for his age. The four-year-old who can't put on his snowsuit, the seven-year-old who can't read, the ten-year-old who can't ride a two-wheeler — these kids suffer in their self-esteem and consequently in their sense of security. Parents should begin early giving children real tasks to perform — helping find groceries in the supermarket (and later shopping independently), watering plants, setting the table, making a salad. It's a good idea, when children are old enough, to let them take on part-time jobs, such as baby-sitting or delivering newspapers. Parents also need to teach basic social skills, the habits of courtesy that will smooth a child's passage through the world. That means not just *please* and *thank you* but how to answer the telephone, how to introduce yourself to strangers, how to wait for a turn, whether to swing or to speak. To become self-reliant, children need to learn good work habits. Make a plan before you begin; be sure you have the necessary materials; don't undertake projects beyond your capacity; finish what you start; put away your tools (paintbrushes, hammers, scissors, whatever). Be punctual. These old-fashioned principles, learned young, become a lifetime source of strength.

SELF-DISCIPLINE: the acquisition of those inner controls which enable an individual to act responsibly in the absence of external checks. This capacity is not swiftly achieved: it develops gradually, through an infinite number of small situations in which parents teach the rules of good and civilized behaviour. "Don't pull kitty's tail; that hurts." "Let's put the clock back where you found it. It's breakable." "We don't taste the grapes when we shop. They belong to the store man." Compassion, care, respect for other people's rights and property . . . with adult guidance, the young learn where their freedom ends and another's begins. Necessary limits can be set without any dampening of a child's energy, his curiosity and his joy in life. It's possible, of course, to keep children in line by power tactics: threats, bribes, ridicule, commands, humiliation, spanking. The trouble with such police methods is that they strike at a child's sense of himself as a good and worthwhile person — and they don't help him to behave well when there's neither carrot nor stick in sight. The surest path to self-discipline is encouraging the child's deepest desires: to please loved parents and to become competent, *grown-up*. The well-disciplined child is not the one who's whipped into shape; he's the one who can control himself. "Good parenting is biodegradable. You work yourself out of a job."

A SENSE OF RESPONSIBILITY. In essence, this involves the

child's realizing that he is not alone on the planet: that he has obligations — to family, to friends, to strangers who are weak or helpless or needy and to his own best self. Children learn responsibility in part from parental models. When mother shops or cuts the grass for an elderly neighbour, when father volunteers his services for the Big Brother program, that tells the child: those who *can* help those who *can't*. His world, originally and naturally egocentric, expands to include awareness of how others feel. But the most important step in learning responsibility is becoming a person who *can*, who makes useful contributions to the many systems of which he is a member (family, school, community, church or clubs). With real work, with a sense of accomplishment, the child experiences himself as a person who counts, who can make a difference. Then he's ready to master the principles of responsible behaviour: Keep your word; honour commitments; consider the other person's point of view; work for what you want. Actions have consequences.

A SENSE OF SECURITY. Self-esteem, self-reliance, self-discipline and a sense of responsibility all contribute to a child's feeling at home in the world. Most important is the trust in family, immediate and extended, as a support system. In an era when church and school have lost much of their old authority, when roughly one in two marriages ends in divorce and the average household moves once every three years, a sense of family is more vital than ever. Children need to feel, not just that (in Robert Frost's words) "Home is the place where, when you have to go there, They have to take you in," but that home is the place where, when you want to go there, they *want* to let you in. Every child needs the assurance of being unconditionally loved by one or two people, of being cherished for what he is, not for what he does or doesn't do. Happy the child who experiences parental passion and parental tenderness. (For the first: the actress Sissy Spacek recalls her father's "Honey, we'd fight a buzzsaw for you!" And for the second: Eudora Welty, after half a century, remembers how, before she wore her new patent leather slippers for the first time, her father took out his thin silver pocketknife and with the point of the blade carefully scored the polished soles all over, in a diamond pattern, so she wouldn't slip as she ran.)

If, in addition to parents, a child can feel part of a whole constellation — grandparents, uncles and aunts and cousins, people to whom he belongs and who belong to him — that's uniquely enriching and strengthening.

INTELLECTUAL CURIOSITY. Children are born curious. Almost from birth, their eyes follow whatever is arresting (a red object), complicated (a checkerboard) or familiar-reassuring (a human face). Creeping and then staggering about, the baby grabs, tastes, listens, smells. Language brings questions — many of them. Three-year-olds have been observed to ask more than three hundred questions a day. There are no figures on how many answers parents produce; probably not three hundred. Of course some questions don't require answers. They're observations ("Baby crying?"), appeals for reassurance ("Mummy stay with you?"), requests for attention ("Want to see me ride my trike?"). With increased verbal facility, children will ask some questions that are serious and important ("Why did Grandpa die?") and others that seem nonsensical ("Why is a cow?"). Silly or serious, all questions deserve consideration. (And who can say which questions are truly absurd? What would parents have said fifty years ago to a child who asked, "Can I fly to the moon?") A child should never be made to feel foolish for asking, just because the answer is obvious — to an adult — or because there's no answer possible. Eli Wiesel puts it well: "Every question possesses a power not found in the answer. A man grows in wisdom by learning to ask the right questions." Research has shown that curious, questioning children enjoy a richer emotional and intellectual life. They do better at school, are quicker at problem solving, more inventive and more flexible. In an atmosphere where questions are welcomed, addressed patiently and carefully, the young move towards confident mastery of their environment — and the formulation of new, larger, more revealing questions.

CREATIVITY. In the sense that he sees the world with fresh eyes, every child is born creative. The three-year-old paints with confident abandon, makes up stories and dances spontaneously to music. He sees new possibilities in old junk: an oatmeal box is a drum, a roller skate the base for a covered wagon. Five years later, many of these original spirits work with pre-assembled kits or push-buttons in a video arcade. A common question now is "How do *you want* me to do this?" The odd child who retains his creative independence is often regarded as precisely that: *odd*.

The decline of creative powers between the ages of four and ten — a decline verified by many researchers — is so general that most parents regard it as inevitable. Those who equate creativity with artistic talent may think the loss doesn't much matter. But true creativity is a quality of mind — inventive, flexible and free. As one prominent art educator says, "a creative child, one who has been encouraged to develop his imagination and ability freely, will bring these qualities to *any* work that he does. The qualities that might make him a creative painter or writer will make him an equally creative physicist or biologist." These same qualities also make him a more complete human being — one who's creative in friendship, parenthood and love. "In the most profound sense," says psychologist Carl Rogers, "to be creative is to fulfil oneself as a person." To be creative is also virtually a condition of survival in a rapidly changing world. How can one equip a child with skills for the future, when no one knows what skills will be needed? In the space and nuclear age, we need what Abraham Maslow called "a new kind of human being who is comfortable with change . . . who is able to face with confidence, strength and courage a situation of which he has absolutely no forewarning."

Parents *can* help children retain their creative powers by

providing a supportive environment. Teach your child to look and really see. ("Look, inside the avocado pit there's a root all curled up. Shall we plant it and see what happens?") Follow the lead of his interests. If he's mad about computers, there's the science museum; if rhythm is his thing, show him how to make simple musical instruments. Encourage original songs and story-telling by using a tape recorder. Provide toys that stimulate imagination rather than electronically operated marvels. Provide lots and lots of materials to work with: clay, paints, crayons, felt pens, spools, buttons, beads, dress-up clothes, many kinds of paper. Respect his privacy; give him time to dream. Show — by displaying his special projects and always displaying interest — that you value his work. Plato said it long ago: "What is honoured in a country will be cultivated there."

DISCRIMINATION: the habit of critical thought. In a world where we are constantly bombarded with high-powered messages — BUY, VOTE, ACT, BELIEVE — the ability to decode such messages is vitally important. Who says this? What is his motive? Where did he get his information? What does it really mean? Critical thinking is not just the habit of criti-cizing: it involves the ability to suspend judgment, to exam-ine before accepting, to consider alternatives before making a choice. In developing this art, children need all the help they can get — and they should get it early. Watching television, for instance, in company with adults, can become a useful exercise in sound reasoning. Your child urges the purchase of Cruncho Muncho, "the dog food dogs like best." How does he *know* about this overwhelming canine preference? Why, just look how that dog goes for it. At this point, parents can encourage the child to think of alternate explanations for the Cruncho Muncho enthusiasm. Maybe the dog hasn't been fed for days; he'd eat gravel. Maybe there's ground steak in that dish — or another brand of dog food. A child led along the path of clear thinking may well come up with his own infalli-ble test for dog delight: "Put a different dog food in each dish and see which one Nicky goes for." In much the same way, children can be helped to understand the complex question of what constitutes proof. "Three out of four doctors prefer brand X." Is that man in the white coat really a doctor, or is he an actor? Who chose these doctors? How many were polled? Children need to learn the difference between a fact and an assumption; they need to be cautioned against after-this, therefore-because-of-this reasoning. ("She used Marvo cream and her pimples disappeared." This does not prove that Marvo solves skin problems. Maybe her diet improved. Maybe she just outgrew teenage acne.) Reckless generalizations, pseudo-authorities (the Olympic champion who knows which breakfast cereal is best), unsubstantiated charges buttressed with appeals to sentiment ("That's un-American!" "It's a communist plot"), false analogies ("Aldous Huxley took drugs, why shouldn't I?") — the multiple varieties of unsound reasoning assault immature minds through print and video images. The alert parent can use such stuff to teach children a sensible, questioning attitude, to detect error and recognize, value, truth.

CAPACITY FOR ACCEPTING FRUSTRATION, DELAYED GRATIFICATION — AND FAILURE. Press a button and choose between comedy, high drama, rock music, cartoons. Pop the frozen dinner in the microwave. Get out your calculator and deal swiftly with astronomical computations. Today's child lives in a world of fast, fast, fast relief and results. To experience a more human rhythm, children should discover early the satisfaction of projects which take planning, patience and time. Could your child have a garden? Choosing seeds, preparing the soil, planting, hoeing and weeding and fertilizing, then harvesting and distributing produce; with supportive parents, such a venture is not only a whole season's pleasure, it's the richest kind of learning experience. When children bake, let it be from scratch, not from a pre-packaged mix. If they want a doll house or a tree house, let that be a shared undertaking in building, taking pains. The ability to wait, to plan for desired goals, to endure disappointment, is a necessary basis for the joy of achievement (as contrasted with the fun of getting something for nothing).

Along with resisting the illusory joys of instant gratification, children need help in resisting our society's obsession with success. Parents ambitious for their children too often transmit the messge of that famous football coach who insisted, "Winning is not the most important thing, it's the *only* thing." This is a scary idea. In the first place, we are not all winners. Some of us will never win so much as a bingo game, and the way to happiness is surely coming to terms with limitations while making the most of our natural endowments. Second, children easily imagine that being loved is connected with, maybe dependent on, winning. What a thought to take to bed night after night, when you're getting Ds in math and failed to qualify for the baseball team. Instead of urging children into the race for success, parents should teach them an invaluable life skill — how to fail with grace and maybe profit too. Success can be a brief and heady pleasure; it may teach one nothing, except that now there's more to lose. Failure perceived, examined, analysed and understood is profoundly educative. On the simplest possible level, such learning may take the form of showing a three-year-old *why* his block tower fell over. "You need some bigger blocks at the bottom. Let's start again. . ." When a beginning seamstress is ready to abandon her project because the scissors slipped, a helpful approach might be, "It's a good idea to work on a hard surface when you cut. Now, what could you appliqué over that hole? A flower maybe? A bit of lace?"

Children need to understand that failure is part of the human condition and that, as therapist Virginia Satir says, "Every person has the *right* to fail." Remember the caucus race in *Alice in Wonderland*, where it's announced that "You have all won, and you shall all have prizes"? Life isn't like that. The young need to learn that no one can be best at everything, no one can win all the time — and it's possible to enjoy a game even when you don't win. A child who's not in-vited to a birthday party, who doesn't make the honour roll or the swim team, feels terrible. He should not be falsely assured it doesn't matter, because it does. He should not be quickly offered a consolation prize or encouraged to shift blame. Rather, he should be allowed to experience his grief and disappointment — and then helped to master it. Failing in this one area doesn't mean he's inadequate. Maybe he can do better next time. If that's not likely, there are lots of other things he can try.

"You are the bows from which your children as living arrows are sent forth" (Kahlil Gibran). If the characteristics I have discussed here are desirable goals, then decisions about early care should be made with them in mind. Can you find, for your under-three child, a form of surrogate care which you trust to nurture these qualities? Conscientious parents inspec-ting a day care facility will amost certainly check things like safety precautions, sanitation. They should also, I think, ask themselves such questions as, "Will these caretakers make my child feel special and cherished? Will they answer his ques-tions, respond to his playfulness and humour? Will they sense his needs for comfort or encouragement? Will they know when to let him be?" That's a big order. Keep your eye on the target. "The object of education at any age," Jerome Bruner says, "is surely broad and plural: to produce competent and zestful human beings who can manage their own lives and contribute to the common good whilst doing so."

Chapter IV

Child Development and Child Care

The question "Is day care good for children?" can't be sensibly answered without further definition. For which children, living in what circumstances — and above all — at what stage? The group care which might be damaging to an infant could be ideal for a three-year-old who has lived closely with one parent and would benefit from a larger social experience.

The Infant

Defenders of surrogate care for babies generally take the position that it doesn't matter *who* looks after a baby — mother or hired caretaker — so long as the child is well cared for. (The baby doesn't *know* his mother, this reasoning goes. So anyone who feeds, changes and comforts will do.) This is such an apparently persuasive argument that it needs consideration.

Do babies recognize their mothers? At a surprisingly early age, they do. Or more precisely, they recognize the look, smell, sound and touch of a familiar caretaker, responding to familiarity as humans do, with relief and pleasure. Research over the past few decades has demolished William James's notion of the baby's world as "a buzzing, blooming confusion." It now appears that newborns are to a surprising degree organized and competent.[1] On the first day of life, they distinguish between regular milk and milk with corn syrup. In the first few weeks they can discriminate the loudness and pitch of sounds and show marked preference for both the human voice and the human face. At five days they will turn their heads in a particular direction in response to one tone rather than another. At this time too, they turn towards a pad soaked in their mother's milk. (Clean pads produce no response.) Between twenty and thirty days they will speed up sucking in order to hear a tape recording of the mother's voice rather than an unfamiliar one. Now they know the difference between her touch and a stranger's. Selective looking comes later than control of other senses, but babies early prefer patterns to random designs and face-like patterns over all others. At about two months, the infant gazes into a parent's eyes — and smiles.

Given that the baby early knows his caregiver (mother, father, or another continuously available person), what has to happen between these two for optimal development? The first thing a baby needs is close, warm, physical contact. (Some cultures employ swaddling, tight wrapping, to satisfy the infant's desire for snugness.) What Alice Honig calls "bodily nurturance" is vital as milk to a baby's healthy development. "Humans are skin-sharing creatures," Honig says. "Infants and young children need laps and breasts and hips to mold into, to drape against. . . . Body-loving promotes secure attachment that fuels courage to be curious, courage to explore."[2]

How does this fundamental need bear on child care provisions? A mother of twins is hard pressed to give *two* babies all the cuddling they want. What can be expected of a caretaker who's in charge of four infants — or six? With the best will in the world, that caretaker will be obliged to give some infants a propped-up bottle, to let others cry while she performs essential tasks. The baby who is left wet or hungry or alone for long periods, says Sally Provence, "can do little to protest but cry, and in time he may not even do that. He may, in fact, retreat into apathy or excessive sleep, which may be welcomed by overburdened or unknowing staff who do not perceive the excessive sleep as a symptom." Some infants in this situation develop the opposite problem: they *don't* sleep. Or they cry inconsolably, vomit, develop rashes or diarrhea — "any of which may arouse concern but may not be recognized as results of care that fails to be truly nurturing."[3]

Babies also need stimulation. An old notion of infant development, implicit in Arnold Gesell's landmark studies of human growth, saw babies as unfolding like flowers. Charting the gradual maturation of the human infant from sleeper to looker to creeper to cruiser and so on, Gesell assumed that this course, programmed from birth, proceeded steadily regardless of environment. New research has shown that, in fact, what the child becomes — whether he develops his innate potentialities or suffers some degree of arrested development — depends greatly on the vividness of his encounters with the world. A baby kept continuously in a crib or playpen, having nothing to play with, nothing of interest to look at, will not develop in the same way as a baby who is carried about by parents and enjoys early adventures with other living creatures and with such things as cups and spoons. A baby who is silently fed and bathed will not show the joyful enterprise of a baby whose parents make even a diaper change the occasion for talk, tickles, smiles, nods and small cheerful noises.

Stimulation is not in itself a spur to growth. It must be the right amount. Babies in crowded chaotic homes, battered by twelve-hour-a-day television and people noises, are stimulated but not helpfully. It must be the right kind — personal, sensitive, loving. In the first flush of scientific excitement over evidence that infants thrived on attention, one project hired "handlers" to stroke institutionalized infants on schedule — ten minutes morning and afternoon, five days a week. Another tried verbal stimulation — an adult counting out loud by the baby's crib, ten minutes at a time. Neither of these exercises produced results. What *does* work is a parent's sensitive response to those moments when the baby is ready, up for excitement or learning or fun. In the first months of life babies emerge periodically from somnolence for a brief state of heightened alertness. (Physiologically, this represents a replacement of the brain's delta waves by alpha waves.) At these moments, an attentive mother initiates the play which is an important part of infant learning — cuddle, croon, pat, rub, blow. Game is adapted to situation — leg-cycling at changing time, for instance, splashing in the bath — and to mood. Lifting a baby high in the air may produce squeals of joy at one moment, panic at another. Only someone close to this baby knows what's likely to be pleasurable. One need not subscribe to theories of mother instinct to recognize a phenomenon duly charted by research: that women in a maternity ward handle their infants at feeding time in highly individual ways. Some spend minutes gazing into the baby's eyes. Some hold the baby close, some hold him out, away from the body. Some move murmurously towards feeding and some, recognizing an eager eater, guide him swiftly to the nipple.[4] What Rudolph Schaffer calls "state reading" is essential to the art of mothering. The more parents respond to states of heightened infant alertness, the more frequently these states occur — and the more strongly the baby develops in that organization of mind and feeling which is central to intelligence. What happens in a day care centre, with other babies waiting to be fed, bathed or bundled into snowsuits? Chances are that the precious wide-awake here-I-am moments will come and go without anyone's noticing. Or that, when a caretaker finds time, she may make a fussy baby more frantic with an ill-timed tickling game.[5]

From the moment of birth, the infant is developing a communication system. "An infant crying in the night, And with no language but a cry": Tennyson was right. The cry is the first language: a complaint, a summons, a demand. Initially, communication between new baby and new mother is primitive, rudimentary and physiologically based. His cry brings a rush of milk to her breast — may even, in the first weeks, produce uterine contractions. So, whether she's frantic or bewildered or confident, she feeds, creating the foundation of what will become an increasingly complex and subtle system of signals. A baby who is well nurtured learns early that his cry brings results: *he has affected his world*, a realization ego-strengthening as well as immediately gratifying. Within a few months, he adds to his repertoire of signals (fretfulness, kicking, arm-waving) the most potent attention-getter — he smiles. Sheila Kitzinger has observed that a baby's whole aspect is calculated to charm: the large head, plump cheeks, fragrant skin and fixed attentive gaze.[6] The smile completes this charm, and though the first smiles may be promiscuous, it's a hard-hearted caretaker who doesn't feel singled out for special favour. (Sturdy, disciplined Margaret Mead, as a young mother, rejected the notion that the chief impediment to work was the fact that the baby cried so much. The problem, she said, is that "the baby *smiles* so much.")[7] In a favourable situation, the more a baby smiles, the more he is picked up, cuddled, talked to, played with. More attention brings more smiles brings more attention . . . a happily self-perpetuating cycle.

As months pass and these two come to know each other, the baby becomes familiar with the frown that means "not a good idea" and the sounds — opening refrigerator door, sloshing milk, clink of spoon on dish — that mean feeding time. The attentive mother, in turn, becomes more adept at reading cues, like the scrunched-up expression which precedes a howl. This two-way communication does more than simplify life with baby. Besides cutting down on fret-fulness and crying, prompt response to signals has been shown to encourage infant activity and exploration; obvious-ly the child who feels *attended to* develops feelings of security which permit him to leave home base.

Gradually, over the first months, the infant cared for prin-cipally by one person develops a primitive sense of causality. He cries, and someone comes; he gurgles or smiles, and some-one smiles back. In the language of psychologists, he learns "that specific activities have signal value," he develops an "effectance motive," the confidence that he can make things happen. For the development of confidence, it is essential that the baby's signals be consistently and promptly reinforced; with six- and nine-month-olds, a delay of only three seconds can prevent or disrupt learning. In other words, the baby needs a mother or mothering person who is more or less continuously available. Dr James Lynch, author of *The Broken Heart*, describing the "dialogue of love" between mother and child, observes that "when a child *goos* or smiles, it is vitally important that someone else say *ga* and smile back. *Someone must respond*. Since no one can predict when a child will *goo* or smile, someone simply has to be there, ready to respond appropriately."[8]

Herein lies the great problem of surrogate care for infants. In a family care home with many children, in a day care centre, it is simply not possible for providers to build up and maintain a reliable system of communication. The morning caretaker leaves half-way through the baby's day, replaced by yet another stranger. And anyway, while she's on duty she has other babies, other chores. Even care at home by nanny or housekeeper, theoretically an ideal solution, may not work. An article on a career mother — "a mergers-and-acquisitions specialist at Paine Webber" — suggests that money doesn't necessarily buy happiness (in this case, reliable child care).[9] This mother went through six nanny-housekeepers in the first six months of her child's life. Number One was arrogant, didn't want to do anything *except* look after the baby. Number Two was a fanatic housekeeper willing to clean and cook and do everything *except* pay attention to the baby. Number Three evidently neglected the child; she "wasn't stimulating him at all" and the infant seemed ominously listless. Number Four, who was just great, left abruptly without notice. Number Five, an *au pair*, spoke no English. The baby stopped gaining weight, and the parents "couldn't communicate with her well enough to find out whether she was feeding him properly." Number Six, a

Haitian woman, spoke English and cleaned up a storm, but she positively disliked babies — and proved paranoid as well. She lasted a week and a half. Number Seven . . . well, at last count, Number Seven was doing fine. A reader of this account can only wonder at the plight of the infant, passed from hand to hand, experiencing a bewildering variety of caretaking styles, meeting and losing all those hands an eyes. Paine-Webber income notwithstanding, he is surely underprivileged.

Insisting on the need for individuality and continuity in infant care, British psychologist Penelope Leach writes, "A baby who does not have anybody special but is cared for by many well-meaning strangers in turn, or one who is cared for sketchily and without concentration, sharing his caretaker with other needful small people, is like an adult who moves from country to country, knowing the language of none."[10]

To say that babies need steady patient support in learning to communicate is perhaps just another way of saying that babies need love. Because *love* is so loosely used, so bathed in sentimental mists, a definition is in order. The essence of love is paying attention: really listening, really responding, really caring about another person. This is not something one can buy by the hour. If mothers have been romanticized through the ages, elevated to pedestals of selfless devotion, it is, surely, because mothering really is in the early years an incredibly demanding role, almost a fulltime occupation. When well done, it brings extraordinary rewards — not the least of which is release from fulltime responsibility. Disciplinarians who caution against "spoiling" a baby miss the point. It is not possible to spoil a baby. Newborns have no control over their behaviour. They cry because they need — food or warmth or dryness or sleep or, most often, loving touch. It is only by meeting these needs that parents help the baby develop what Erik Erikson calls "basic trust," confidence in the world as a good place. Truly "spoiled" children — whiney, clingy, demanding, querulous — are those whose needs, in infancy, were never met. Only the child who has been sufficiently gratified early can learn, later, to delay gratification. Only the child who has been granted an appropriate period of total dependence will be ready in a few years to begin the journey towards independence. Margaret Mead puts it well. "The child who has experienced safety, warmth and comfort in its mother's arms carries with it a sense of personal worth and of trust in human relationships that makes tolerable the tasks and difficulties that must be faced later in life. . . . We do not know — man has never known — how else to give a human being a sense of selfhood and identity, a sense of the worth of the world."[11]

To these psychological-emotional considerations must be added a harsh practical concern: babies are terribly vulnerable. They cannot tell us what's wrong, they cannot report harsh treatment or neglect. Edward Zigler observes that physically, infants have fewer defences, fewer immunities against some infectious diseases than they will have even a year or so later, as toddlers. Infants are often asymptomatic, without symptoms, even when developing serious disease. In group care, potentially dangerous conditions may go undetected until the damage has already been done.

The Toddler

Louise Kaplan's study of a child's "psychological birth," *Oneness and Separateness: From Infant to Individual*, might well serve as a theme for the first three years of life. From a blissful early symbiosis with the mother, a boundaryless union in which the infant has no sense of either himself or mother as a separate being, he develops gradually a sense of otherness. He finds, he experiences, *his* fingers, *his* toes; he becomes aware of mother's breasts and hands as out there, separate. Some time during the second half of the first year, he discovers that he can move away from mother under his own steam. This is heady stuff. He creeps, stands, totters, falls, staggers away, experiencing simultaneously the ecstasy of independence and the terror of being unsupported, alone. For months this divided impulse — to hold on and to get free — will make his life, and caretaker's, a whirlwind. The well-known characteristics of the terrible twos — the tantrums, the tears, the unreasonableness, the demands, the positive assertions (Me do it!) and the steady negativism (No, no, No!) — are all expressions of the conflict which drives and periodically overwhelms him. He fights restraint, but becomes frantic if the restraining presence disappears from view. He clings; he hammers at the bathroom door. At six months he beamed seraphically when held by a friendly stranger; at a year a stranger's mere approach may provoke howls. At eighteen months, left in other-than-parent care, he throws himself on the floor and weeps inconsolably. Now for the first time he knows a feeling which will recur with more or less violence over the years — starting school, going to camp, leaving home to create his own base, losing friends or lovers . . . Psychologists have a word for it: *separation anxiety*.

Though young children continue for years to protest parental absence, they are particularly prone to separation anxiety during that period when *gone* equals *lost*. This fear first crystallizes during the second year of life, intensifying and reaching a peak around eighteen months — after which it begins to level off and decline. So the period between roughly ten and twenty-four months is particularly unfavourable for entrance into any kind of surrogate care. Until language has organized his thoughts, until experience has demonstrated (over and over again) that the absent parent returns, the small child has no way of knowing that the mother who waved "bye bye" has not disappeared forever. He has no sense of time. What he does have is a sense that his safety and comfort depend absolutely on that one familiar figure who has now inexplicably left him in unfamiliar hands. He may for brief periods play happily with substitute caretakers. But at critical moments — naptime, mealtime, waking from sleep, feeling sick or frightened or hurt — he wants his mother. William and Wendy Dreskin, pre-school teachers whose centre care experience convinced them that day care violated children's best interests, offer a rule of thumb for tolerable separation.[12] Up to age five, they feel, a child can comfortably handle, on a daily basis, one hour a day for each year of age. So a two-year-old can accept two hours a day away from parents, a three-year-old three hours. More than that constitutes stress. Eight to ten hours, the usual length of a day in care, creates intolerable strain. The directors of Yale's Children's House report that the feelings of children in care range from a sense of bewilderment to acute longing for mother and home and that their adaptive capacities are increasingly overtaxed as the hours lengthen.[13] That's a model centre, with small groups, a favourable staff/child ratio and a high quality program. What is a ten-hour day like for the two-year-old in a large group, battered by noise and confusion, with overburdened caretakers who themselves grow increasingly tense and weary as the hours pass by? Years later, children will not remember these early events. What they remember or preserve, says child psychologist Selma Fraiberg, "is anxiety, a primitive kind of terror, which returns in waves in later life. . . . What is preserved may be profound moodiness or depression in later life, the somatic memory of the first tragic loss. . . . What is preserved is the violation of trust, of the ordered world of infancy in which love, protection, and continuity of experience are invested in people."[14]

In an ideal situation, the child remains in his parents' care until, by the age of three, he has developed confidence in them and in himself. By three, he has sufficient command of language to ask questions and to understand parental assurances. He has now some general understanding of time — not "Daddy will come for you at six o'clock" but "You'll play, and have a snack, and go outdoors, and have lunch, and nap and play a little more, and *then* Daddy will come."

He may still protest and be sad at parting, but he has developed the inner resources for coping with disappointment. He is able, now, to wait. He's also old enough actively to enjoy playing with friends. If, on the other hand, he is prematurely deposited in an alien world, with changing caretakers and many other needy little strangers, the natural developmental rhythm from infant to individual is rudely interrupted. "The cumulative nature of the stresses introduced [by a day care situation] makes one fear the final outcome if such child-rearing practices become widespread," says an American psychiatrist. "One thing seems clear: we will produce a different type of child and for all we know one that is liable of multiple handicaps for adaptation, given our social organization and needs."[15]

The toddler's most challenging developmental "task" is the acquisition of bowel and bladder control. This, as Philippe Muller observes in The Tasks of Childhood, constitutes a double challenge.[16] He must substitute voluntary control for a reflex activity — and must submit to social control a source of intimate satisfaction. How this feat is accomplished will powerfully affect his sense of self. If toilet training becomes a battleground, if it is accompanied by shame and punishment and repeated failures, the child may feel baffled, resentful, diminished, betrayed by his own body. If on the other hand, he is lovingly supported in this learning, he approaches the next tasks, as Muller says, "with a certain feeling of autonomy." So adult consistency in this area is vitally important — a consistency hard to achieve if toilet training is divided between parents and day caretakers. Interviews with working mothers around the United States reveal, not surprisingly, evidence of frustration and anxiety.[17] Here's a mother determined not to push — but the day care centre policy is to toilet train together all children of a certain age. Here's a family care mother teaching a small boy to urinate outside, and another spanking for accidents. Here's a centre declining to support a mother's training efforts with her two-year-old, though the child has already achieved considerable success. In a reverse situation, the centre says *training pants* when a harassed mother prefers the convenience of diapers. In all these situations, the child receives, in a crucial life area, mixed signals.

The toddler fears and mistrusts strangers — he is absolutely not a team player. Driven as he is by passionate impulse — "I want!" "Mine!" — he is unapt for groups. But the day care setting requires, to prevent chaos, some degree of regimentation. There is a time for juice and a time for pottying; there is no time to finish a puzzle or a picture if the schedule says "Now we go out to play." All this is frustrating and mysterious. It is true, of course, that at home too the child must at times conform, against his will, to family rules or simply to his mother's moods. The important difference, as Otto Weininger points out, is that home interruptions and limitations "usually do make some immediate practical sense which the child can perceive, and which are crucial in teaching the give-and-take, compromise patterns necessary for life in families and in society." The imperatives of a day care program make so such sense to him, and they cannot, in the nature of the situation, be adjusted to *his* rhythms. Some children like long naps and some like short naps and some don't like naps at all, but in the centre all naps are a prescribed length. The young child will, in time, learn to conform to the rules of group life (the survival instinct is strong) but surface conformity frequently conceals a lack of emotional and intellectual readiness. In a group situation normal playfulness and spontaneity may be labelled "uncooperative" and be repressed in the interests of disciplined order. The bright, imaginative, lively two-year-old is in this context a problem; parents may be informed that he's hyperactive.

The basic life-task of the pre-school child is the achievement of autonomy — that is, not just separateness but *confident* separateness. Playing or working (at this age, they are the same), he moves towards the condition of the astronaut who carries his own oxygen supply. The caretaker's job, then — to carry the image a bit further — is readying him for life in space, accustoming him to the novelty of weightlessness and the blast-off stress. This can only occur if the child is given considerable freedom to explore, experiment — and take risks.

Abraham Maslow describes the process of human development as an ongoing tension between the desire for safety and the desire for growth. "Every human being," he writes, "has both sets of forces within him. One set clings to safety and defensiveness out of fear, tending to regress backward, hanging on to the past, afraid to grow away from the [mother], afraid to take chances, afraid to jeopardize what he already has, afraid of independence, freedom and separateness. The other set of forces impels him forward toward wholeness of self and uniqueness of self, toward full functioning of all his capacities, toward confidence in the face of the external world at the same time that he can accept his deepest, real, unconscious Self."[18] The child at home, with a loving patient mother who understands his needs, extends his capacities and his daring in the course of everyday domestic life. His mother knows when he's ready to chop apples with a not-too-sharp knife; watching but not interfering, she accepts the risk of a cut finger. That's a small price to pay for the freedom to venture and to grow in a sense of accomplishment. She watches him struggle to hold the kitten — which may scratch. He will learn, on his own, something about holding kittens. She allows him to push a chair up to the counter, then climb on the chair to reach a cupboard for his special cup. She lets him find his own playthings and games as he follows her about the house. Ultimately he will learn that brooms are for sweeping. Meantime, he's free to ride the broom, to push it for a pretend lawn-mower or to use it as a source of straws. In the day care setting, free exploration of this sort is constrained by the artificiality of a child-oriented world and by the caretaker's role as teacher-custodian. Keeping small charges safe is, understandably, a high priority here; nobody wants to send a child home with bandaged finger. It is also sadly true that day care personnel often see their job as teaching children how to do things *the right way*, a notion which leads to intrusiveness and may cut off creative exploration. Here, for instance, in a commercial centre, a three-year-old has taken out the block tower — vari-coloured nesting cylinders of graduated size designed to fit each other in predetermined ways.

> Caretaker: That's a baby toy. Why don't you get a puzzle?
>
> Child, without responding, shakes out the cylinders and begins what is clearly an experiment. She takes the small cylinders as a base, proceeds — very delicately — to balance the large ones on top. It's a new, challenging game.
>
> Caretaker: Oh, you've got it all wrong. The big one goes on the bottom . . . (demonstrating) Then the yellow one . . . Now, which one comes next?
>
> Child, in a fit of temper, kicks over the tidy correct tower.
>
> Caretaker: That's very naughty. Pick up the blocks and put them back on the shelf just the way you found them. And get yourself a nice puzzle.

The only lesson learned here is that the safe way is the adult way. Do what you're told.

In their sensitive observation of British day nurseries, Caroline Garland and Stephanie White distinguish two kinds of independence.[19] There's the obvious kind involving physical care: children in a group facility are encouraged to go to the toilet and wash their hands unaided, to blow their noses, to dress and undress themselves, to set or clear a table and put away their toys. This constitutes a very limited kind of independence — the adult's rather than the child's, since it frees the adult from prosaic caretaking tasks. Adults most diligent in promoting this physical independence, Garland and White observe, "reacted with dismay to a search for a different kind of independence — that involving choice, decision, and eventually autonomy." The child's sought-after freedom is of a different order. It's freedom to play with whom, when and how he chooses — or not to play at all. "Routes towards this goal must inevitably involve exploration, and the discovery of one's own as well as the adult's limits." They are difficult to pursue in a group, under the constraints of a fixed schedule, and in the care of someone other than mother who has seven or eight other children to control.

The problems of toddlers in groups are legion. Unreasonable, unpredictable, at times all but unmanageable, the toddler really needs the attention of one devoted, humorous, infinitely flexible adult. "Adults having such qualities are, in our experience, especially hard to find," *The Challenge of Daycare* notes.[20] It's not that the two-year-old is someone only a mother can love: he's enchanting, terrific, as well as terrible. But it may well be that he's someone only a mother (or father) can live with happily. Toddlers are just old enough to fear that their consignment to surrogate care constitutes rejection and may indeed be punishment. Intensely egocentric, they are unapt for group play. Some push, snatch, hit. Others, the timid ones, are pushed and hit and snatched from, a situation unhealthy for both aggressor and victim. In a large group some pre-schoolers learn how to fight their way to the top of the heap; others retreat to the edges, where they may stand unnoticed, clutching blanket or bear, while life swirls by. Penelope Leach concludes her survey of such problems with a categorical imperative: "No form of group care is appropriate for toddlers."[21]

Supporters of early day care complain that home care advocates employ false, sentimental contrasts: the coldness of centres as compared with the warmth of Mom's kitchen or the regimentation of group situations in contrast to Mother's stimulating creative play. Sandra Scarr, author of *Mother Care/Other Care*, scornfully dismisses "the glowing legend of all those happy mothers at home, baking cookies and singing as they do the dishes."[22] Fair enough. It's true that lots of mothers buy their cookies at the supermarket, are more involved with soap operas than with Tinkertoys and complain bitterly as they do the dishes. It may even be true, as social psychologist Lois Hoffman claims, that the average fulltime mother spends less than ten minutes per day playing or reading to a pre-school child.[23] None of this alters the basic reality that in one case the child is at home, in familiar surroundings with his own possessions and his own mother somewhere about. In the other, the child spends most of his day — eight to ten hours, an unimaginably long stretch of time for some young children — in an other-care setting with other-caretakers whom he must share with other needy children. At home with a busy or indifferent mother, the child may be bored but not, probably, stressed. The very activity of a quality centre may be too much for under-threes. Here is the director of a highly rated New York day care facility: "We focus on education and development. Often children spend all day at home — but half the time the parent may be in the next room or watching TV. Here, the children's time is always occupied, their development is always being fostered."[24]

Always occupied, always having one's development fostered, from 8 A.M. to 6 P.M. Imagine.

Part 2

The Options

Chapter V

The Kinds of Care

The Day Care Centre

"Let's assume that all types of child care are available to you and that money is no problem," researchers at the University of Regina proposed in a recent opinion survey. "Given that situation, what type of arrangement would you prefer for your children?"[1] Most parents with children aged between nineteen months and five years said they'd choose a day care centre. A *Family Circle* survey of 10,000 American parents found a similar bias: forty-four percent thought group care was the best choice for pre-schoolers.[2]

This widespread preference for centre care is not hard to understand. To most working parents, the centre represents stability. "Barring sudden death or a national emergency, I absolutely *have* to get to my job, five days a week, nine to five," a single mother says. "So I can't trust any arrangement that depends on just one other person, whether it's a sitter or a family day care mother." The centre offers other kinds of reassurance too. If it's licensed and government-approved, parents assume superior care. The presence of a sizeable staff, a supervisor, a regular schedule of activities and, in a good centre, supplementary health and whole-family services — these contribute to parents' feeling, when they drop off the kids on the way to work, "That's taken care of. They're in good hands."

Day care centres come in many sizes and types. The commercial centre is a for-profit operation, usually but not always licensed; it may be a single, privately owned facility or part of a large franchise operation. Not-for-profit centres include: co-operatives, directed and partially staffed by parents; workplace centres, on-site child care provided by employers under some kind of subsidy arrangement; community centres run by the local boards of charitable organizations, social agencies or churches; public centres, licensed, owned and operated by a municipal, state or provincial government. In the United States about nine percent of day care centres receive direct government funding. In Canada the proportion is about eight percent. Only Ontario and Alberta maintain publicly owned day care centres. The Canadian government, under CAP (the Canada Assistance Plan), shares fifty percent of day care costs with the provinces for families considered to be "in need." Families who meet qualifications for social assistance benefits after taking a "needs" or "income" test — or a combination of the two (depending on the provincial government's requirements) — may apply for a subsidy towards day care costs.

For all others, the only federal assistance takes the form of an annual tax deduction of up to $2,000 per child to a maximum of four children and a modest child care tax credit. In the view of day care activists, this makes good day care "financially accessible only to the fairly affluent and to those poor enough to qualify for subsidy." So day care remains essentially a welfare service. In the United States subsidy arrangements are more available and more various; the states set their own qualifying standards. There is a federal income tax child care credit and, in some states, an additional child care tax credit.

In spite of organization differences between types of centre care — and individual differences within a single type — centres have a good deal in common. They open and close at fixed hours: from 7 A.M. or 8 A.M., as a rule, to 6 P.M. All are literally child-centred: physical facilities are especially designed or adapted for child needs, and the staff's chief occupation is child care. (Contrast this with the family care mother, cooking and cleaning her own house while caring for young charges.) If licensed, they have presumably met at least minimum standards regulating physical plant, staff/child ratio, nutrition, safety and fire law precautions. Most — not all — employ trained caregivers. Most profess to offer some kind of program that fosters intellectual development. Most have more toys, books, games and outdoor equipment than the child has access to at home. Some offer unusual freedom to explore.[3] All, by virtue of their nature, offer a social experience, in small doses valuable even for the very young. Day care advocates claim that at the centre the child learns to play, to share, to get along with others — and to rely on adults other than family members. Presumably, then, the centre care pre-school child is less likely to be lonely, isolated, bored.

Some of these apparent advantages are double-edged. Because the centre opens and closes at fixed times, it presents problems for parents who work irregular hours, or who might on occasion be kept late on the job. It is always open at prescribed times, but will not necessarily accept the child who's sniffling or looks feverish. Parents who use centre care must be prepared with back-up arrangements for emergencies. Precisely *because* it's child-centred, it places the child in an artificial environment, isolating him from the real world where lots of fascinating things go on that have nothing to do with him. As for licensing — it is in fact no guarantee of quality; without adequate funds official ratios and training requirements can't be enforced. Cut-backs in government funding affect every aspect of centre management. Old furniture and equipment are not replaced, important repairs are not made. When staff is laid off, vacancies remain unfilled; college graduates hired to work with children double as cooks and cleaners. Rock-bottom salaries (as low as $677 a month in 1981) mean that individuals with dependents can't afford to stay on. The resulting high turnover rate — in Toronto in 1979, for example, fifty percent a year — disrupts personal relationships and the whole program operation.[4]

Centre programs tend to be standardized, not adapted to perhaps erratic individual needs, and schedules may be rigid. The social experience may be too much, over-stimulating and tiring, for the young child who spends an entire day in the buzz. Some day care children spend ten hours away from home. That is a terribly long time for anyone, doubly strainful for a child who will experience, during that period, several changes of caretakers. Maybe these children are not lonely, but many must long for quiet and a private space.

Non-Profit Community or Government-Sponsored Centres
Ideal day care, says an urban studies expert, "should of course care for and protect our children; it should connect the child's worlds of home and day care; it should provide an environment that fosters his development with a sense of self, self-worth and security, and his ability to get what he wants and needs from the environment around him; and one which stimulates and develops his cognitive and sensory abilities."[5] This is a large order. Given the resources available in the real world, few centres can realize all these desirable goals. Some very superior ones, however, offer an inspiriting vision of what's possible in a less-than-ideal world.

Victoria Day Care Services in Toronto is one of three centres operated by The United Way. In 1984 it served 143 families, of whom only 27 were full-fee paying families that might be described as traditional: "two parent, non-adolescent non-newcomer families not in need of extra resources." The rest consisted of single parents (almost half the number), recent immigrants, adolescent parents or families whose limited means qualified them for public assistance. In addition to caring for the children of these core families, Victoria also supervises 75 family day care homes, a job which includes not only placement but also a provider training program (everything from emergency first aid to language development and infant learning through play). Because of its many new-immigrant families (from 30 different countries) the centre makes a special effort to relieve the stress and anxiety of families adjusting to a strange world. Staff members see their heterogeneous community as an opportunity to broaden their understanding of differences in child-rearing patterns and cultural behaviours: the Pakistani image of a "good" child is different from the Chinese, from the Jamaican, from the Rumanian. Even menus are composed with an eye to the group's various traditions. Middle Eastern curry and yoghurt, Caribbean yams, are featured along with Canada's hamburgers. In addition to helping new Canadians adjust to a new culture, this sensitive approach to difference enriches the experience and awareness of *all* centre children. "Everybody don't use forks," a four-year-old explained earnestly. "Some kids use fingers and some kids use tortillas, because that's how they do it."

Victoria's staff is well paid (by day care standards): from $16,000 to $20,000 a year, as compared with an average $9,000. A natural happy consequence is low turnover; in one typical year, two out of seventeen workers took maternity leave, four others moved away. So centre children, centre *families*, have a real chance to form bonds with their caretaker. To cement the family connection and promote the best possible child care, there's a fulltime worker whose job is to connect centre and home. "If our goal is healthy development of the child," says family worker Mary Ellen McDonough, "then we must concern ourselves with stable family life." McDonough takes part in the interviews which precede every admission. Where was this child born? What is his position in the family? Any health problems? How are his relationships with siblings, other children? Have the parents any special concerns? She gets to know each family, keeping an eye on problems (is Mother's boy friend competing with the children?) and finding each parent's special strength. Whatever concerns the family concerns her: she locates scarce housing, instructs families how to proceed against an exploiting landlord, helps with budgeting. Above all, she provides guidance in the family's life with the centre child. If a mother from an early-dry background worries that her toddler is still in diapers, the family worker can provide reassuring explanations of normal child development. (*Late* is not bad or retarded. It's just later than some.) When a parent reports eating problems, she suggests things to try. "Put just *one* bean on his plate" or "Have you offered vegetables from the cabbage family? Here at the centre, he loves broccoli." From her office near the front door, McDonough can see arriving and departing parents, observe signs of stress or change. If a normally well-put-together young woman comes in bedraggled and puffy-eyed, the family worker makes a tactful approach. Over a cup of coffee, the problem may emerge: a lost job, an impending divorce. In that case, the family worker becomes a guide to community resources: free legal aid, unemployment insurance, emergency child care, whatever. "Our primary concern is with the child, yes," McDonough says. "He's close to his mother's moods and feelings. If she's depressed, he may be abused. Everything that has to do with family life has to do with this child."

Sometimes it's the worker who spots a problem and must alert parents — again, tactfully, in a non-threatening way. Working class families, particularly when they've had experience with welfare agencies, are often ill at ease with middle class professionals who "think they know all about what's good for kids and how they're supposed to act."[6] So the family worker intimates gently her unease about this four-year-old. He doesn't seem able to follow directions, can't play happily on the playground, strikes out with his fists when frustrated, cries easily . . . The centre would like to call in a psychological consultant — for assessment only. There'll be vision and hearing examinations, some general testing. "We're looking for more information, help. We won't do anything without your permission. The specialist will tell us what he thinks, and then you make the decision." By this process a child might be referred for play therapy or speech therapy. Or he might, with parents' consent, be placed in a family day care home where he'll get appropriate individual attention.

Because Victoria is a medium-size centre with a good staff/child ratio (infants and toddlers, one to five and two-and-a-half to five, one to eight), individual attention remains the not impossible dream. Except where a child's needs are so special that they can't be served in a group setting, the centre makes extraordinary efforts to adapt. Take the matter of meals. One cook, eighty-three children — but the cook will see to it that Kevin, who's allergic to corn and dairy products, will get a peanut butter sandwich when the other kids are eating cheese; that Rivka will be served specially slaughtered kosher meat; while Sharin, from a vegetarian commune, will never be offered foods containing meat. Staff members try to follow generally approved centre guidelines without offending individual family values. "When a parent says 'The world is a jungle. My kid has to fight his own battles,' we say 'I understand. But here we don't allow hitting.' Then we try to suggest ways of helping a child control his aggression — giving him a pillow to hit, or maybe giving him time out from the group until he's ready to come back and be friends."

This kind of connecting home with day care is the heart of a good centre program. "We are not taking the place of parents," director Renee Edwards says. "We care for children while their parents are absent — we try to help parents with their job as caretakers." Adolescent mothers and recent immigrants learn from coming to the centre how to play with children and how to cope with tantrums; they pick up new ideas about family management. They become familiar with child development norms. The centre posts assessment goals regularly, without age limits, to give an idea of usual patterns. (For infant-toddler gross motion development, say: "Lifts head and upper chest without supporting on elbows or hands . . . Rolls from back to stomach . . . Crawls on all fours . . . Moves holding on to furniture . . . Stands alone.") Above all, parents get from the centre, as the children do, a feeling of being supported as they find their own strengths.

This is a real, good centre operating with the usual practical-financial constraints in the real world. More typical is the centre where the caretaker-child ratio exceeds the legal limit, where an underpaid staff changes constantly, where safety and sanitary provisions are casual and children are either regimented or left to wander aimlessly. For a glance at the possible-ideal, there is the plan proposed by Action Day Care for universally accessible, publicly funded day care in Canada. This model features as its hub a "neighbourhood resource centre" offering all-day group care, health care, a half-day nursery school, a parent-child drop-in centre, a toy lending service and an education centre for both parents and providers. Radiating out from this core, like spokes from a wheel, would be allied services: emergency care for sick children or families in crisis, supervised private home care, workplace day care, overnight care for children of shift workers, support for parents at home with children. Almost everyone agrees this would be splendid. Everyone, including the proponents, knows it would cost a great deal — approximately ten times, in public funds, what is presently spent on day care. Which means that the scheme, however noble, has no bearing on the decisions of parents who have young children *now*.

Commercial Centres

"Kinder-Care knows that you want the very best for your pre-schooler," says an advertisement for North America's largest commercial day care chain (750 centres in the United States and Canada). The promise is seductive: nutritious meals ("prepared under the supervision of our nationally recognized dietician"), the finest educational and recreational equipment available, specially trained staff, an individualized curriculum designed to promote intellectual, social and emotional development . . . All this and tender loving care, at a bargain price — in 1985 an average $80 per week, as compared with $100-$125 per week for a non-profit centre. *How do they do it?*

The answer to that question depends on whom you ask.

President Perry Mendel says the secret is efficiency, know-how, along with the huge savings made possible by standard-ization and mass marketing. Certainly, when it comes to marketing, Kinder-Care knows how. The already familiar buildings — orange tile steeple with black plastic bell — are located in young-family suburban areas "on the morning side of the street" (to simplify drop-off on the way to work) or in large apartment complexes. Frankly not an educator but a businessman (with early experience in real estate and auto parts), Mendel enthusiastically applies to child care the mer-chandising techniques of the fast-food chains (a comparison he welcomes). "Kinder-Care is going to take its place along with chains like Holiday Inn, Howard Johnson's and McDonald's," he predicted in 1978. These hopes have been abundantly realized, both in the expansion of his empire — absorbing competing chains like Mini-Skool and Living and Learning — and in soaring profits. In 1983 the company had revenues of $116 million and earned $14 million in profits; in five years its earnings per common share rose more than 700 percent. Public pronouncements play down the economies which produce such results, focusing rather on Kinder-Care's triumphant march towards ever greener pastures. "I look upon Kinder-Care eventually as a great mail-order business," the president says. Children are, among other things, con-sumers. With a steady eye on his captive market, Mendel already sells, through centres, Kindersuits, Kindercaps, Kinderbibs (no consumer too young) and Kinderlife-insurance policies, cradle to grave. "We're two or three years from the numbers it would take to allow us to go into marketing merchandise. I just can't push the calendar up fast enough."[7]

Women's groups, unions and day care activists take a dim view of these exciting goings-on — particularly when a com-mercial chain applies for a share of tax dollars. The central charge against Kinder-Care is that the company amasses pro-fits at the expense of workers and, ultimately, the children it professes to serve. Salaries at Kinder-Care satellites are almost universally lower than those paid by not-for-profit centres. They represent forty percent of total operating costs, as compared with eighty to eighty-five percent in non-profit centres. Both American and Canadian Kinder-Care centres start workers at or near the minimum wage. In 1983 striking workers at a Mississauga, Ontario Mini-Skool (just before its absorption by Kinder-Care) were paid $4.08 an hour, fifty-eight cents above the minimum wage. Meanwhile, unionized day care workers in Metro Toronto were being paid $9.28 to $10.26 an hour. One striking worker reported that the company's rock-bottom wages were not always forthcoming; on days when enrolment fell, she was sent home. The guaranteed minimum of four hours, pay daily was often not produced unless she pressed for it.[8]

An almost inevitable result of depressed salaries is depressed workers and high staff turnover. Since "specially trained" caregivers are not usually available for the cost of a short-order cook, Kinder-Care takes what it can get. In 1977 a company executive claimed that maybe a third of his people had "a degree" and the rest "some education."[9] It is, of course, perfectly possible that a worker without a degree may give superlative care. It is not likely that *anyone* gives superlative care on near-starvation wages in a situation where, as frequently in commercial centres, the proportion of caretakers to children is very low. Kinder-Care has lobbied everywhere to reduce legal standards for day care centres (they want more kinder per carer), and critics claim that existing standards are ignored.[10] During the Mississauga strike a worker reported that two staff members were assigned to twenty-five pre-schoolers. (Legal limit: one to eight.) "It's hard to supply quality care," she observed, "when you spend all your time trying to stop the kids from killing each other."[11]

And sometimes — when there's not enough staff or competent staff — the unthinkable occurs. In 1983 a five-year-old was killed at a Woburn Kinder-Care centre when a storage

cubicle fell on her as she napped, causing massive head in-
juries.[12] Various parents interviewed after the disaster insisted that no, they would not withdraw their children from
the centre. Where else could they go? "It was a terrible, terrible accident," one mother said. "It could have happened any
place, any time." Investigating authorities thought otherwise.
An emergency order from the Massachusetts State Office for
Children, requiring the company to hire a *qualified* co-
director immediately — and to bolt down all storage cubbies
— noted that this was not a freak accident (any place, any
time). The cubbies were not adequately supported, were not
anchored and were positioned perilously close to sleeping
children. On three previous occasions a cubbie had fallen
over — in one instance, breaking a table-top when a child's
tantrum set up toppling vibrations. "The director knew, or
should have known that the cubbies posed a hazard. The
director and staff failed to exercise good judgment to protect
the health and safety of children in the center by failing to
take immediate action." Meantime, Kinder-Care's national
director of public relations, queried about the company's staff
and safety requirements, responded, "We have expressed
very sincere sympathy and compassion to the family. We are
not going to make any statement at this time." In the ensuing
publicity it was revealed that the State Department of Social
Services, which arranges day care for children under its protection, had some months previously dropped its contract
with the Woburn centre (and others in the state) because of
"programmatic concerns." Though the meaning of this
opaque charge was never spelled out, a department source in-
timated that the basic concern was high staff turnover.

In addition to practical issues like turnover and caretaker-
child ratio, critics of the commercial chains raise the larger
concern of standardization and its effects. To make a profit,
to keep shareholders as happy as they are now (eighty-seven
cents-a-share dividend in 1981), Kinder-Care must sell the
same product in Kentucky and California — and in Canada

too, where the company operates sixteen centres, mostly in Alberta and Ontario. So there's no question of adapting to individual or community needs or of soliciting parent preferences. (The official view is that working parents are too busy for that sort of thing — and alas, it may be correct.) So the same learning kit goes out to every centre in America — a collection of mostly busywork activities designed for children from two-and-half to six, the idea being that caretakers will make necessary adaptations according to age. Daily menus are dispatched from the central office, as are weekly and monthly program activities. Of course individual variations occur, as in all things human: caring for children is not like turning out hamburgers. But the aim is uniformity and the result, inevitably, a dampening down of creativity and enterprise. The children are — have to be — *managed.* A *Chicago Tribune* writer comments on the likely effect of child-care-as-big-business: "Over and over, anecdotes from observers report that children are kept in groups, herded from one line at the swings, to another for juice and crackers. As one psychologist puts it, maybe no one in these centres tries to teach children anything, but that doesn't keep them from learning a lot: conformity, submissiveness, passivity and hostility."[13]

But the commercial centres are thriving, the fastest growing section of day care. In the United States, they constitute about one-third of available centre care, with chains like Kinder-Care, Mary Moppet, Children's World and La Petite Academy in the lead. Kinder-Care currently handles about 100,000 "units" in forty-two states. (A "unit" is a child.) In Canada about forty percent of licensed day care spaces are found in run-for-profit operations. To be sure, not all of these are chains. Individually owned mom-and-pop centres often do a gallant job. So, it appears, do some off-beat franchise operations. Ellen Galinsky, a teacher at the Bank Street College of Education, describes one such exception, the Children's World Center at Mesa, Colorado Springs, where children learn and play freely in surroundings of great natural beauty.[14]

Do parents distinguish between routine and imaginative caretaking? Are they sensitive to the difference between child care as business and child care as vocation, even dedication? Not always. When Donna Lero, a professor of family studies at the University of Guelph (Ontario) interviewed working mothers about their child care choice, she found very little shopping around. Forty percent of those using centres simply chose one they'd heard about. Of the remaining sixty percent, almost half visited a single centre and chose that; less than one-quarter made any real attempt to compare offerings. In general, Lero found little awareness of the difference between private and non-profit day care.[15]

The answer appears to be that, in a stress situation, people do what they can. Take a family with young children and two working parents or one parent (working). The need for care arises, maybe suddenly. Aunt Gertrude just said *No more*, or the family day care mother got sick. They rush out to look. And there stands a handsome new building of familiar design — broadloom on the floor, playground asphalt barely dry. (Commercial chains tend to put their money where it shows, in buildings. Equipment, on the other hand, is frequently stinted — as much as thirty percent less outlay per child.) There are brochures, logos, perhaps an expensive gimmick to charm the innocent — a model cow that moos, numbered squares that light up when a child steps on them. Everything looks efficient and clean and safe. They sign on. They try not to worry. ("I'm very comfortable here," said a parent at the Woburn Kinder-Care days after the fatal accident. "These people have done wonderful things for the children." Other voices: "I don't have any qualms about bringing my son back." "Kids can get hurt at home.") Certainly parents are not likely to ask themselves whether a business set up for profit is going to put children first. So the experts deliver their opinions — "I have never seen a franchised run-for-profit infant or toddler program that I felt was truly good, nor have I read about one in any reliable source"[16] — and the parents do what they can.

Some centres defy classification. Often run by graduates of Early Childhood programs, they are not subsidized, neither are they commercial in the usual sense. The directors draw a salary, hope to make expenses with a bit over, work hard just to make ends meet. The centres are usually small (from twenty to sixty children) and — since there are easier ways to make money — tend to be run by genuinely idealistic individuals. William and Wendy Dreskin, authors of *The Day Care Decision*, started their first pre-school centre with a hope of transforming society from the inside, building on the openness and honesty of the young. In the face of rising costs, without the savings made possible by large-scale operations, it is hard to make a go of such ventures. Rent, taxes, utilities, salaries, equipment, insurance, food . . . Where are profits to come from? Unless they raise fees to an almost prohibitive level, small operators must skimp on food, play equipment — and staff. The choice may be between lowering program quality (fewer caretakers, poorly paid and overworked) and bankruptcy.

Co-operative Centres

Because the essence of the co-operative is volunteer work, it seldom meets the needs of parents with nine-to-five commitments. (When are they to help out with the children or sand the floor?) Early co-opers, in the 1970s, tended to be students with left-wing sympathies, and students still constitute the bulk of co-op families. Co-op day care is also possible for parents who work part time or have flexible hours. More than any other day care arrangement, the co-operative is fuelled by a central philosophy focused equally on parents *and* children: sharing, social commitment, love, peace and mutual support. The typical co-op is very much a group of kindred spirits against the system (which it defines as regimentation, sexism, materialism, racism, competition). So there are lots of meetings (often, one parent reports, "going nowhere"), lots of family occasions. Reflecting group beliefs, programs are generally open and free; "structured" is a dirty word here. Food is either brought from home or prepared on the premises by a cook who works miracles with soya beans and tofu. (Most co-ops have a high vegetarian component.) Discipline emphasizes independent problem-solving. Writing in *Good Day Care* about his experiences with a University of Toronto co-operative, a father admits that the group was obliged to relinquish its dream of letting kids work out disputes without adult interference. In actual practice the kids fought it out — and the boys, generally bigger, stronger than the girls, ended up winning. So what had started as an egalitarian non-sexist idea "that boy and girl children should be encouraged to solve their own problems turned into a situation where the children's behaviour was worse than the social norm we had tried to change."[17]

Other co-op dreams frequently fall by the wayside in real life. Despite an official requirement of equal work-sharing between male and female volunteers, the women tend to cook, diaper and clean while the men rough-house or fix broken chairs. Some parents are distressingly casual about their responsibilities, with the result that the centre is understaffed at times. "There are always more people who want to play guitar or plan demonstrations than to do the dishes," says a former co-op parent. Disputes are common. One element will be all for social adjustment, getting kids to share, while another pushes for academic preparation. Some see the co-op as a place to raise children free from sexual hangups, others want to concentrate on peace and nuclear disarmament. The co-op is almost always a lively place, generating a certain cheerful chaos. It's not every parent's cup of tea.

Very few co-operatives are pure co-op, staffed only by

parents; those which come into existence are usually small and short-lived. More typical is the arrangement involving one or more hired staff (not necessarily the Early Childhood Education variety) and a rotating group of parent aides. Parents play a major role in centre policy. They decide admissions criteria, choose teachers, monitor health and safety requirements, consult on menus and raise funds. They *are* the centre — a fact which makes for both the strength and the weakness of co-ops. Since children seldom stay more than three years at a centre, the turnover of parents is constant — with predictable effects on policy and practice. One model co-op, The Family Centre at Bank Street College of Education in New York, attempts to meet this problem by requiring that new admissions be children under one year of age; that way, the parents will have three years to learn co-op ropes. The steering committee, responsible for major decisions like hiring and firing, always includes at least one parent of a very young child; this ensures smooth transitions and a consistent direction.[18]

One problem, really insoluble, with co-op centres is the confusion introduced by volunteer care. When each parent helps out for just a few hours, one or two days a week, children are exposed to a constantly changing parade of faces, voices and caretaking styles. Co-op enthusiasts say it's good for them to know and relate to many different adults, and in the long run that's true. But before a child can trust many, he must know and trust one in a close, ongoing relationship. In a busy catch-as-catch-can co-op, that single necessary bond may be lacking, as the child passes from hand to hand. There will be, too, considerable variations in the sureness of those hands. Being good with one's own offspring is no assurance of doing well with someone else's. As for those occasions when the child's own parent is present and helping, that's mostly confusing. Why is Mom here today and gone tomorrow? Why is Dad playing with the other kids and not me? These are troubling questions for a pre-schooler.

Depending on the amount of volunteer work provided by parents, co-ops tend to have lower fees than other kinds of centre care. But they cost a lot in time and energy. A single mother who took her son out of a co-op after the first year says, "Liam really loved the place. I did too. The group had a warm, supportive feeling, like family. But I couldn't manage all those meetings — sitters two nights a week, sometimes while we argued over whether we should serve chicken or who would take the kids to the zoo. In the long run I just didn't have the energy. I work hard, I have a long day. I want to drop my son off at a centre and feel that nothing will be required of me beyond paying the fees and picking him up on time."

Day Care in the Churches

Surveys of available centre care have, up to now, ignored a major source, one might almost say an underground, of child care services — the programs sponsored by local parishes. In church basements and empty meeting rooms across the land, thousands of children have been cared for since the beginnings of the women's back-to-work movement. Only with the National Council of Churches' extensive survey (1981-1982) did it become apparent that about one-third of all churches provide or allow some sort of day care on their premises and that church-housed programs probably constitute the largest group of day care providers in the nation.[19] This extraordinary development, a true grass roots phenomenon, is not the result of any church hierarchy decision. Indeed, one of the notable features of day care in the churches is the total lack of central organization or coordination. What has happened, repeatedly, is that a local church responds to a local need. The churches of a Montana resort community with high unemployment banded together to provide full-day child care during the short tourist season when jobs were available. A New Jersey congregation offers care fourteen hours a day, six days a week for the three months during which berry and corn crops are harvested. An Oklahoma City parish uses a volunteer staff to offer "respite care" for mentally retarded and emotionally disturbed children. A Florida church enlists elderly men as grandfather-caretakers. A rural church in the Rocky Mountains foothills gathers up the small children of cherry pickers (they used to be left in cars, from 4 A.M. on, while parents were in the orchards) and takes them to the church for supervised play and a hot noontime meal. In this haphazard fashion good Samaritan impulses have built up a network of child care services across the country. Sometimes the congregation itself runs a program, sometimes (roughly half the time) the church acts as benevolent landlord to an independent group.

Why have the churches become so deeply involved in child care? The physical, practical reasons are obvious. As a major property owner, the church has available space. During the lively construction era (the 1960s), many churches added classrooms, parish halls and all-purpose rooms. Facilities originally designed for Sunday school have child-sized fittings — the chairs, tables, toys and changing tables essential for child care programs. Start-up costs are greatly reduced because the church already has, in addition to equipment, insurance and garbage collection. The church's tax-exempt status lowers operating costs. Finally, most important, churches have traditionally been located in the heart of their communities, either close to public transportation or along main roads. Churches are easy to get to.

Beyond reasons of convenience lies the social, moral impulse sometimes called "mission theology." This embraces not just a commitment to Christian education, but a wider concern with social justice and community service. As a New Jersey pastor wrote, explaining to the National Council of Churches his congregation's decision to provide child care: "It is a part of our sense of being good neighbors. We want to offer our neighbors help in any way we can. Right now they need a place for their day care center."

Asked about goals, church centres overwhelmingly cite a desire to provide love and warmth, along with basic care, for the children of working parents. Also high on the list are independence/self-reliance, positive self-image and sharing/co-operation. Interestingly enough, both school preparation and spiritual development are way down the list, in seventh place. Few programs include specifically religious material; ninety-nine percent of the church-sponsored centres are open to all members of the community, regardless of race or religious belief. There is a widespread effort to serve lower-income families by offering scholarships and a sliding fee scale.

By the usual criteria of quality, church-sponsored centres rate high. Fully eighty-seven percent of the directors hold college degrees — well above the national average; over ninety-one percent of the teachers have had some training in early childhood development. Group size is kept low, usually under eighteen children, and the adult/child ratio is generous (ninety percent of centres report ratios between one to two and one to six).

The church's problems in offering quality child care are, by and large, those of all centres. Money is number one. "Quality day care that provides salaries that insure stability and a decent quality of life to staff is a hard juggling act," writes a Massachusetts centre. An Iowa group, reporting that they have never turned down a child, expresses a special concern: "It is difficult to keep the tuition down so that the lower-middle class can take advantage of our program. We have felt this is the 'neglected class.' " Qualified caretakers are scarce: "Low pay and high burnout are forcing many child care workers into other fields." Because church centres seem curiously cut off from the child care mainstream, there are many expressions of unease about inadequate knowledge or materials. There are the predictable difficulties with unsympathetic parishioners: "The older people don't want their church filled with little black children dirtying their church walls" and "The local church is fearful that the centre may cost the church money and is still waiting to see it fail although it's in its fifth year." A typical, very current problem comes from parents with some basic misconceptions about the role of pre-school child care: "We face constant pressure to push kids faster and faster into formal sit-down reading and writing activities." In spite of these strains, in spite of government cuts in subsidies and food programs, the church centres clearly experience a gratifying sense of accomplishment. "For many of our children, we are the only stable thing in their lives, and the food they get from us is all they may get." "We are training the children to work with groups and to give and take successfully." "We are offering quality child care to all age groups in a rural environment where this has never been a concern, making the community aware of the specific needs of infants, toddlers, preschool-age children."

Workplace Day Care

When General Mills conducted its 1980 nation-wide survey of double-income families, eighty-seven percent of both parents and labour leaders and eighty-six percent of social workers endorsed the principle of employer support for child care arrangements.[20] This figure suggests a surprising unanimity among groups with very different concerns. The employer's interest in workplace day care is practical-economic. On-site child care — not free, but subsidized — constitutes a major job attraction, particularly for women, who bear the major responsibility of caretaking arrangements. During the 1970s, for example, when nurses were in short supply, hospitals met the problem by providing round-the-clock care for staff children. In both Canada and the United States, hospitals continue to be major providers, accounting for approximately fifty percent of all work-related day care programs. Most offer on-site care. Toronto's Riverdale Hospital, for example, maintains a centre for its employees on the hospital grounds; it is open eight to eleven hours daily and cares for children three months to five years of age, at a fee somewhat below the going rates. The hospital assumes responsibility for food, accounting, housekeeping, laundry and general maintenance and also for small daily medical matters — the cut knee or sudden fever. Winnipeg's Health Sciences Day Nursery (Manitoba) began with space for eighty children in a nearby public school; with the help of government grants, it has taken over the entire building and accommodates 124 children, about fifteen percent of them infants. A special feature of this nursery is emergency care for the children of hospital patients.

Hope of attracting more female workers has always been the primary push behind employer-sponsored child care. Under ideal circumstances this motive may serve all parties well. During World War II, in order to meet heavy construction demands, the Kaiser Shipyards in Portland, Oregon hired 25,000 women and established a round-the-clock, 365-days-a-year centre to care for their children. Apart from its huge size (2,250 children in two complexes), the Kaiser centre was in many respects a model: a well-paid, thoroughly professionial staff; the best equipment available (everything from unbreakable juice glasses to easels and scooters); an infirmary staffed with fulltime nurses; provision for immunizations to save parents from time-consuming visits to the doctor; a special service room for temporary care of children not enrolled in the centre; carefully planned, nutritious meals and snacks. The centre even operated a pre-cooked food service: a worker could order her family's dinner in the morning, from a standard menu, then pick up the salmon loaf and avocado-lemon gelatin salad when she collected her child at day's end. The centre distributed a bi-weekly newspaper describing the children's activities, sent out booklets on child care, toy selection, holiday activities and shopping ideas. It maintained a lending library of children's books, at one time even ran a mending service. There were plans for a mother and infant dormitory, a shopping service, provision for haircuts and photographs. "We thought that anything that saved the working mother time and energy meant she would have more to give to her child," recalls James Hymes, Jr., who served as on-site manager.[21] With war's end, the centre closed. Nothing remotely like it has since appeared on the North American scene.

From an employer's point of view, workplace day care has to pay its way — if not in cash savings, at least in other more or less measurable respects. One large study recommends that companies subsidize their own day care centres only if they meet these three conditions: a large labour force located in one geographical area and utilizing about one thousand female employees; above average turnover and absenteeism costs; a continuing need to attract new recruits.[22]

Given the perennial difficulty of finding good child care, it is certainly true that women will give first consideration to firms which offer satisfactory arrangements and will think more than twice before moving to another job. "I could earn $50 more a week with another company," says a mother employed by a large insurance firm. "But I have three kids here at the centre. If I had to put them somewhere else, that money would be used up in no time." By cutting down on staff turnover, a company also reduces the costs of training employees — a saving which may more than compensate for the investment in workplace care. Intermedics, a Texas electronics firm, established its child care centre out of concern over high turnover. Since the company produces heart pacemakers and other medical devices involving precise workmanship, a stable and highly skilled work force is crucial. In 1979 the firm opened a child care centre four miles from the plant; its 260 places were filled on opening day. Serving children from six weeks to six years of age, weekdays from 7 A.M. to 6 P.M., the centre gets four-fifths of its funding from Intermedics; the balance comes from parent fees, a modest $25 per week in 1984. Within two years of the centre's opening, employee turnover was down sixty percent.[23] That dramatic improvement, plus greatly reduced absenteeism, saved the company during the same period some 30,000 work hours and two million dollars. Tardiness has gone down too; foremen hear fewer sad tales of the no-show babysitter or the day care provider's sick child. Considering that the child care centre costs just $500,000 per year (less employee payments), Intermedics would seem to have caught two birds with one stone, and its low paid jobs are now in great demand in spite of an isolated rural location which once discouraged applicants. In five years the firm has doubled in size (from 1,000 to 2,000 employees); plans are under way to build another centre to accommodate another 500 children. According to the child care centre director, the company is convinced that the centre "gives more benefit to the company per dollar than any other employee benefit."

Other benefits reported by firms which have instituted workplace care are an increase in the number of employees available for overtime and shift work (assuming an extended day care day) and the increased participation of women at all levels of the company. In a 1982 survey conducted by the National Employer-Supported Child Care Project, forty-nine percent of companies visited reported that provision of some kind of child care assistance had boosted productivity.[24] ("People using child care work harder and do better because they want to keep their jobs.") Some firms said they had fewer accidents, presumably because workers are happier, less anxious. (Stress over child care problems was identified as a factor in industrial accidents by forty female assembly line workers at a Toronto auto-workers' conference.)[25] The president of Neuville-Mobil Sox, a North Carolina hosiery mill, claims that its on-site child care centre has notably improved worker morale. "It adds an extra dimension to working. I think everybody is a little happier. The kids are around laughing and the mothers don't divorce themselves from their families during an eight-hour work period." At PCA, a North Carolina photography company, the child care centre is credited with the high work satisfaction reported in an employee opinion survey; parents using the centre ranked their job satisfaction at four out of a possible five. "Parents of a young child feel guilty if they must go to work," the centre director observes. "When they can see their child during the workday, it relieves some of the guilt and anxiety." Along with these very real gains, the employer who suffers the little children to come unto him enjoys a greatly enhanced public image and improved community relations. An official of an Illinois airline guides company, describing its on-site day nursery as "successful in all regards," notes particularly the fact that it has generated "a tremendous amount of free publicity. Those employees who have no need for the centre seem as enthusiastic about it as those who use it, and it has enhanced our image in the area as a progressive, employee-centered company."

Employee pride in a model centre is cited as one considerable dividend from Boston's Stride Rite development, opened in 1971 to provide child care for the shoe company's employees and the surrounding community. Costs are shared by the company, the Massachusetts Department of Public Welfare and the parents, who pay ten percent of their gross weekly salary for each child enrolled. The centre cares for about fifty children, maintains a permanent staff of ten mostly college educated men and women and gets a good deal of assistance from student volunteers. Staff turnover is minimal; the director says that the presence of a well-known, well-regarded child care facility helps "to recruit and retain stable, family-oriented people." The centre has access to all company facilities — the cafeteria, repair shops, accounting department, computers — and a bonanza of scrap material useful for crafts and building projects. (Cloth, leather, buckles, buttons, wood scraps, braid. . .) Parents are involved in both centre policy making and hands-on activity; the adventure playground was put together entirely by parents with lumber, rubber tires and hardware oddments donated by the plant and the community. What works for the families works for the company too. Stride Rite's president says, "This shouldn't be construed as do-gooderism or tokenism because it's really self-serving. There's a need for corporate management to begin to appreciate the economics of something like quality day care. Fifteen per cent of American households are below the poverty line, and if business can get them to contribute to the gross national product, business will benefit."

What about parents and children, the most important parties to this arrangement? Does workplace care work well for them? In theory the company centre eliminates usual caretaking hassles. To begin with, the child has somewhere to go, an assured place; that is an advantage not to be lightly dismissed, particularly where the child is an infant. He can travel to work along with parent or parents. (Some optimists see this as a possibility for more "quality time.") Perhaps he can have lunch with them. A nursing infant can be fed during breaks. Parents enjoy the knowledge that their family is near by; presumably they can talk to caregivers, keep close tabs on their children's development, become intimately familiar with their daily rhythms. The children, in turn, see and come to understand the parents' work. In an emergency mother or father is *right there*. Parents spend less time and money transporting children to various caregivers. Children can sleep in a little longer in the mornings, get home earlier and so have more time for play and family talk. On a loftier level there is always the hope, expressed by Toronto's Social Planning Council Task Force report, that "on site or near site day care can help to humanize the workplace. Parents and nonparents alike can be uplifted by the presence of children and the creation of a family atmosphere."[26]

All this sounds so good that the relatively small number of workplace centres comes as a surprise. Canada has never had more than a scattering — in 1984, about seventy, most of these in Ontario and Quebec and ninety percent associated with either hospitals or government agencies. In the United

States a 1984 report by the Bureau of National Affairs estimated that 1,000 employers were providing some form of
child care assistance to employees; most of this assistance,
however, takes the form of cash subsidies, vouchers to be
applied against child care costs at designated centres, information and referral services, employee seminars on parenting
and family life, arrangements for flexi-place (work at home)
and flexi-time. Though the number of employers involved in
child care plans doubled between 1982 and 1984, business
continues to harbour serious misgivings about on-site centres.[27] In 1982, for example, the National Employer-
Supported Child Care Project found that of 385 employers
providing child care benefits, fewer than half did so with an
on-site centre. The proportion of employer-supported centres
is declining — and some ambitious projects, like a Minneapolis consortium (half a dozen downtown firms sharing a
centre), have reverted to community ownership. Industry
explanations for lagging interest — and closings — vary.
Expansion was needed but impractical; outside funding
evaporated; the space had to be allocated for more pressing
purposes. Costs are high — start-up costs often in the
$100,000 range, with annual expenses of $2,000 to $3,000 per
child. Alfred J. Kahn of the Columbia University School of
Social Work insists that "almost everyone who knows anything about the field doesn't think on-site centres are good
ideas. On-site care scares the hell out of employers. They
have to build facilities for the employees they have today,
but their labor force is changing." The opposite situation, an
unchanging labour force, also creates problems. When
employees remain with the same company for years, they
grow beyond the world in which pre-school care is a concern.
(A major factor in the phasing out of the Minneapolis consortium, Northside Development Center, was an aging work
force and few children young enough to enrol in the centre.)
Other anxieties about on-site care focus on legal liability —
some employers worry about children in the workplace —

and equity in the case of parents who choose not to use the centre or can't afford to. Finally — the real bottom line — the proportion of a work force which uses an employer centre turns out to be less than four percent.[28]

Why don't more parents use on-site care? Families who have tried and rejected the company centre complain about food, cost-cutting, general atmosphere. "It's just too big — over a hundred kids milling around in an enormous room." "An outside catering service did the lunches: macaroni with processed cheese, cardboard pizzas, canned vegetables and Twinkies for dessert. I want my kids to have fresh fruit and vegetables, high quality protein." "I'd get off *my* assembly line job and there were all the little duffers on *their* assembly line for juice or bathroom. Two is too early for that kind of regimentation." "I tried to talk to the supervisor about my son's tantrums, and she cut me off. They give me the feeling I'm lucky to get cheap care and should shut up." "The drive to and from work with the kids, at rush hour, was a nightmare."

Behind such particular complaints lies a larger and ultimately definitive concern: that this child care facility represents The Company, and its interests are inevitably very different from the parent's. The reality of this concern is on occasion made evident by official pronouncements. Commenting on the establishment of a day care centre for the use of Ohio Bell Telephone employees, a company spokesman said, "We want to be sure . . . that we're at least not harming the children. A positive effect on the children is a nice fringe benefit. But let me restate that the whole purpose of these programs is to determine whether industrial child care saves us money in the areas of hiring, training, absenteeism, tardiness and attitude." This is not the kind of reassurance likely to lift the hearts of working parents. In some jobs, there are understandable anxieties about the work environment — an inner-city location with poor playground facilities, noise and air pollution. (The Port Authority of New York and New Jersey plans a non-profit centre at JFK airport for the children of Port Authority and airport community personnel. How many parents would want their children to play in an atmosphere of arriving and departing planes?) There are disenchantments: lunch with one's pre-schooler uses up precious time — and may defeat the purpose of some working women, which is to escape domesticity and enjoy a freer, adult climate. Visiting a two-year-old during the day may provoke not rapture but howls and clinging. ("I don't go to see my little girl during the day any more. It just upsets her.") Some parents feel strongly that a child should be cared for in his own neighbourhood, where he can be with familiar playmates. Some resent the power which workplace care gives the employer. "Let's face it," says a single father with two children in company care. "Using the plant centre — which is handy, which is cheap — ties me to this job. Am I going to complain about work conditions, am I going to *strike*, when the end result might be two little kids with no place to go?" Above all, always, there's the fear that accepting what appears to be company generosity will cost too much. "The employer's commitment is not to the children but to increased profits and productivity," writes Barbara Joan Freedman, a teacher and community education worker. "Therefore the employer will do everything possible to cut costs. This may mean decreasing the staff/child ratio, or skimping on food, equipment and program materials." Though workplace care appears to meet women's needs, she concludes, "in practice it will likely be used simply to extract more work, with more compliance, at lower pay."[29]

What's the answer? Much depends on the employer's goodwill and on parent involvement. Research suggests that failed workplace centres are often those with little or no parental representation. Successful ones — like Stride Rite's, like the Hester Howe Day Care Centre at Toronto's City Hall (for the children of municipal employees) — include parents, day care staff and often union representatives on the board of directors. Still, however well run the on-site centre, many families prefer a more open type of employer support. This might take the form of a completely separate employer-run enterprise; examples are Toronto's Orde Street Day Care Centre, operated in a public school building for Board of Education workers, and Montreal's Lavalin Garderie Enfanfreluche, which cares for children of Banque Nationale employees in a renovated downtown coach-house. Some companies purchase space in private centres: in Toronto, the Manufacturer's Life Insurance Company obtained priority for employees' children in return for a $12,000 forgivable renovation loan and mortgage assistance. Some companies offer voucher plans. The Vancouver Y.M.C.A. issues vouchers for short term or emergency child care at a specific centre (Granny Y's); the Toronto Y.M.C.A. grants cash allowances towards employees' day care expenses.

The further one travels from on-site care, the more employer-sponsored assistance melts into the familiar world of day care, becoming a financial aid, not a special provision. Perhaps Debbie King, a Connecticut official of the Hospital and Health Care Employees union, is right in concluding: "The feeling we got from surveys of our members is they wanted big wage increases more than they wanted child care."[30]

Family Day Care

Family day care is a very attractive idea. If a child can't be looked after by his own mother, then another mother, living nearby and happily involved with her own little ones, is surely the next best thing. Not a centre but a home, this day care setting holds out the promise of everything a child needs to feel safe and loved: playmates, familiar reassuring domestic routines, a kitchen with cooking smells, a yard and garden, a father figure for occasional rough-and-tumble, a mother figure for comfort and affection. Maybe even a dog, a cat and a canary. Real toys (battered trikes and chewed blocks, as compared with the special educational materials of a day care centre), real-life activities. The *realness* of family care is a chief attraction. Freedom. Spontaneity. It's easy to understand why so many professionals promote family day care as offering "a wide variety of daily experiences of the world around the child and the opportunity to grow up in an adult world and share adult experiences."[31] Presumably, too, the intimacy of the arrangement answers the child's deepest needs, a support system of those "close, personal, continuing relationships that are so essential as the foundation of sound emotional development."[32]

Family day care does indeed offer some unique advantages, the chief one being its high ratio of adults to children. The legal limit for numbers of children per caretaker is never higher than six. Since, in actual fact, many day care homes take only one or two, there should be enough love and attention to go round. Small size makes family care particularly suitable for children with special needs — the shy, the backward, the difficult and the handicapped. The day care home is very likely to be in the child's own neighbourhood — in the same high-rise development, or just down the road. A Canadian study found the average travel distance to be six blocks.[33] This reduces time pressures and spares small children the weariness of an early morning trudge or a long ride on subways and buses. It also means that neighbourhood friendships continue without interruption, and that the child, going to shops or laundromat with his daykeeper, sees familiar figures — the grocery man who hands out Oreos, the bank teller who greets him by name. Penelope Leach, not a day care advocate, feels that if a child must be "minded," he should remain part of his own community, "able to benefit from whatever it can offer."[34] From the mother's point of view, there appears to be some psychic benefit in knowing that children are close to home, near friends and older siblings after school hours.

The flexibility of family care homes represents an enormous advantage to most working parents. Centres open and close at precise hours and often impose stiff penalties on parents who show up late to collect their young. (Five dollars for every fifteen minutes late is not uncommon.) Day care homes don't close. Though they might prefer, after hours, to start supper and attend to their own children, family care mothers will provide soup and Sesame Street for the toddler whose mother is delayed at the office. They will also, often, adjust their hours to accommodate parents who don't work the standard nine-to-five shift; they may take children evenings, weekends and even overnight. Since the caregiver has her own children for spring break, no-school days, Thanksgiving and Christmas, she can, if necessary, fit her little charges into family holiday rhythms. A special advantage is the willingness of most family care mothers to look after a child who has, not measles or strep throat, but stomach upset or the kind of drippy sniffles unacceptable at a day care centre. And there's what might be called reverse flexibility. Many mothers would hesitate to interrupt a centre care day by picking up a child at an unaccustomed hour. ("But we've just started rhythm band!") They can be reasonably sure that the family caretaker will have no objections to early collection.

For some parents family care offers the happy possibility of placing siblings in a single location. Two pre-schoolers can then be delivered and picked up together, each presumably cheered by the presence of the other. Older school age brothers and sisters can come to the home later for milk and cookies and after-school care. Even where there are no siblings, the mixed ages of a typical home care group create a normal family atmosphere; older children can serve as models and guides for younger ones, with everyone enriched by a friendly learning relationship. Bryna Siegel-Gorelick, a child psychologist at Stanford University Medical Center, says that a mixed-age group inspires more mature forms of play;[35] other researchers have pointed out that it fosters more affection and less competitiveness than the typical push-and-gimmee of same-age children.[36]

Proponents of family day care value its *family* aspect. Becoming part of a real family, they say, children are caught up in the rhythms of normal household activities which, though not formally "educational," will be very instructive. In a day care home the child may learn to chop apples, set the table, water plants, sort laundry, answer the phone and feed the cat. He talks to the mailman. He learns to follow directions. ("Go *upstairs* to the *front* bedroom and bring me a towel from the *bottom* bureau drawer. . . .") Since naps, meals, indoor and outdoor play are not strictly scheduled, a lot of the time he is free to do as he pleases.[37] The fact that the day care mother is not actively "caring" all day, that she's occupied with her own domestic tasks, may be a positive advantage. "The children are spared that combination of adult over-attention and adult boredom which is typical of settings where there are no grown-up activities except child care.[38] The home atmosphere is likelier to be cosier and more intimate than that of even the friendliest centre.

What about the relationship between day care mothers and the children's own mothers? An optimistic, ideal view holds that, as a connection between mothers, not expert and client, it is likely to be good. Penelope Leach sees the child-minder as a woman surely motherly (why else has she chosen to stay home with her own offspring?) and so, sensitively aware of the other mother's anxieties in leaving children while she goes to work. According to this view, the minder will be more emotionally involved than a professional day care worker and more ready to discuss issues involving the child's happiness. Ideally, too, in home care it should be possible to achieve a close match of values, language and life-style between families and providers. The result, then, might be a genuine friendship which benefits everyone and might well outlast the day care arrangement.

Children in family home care are exposed to fewer infections, particularly the respiratory infections which frequently sweep through a large centre. When they're only mildly ill, they can usually be isolated in a spare bedroom, leaving parents free to go to work. Many home caretakers will also accept responsibility for doctor and dentist appointments. Finally — for parents this may be the definitive advantage — home care is very much less expensive than centre care.[39] In the United States the average national cost of family day care in 1983 was 89 cents per hour, as compared with an average of $1.25 per hour for centre care of children under two.[40] In Britain 1976 figures show child-minding as less than one-third the cost of day nursery care.[41] In Canada the 1980 average weekly cost for family care was $35 a week; centre care for the same year averaged from $50 to $75 a week. In actual fact, however — and this may be true elsewhere — Toronto's Project Child Care study found that in fifteen percent of cases, no formal payment system existed, and sitters received no money for their services.[42] A bottle of Scotch at Christmas, clothing (new or used), toys, cigarettes. . . These were all considered by some parents appropriate recompense for child care. One sitter recalled parents who had given a rose-bush. As Johnson and Dineen observe, "It's hard to tell what level of care would be the right return for a rose-bush."[43]

Here, then, is the (affordable) ideal: "At its very best, family day care can provide a child with warm personal care from a capable, responsible and loving adult in the comfortable and familiar surroundings of a home. It can be a happy place to go after school or for the day, and it can be a place to learn and play and feel accepted outside the family."[44]

It can be.

It most often is not.

The central hope held out by family day care mythology — a home away from home, another mother — is simply not supported by existing evidence. Set aside the horror stories: thirty-nine young children sleeping on mattresses on the floor, attended by one (unqualified) adult;[45] forty-seven children in a licensed "home," some strapped to high chairs, others huddled before a basement TV and the rest in a fenced yard; a home care service where children were sexually abused by the proprietor, a convicted child molester, and his wife.[46] These are certainly not typical. What does appear to be typical is an atmosphere neither warm nor personal nor stimulating, with care by an adult who may be capable in a purely domestic sense but who assumes no responsibility for the child's emotional security and intellectual development. Two major research projects, one in Canada and one in Britain,[47] arrived at substantially the same conclusion: that family day care in the real world (as distinct from ideal projections of what might be) is a merely custodial arrangement, baby-sitting on a larger scale. Because it *is* primarily baby-sitting and not a child-centred, child-concerned arrangement, fantasies of delicious nourishing home-cooked meals seldom materialize. At a public day care forum in Thunder Bay the mother of a two-year-old described her son's daily fare. "In my son's short life he was fed starches and sugars because they keep children quiet and were cheaper than fruits and vegetables. He was plunked in front of a TV instead of being provided with stimulating play."[48] (A child overdosed on sugar is no doubt more placid, easier to manage.)

Why do minders mind? Evidently the world has not changed much since Dickens presented, in *Our Mutual Friend*, the no-nonsense reasoning of a professional minder: "I love children, and fourpence a week is fourpence." In the beginning (and the middle and the end) is the money. Not much, to be sure, but in the view of run-of-the-mill caretakers, a nice little extra, the price of a blouse or a pair of shoes, with no effort expended. Most home caregivers claim to enjoy children. "It's company. I like young children's company." "My kids like having the others here. So do I." Rather less positive, but still, presumably, an item on the enjoyment scale is "It gives me something to do, fills the day." Many women fall into the job as a favour to friends or relatives. "They asked if I'd take her and I couldn't think of a way to say *No*." (This minder wasn't sure of the mindee's age. Three? Four maybe?) For some, the day care enterprise is not so much choice as the only possibility of work, however ill paid: these are the women who have very limited education, don't speak English or — a fact to give one pause — are not well enough to do "real" work. The Canadian interviewers found that almost one-quarter of home caregivers suffered from chronic health problems: arthritis, rheumatism, bad backs, kidney ailments, failing sight, ulcers, deafness, not to mention "bad nerves" and headaches. The same proportion, one-quarter, gave money as their chief reason for taking in children. British caregivers seemed somewhat more high-minded (much mention of doing something worthwhile, performing a service), but money and freedom, the two doubtless connected, emerged as major motives. Few women had anything like a career attitude. Some "wouldn't do it a minute longer" than they had to; others, less testy, merely said that *of course* they'd stop when their circumstances changed for the better, or when their own children entered school.

That such attitudes produce inferior caregiving is not surprising. Exceptional day care mothers play with children, take them on outings, read and talk and sing and respond sensitively to individual needs. The great majority assume that their only responsibility is physical care. So what they provide is meals, naps, toileting arrangements and, almost invariably, lots of television. (Asked whether she had purchased any special materials or play equipment for her charges, one caretaker said indeed yes: "I bought a colour TV.") As for the stimulus value of normal domestic activities. . . It's true that a day is often varied by the caretaker's regular round of errands, shopping and visits. A trip to the dry-cleaner's or the hardware store could be diverting if accompanied by talk and awareness of the child's presence. ("Would you like some paint-colour sample cards?"

"This fluffy stuff is insulation. People put it between the walls to keep a house warm.") If, however, the child is dragged along reluctant or transported like a package, the end result is weariness and bad temper.

Now it's true that there are also many mothers who don't play, read, sing or initiate creative activities. But leaving a child to his own resources on his own turf, with his mother, is very different from dropping him onto strange turf and expecting him to entertain himself. The British research team speculates that the way children are left with minders — often abruptly, with little preparation and no adjustment period with mother staying on — may lead to anxiety and ultimately resignation or depression. And since an anxious, depressed, apathetic child is not likely to elicit affection, the sense of isolation may increase over time. Another uneasy-making speculation is this: that perhaps there is something in the home care situation — the procession of other mothers' children who come and go — which inhibits the forming of close emotional ties. For whatever reasons, it seems clear that the relationship between a day care mother and her charges is seldom a rich, loving, satisfying bond. "While, at its best, minding can offer this, and did to some of our children," the British observers conclude, "it did not do so most of the time to most of the children (and this in spite of the fact that most minders were warm-hearted, caring, kind). Three out of five children seemed abnormally quiet and detached, or at least not very involved with the home care mothers. One in four children was openly disturbed or depressed or had impoverished speech.[49]

Inevitably, the day care home will involve some constraints different from those imposed at the child's own home. At his house, say, he's allowed to use felt tip markers at the dining room table; not here. Or modelling clay is off bounds in the day care kitchen. Differences there are bound to be, some puzzling or perhaps frustrating. The toys here are not *his* toys, the mother is not *his* mother. There may be, in residence, another small child who enjoys superior privileges and whom he must appease. (Though minders' children often welcome a little playmate, they are just as likely to resent his intrusion and to let him know in no uncertain terms.) In addition to these gross, obvious constraints, there may be a subtle pressure exerted by the kindliest of home care mothers, the pressure to be "good," which in this context means undemanding, uncomplaining, *quiet*. When the British research team observed children both in their own homes and in the day care setting, they found that children were far livelier, more active and energetic, at home. At home children rushed about, played with siblings, talked to parents. At the minder's they often engaged in solitary repetitive play or just *sat*. Doing "little or nothing" was four times as likely there. Often the child in day care appeared transformed, unrecognizable. The bright, energetic, rather cheeky little girl observed scampering about her house and garden became passive and melancholy. "She spent some of the time sitting on the minder's knee, but when put down she sat limply on the sofa sucking her thumb and looking dreadfully miserable."[50] Withdrawal of this sort was frequently noted in the very children who most needed support, those from conflicted homes. Both British and Canadian studies comment with concern on the amount of time some children spent *sleeping* in day care homes, evidently waiting for time to pass. No wonder, Johnson and Dineen say. In the typical day care home, activities are bland or boring or negligible, watching cartoons and soap operas being the chief thing to do. "Like the packaged instant macaroni and cheese dinners that so many of the surveyed caregivers offer their charges, their programs lack enrichment and variety."[51]

If the problem with home day care were simply programming, then better programming, training of caretakers, might be the answer. Some day care activists see hope in the possibility of education for child-minding: courses, workshops, professional supervision, support from day care centre staff. There is talk of a "satellite" system, with family day care homes organized around a neighbourhood group centre, having access to centre materials and guidance. Toy lending libraries and drop-in centres might enrich home programs and alleviate the isolation of the home caregiver. Trained caregivers could be given employee status along with centre counterparts, enjoying similar benefits and pay.

These are all possibilities. In view of what is known about family day care, however, it seems unlikely that such developments would produce major change. Few providers see home care as a permanent or even relatively long-term career; it's just what they do until something better comes along. As a British specialist pointed out in a paper rejecting the possible value of training: "Most childminders do the job for their own convenience — and often short term — because it fits in with their domestic commitments, not out of informed, caring interest in children. . . . So training schemes carried out by local authorities are unlikely to affect the attitudes of those currently minding, who have nothing to gain by improving the way they 'mind' children.[52] Nor, incidentally, is there any evidence that lectures and discussions raise the level of family day care. In a study carried out by B. Mayall and P. Petrie, "trained" caretakers showed in practice no special knowledge or skills.[53] When caretakers themselves are consulted, the few who show interest in training want courses in health, safety and above all, first aid. It is not likely that learning to give artificial respiration will raise the level of home care. Even courses in making things with children, an occasionally expressed interest, will have no effect if the caretaker is typically occupied with cooking, cleaning, laundry, shopping. Apart from raising pay to levels which would make home care as costly as centre care, there is no escaping a built-in limitation. The caregiver's primary commitment is to her family and her home, and other people's children must fit in as they can.

Unchangeable also by either training or better pay is the

natural chasm — of attitude, belief, life-style — between working mothers and caregivers. Any fantasied closeness between these two women as parents, meeting on equal ground, has little basis in reality.[54] Home caregivers are almost always less well educated and less well off financially than the mothers they serve. They tend to be older, more rooted, more traditional, to have larger families and to be far more domestically oriented. Inevitably, then, they view with suspicion, disapproval or envy the woman who leaves her child to take a job more gratifying than the minder's. Working? "I don't think it's fair to the children." Three-quarters of the providers interviewed by Project Day Care thought mothers of pre-school children belonged in the home.[55] "I never palmed my kids off. I wouldn't do it — only if I really had to money-wise." These typical caretaker statements suggest some hostility towards the working mother — an attitude that might well influence care.

Given the differences between minders and mothers, it's understandable that day's end, when the child is collected, brings few heart-to-heart chats. The minder suspects, often correctly, that the mother is tired and does not want to hear about problems — particularly not at 5:30, with a supermarket stop on the way home and dinner to prepare. The minder has also by that time had enough of child difficulties — some children stay ten hours — and is eager to get on with her life. Add to this mix the mother's anxiety (What if this arrangement doesn't work out?) and the minder's irritation. Conditions do not favour a leisurely exchange of information or advice.[56]

Probably both parties to the day care contract have some sense of potential differences. The mother who would like her child to have home-made soup and fresh fruit and vegetables may suspect that the usual fare is Alphagetti, potato chips and Twinkies; best not to rock the boat. She may be troubled by evidence that the caretaker's TV is on constantly, bathing the children in a confusion of rock music, commercials and cartoons. But this is not *her* house, and probably her child is not the only child being cared for. How can she impose conditions or request special treatment? This is true even in the touchy, crucial area of discipline. Differences in social class, background, age and culture mean that the two women will often have vastly different philosophies of child raising — the minder more often than the mother relying on slaps and spanking. Project Child Care interviewers found that almost half of their 281 day care mothers used physical punishment to keep charges in line. A child who spilled talcum, pulled pans out of a cupboard or (heaven save us) "touched things" in a bedroom was disciplined by smacks, spankings or a dose of his own medicine. "If a kid hit me, I'd hit her back harder, so she knows it isn't nice. I'd do the same if she bites — bite her back." A mother who disapproves of spanking may simply not dare raise the issue. What if the caretaker, offended, says, "Take your kid!"

The Nanny

"A unique and curious way of bringing up children, which evolved among the upper and upper-middle classes during the nineteenth century, flourished for approximately eighty years and then, with the Second World War, disappeared for ever." That's how Jonathan Gathorne-Hardy describes nannying in a 1973 book chronicling the rise and fall of the British nanny.[57] Were he to survey the scene today, Gathorne-Hardy would be surprised. The traditional nanny, a Norland training-school graduate in crisp brown dress and sensible shoes, pushing her Regal pram and leading an ambulatory charge on white hygienic Clippa-Safe baby harness, may have pretty much gone the way of Tyrannosaurus rex. But a new breed of lively young nannies is springing up on both sides of the Atlantic. These new nannies, with their jeans and long hair, may in the park or supermarket be indistinguishable from the mums. They no longer see themselves as defenders of sacred upper class privilege. ("Excuse me," says the nanny with gold-crested pram to a plain-pram colleague in Hyde Park. "This bench is reserved for titled mummies' nannies.") They no longer purvey the snobbish upper-class wisdoms (it is *common* to whisper, to eat dripping, to say Hip, hip, *Hooray*! instead of *Hurrah*!) For them, Piaget and Montessori have replaced the maxims of traditional nannydom ("Always bread and butter *before* cake," "Children should be seen and not heard," "No pickings or choosings, take the first that comes" and "Always pick blackberries *above* dog-lifting-leg height.") They do not, like nannies of old, view their profession as a lifetime commitment; the North American nanny, as a rule, is a young woman who is caring for other people's children until the real thing comes along. But like their predecessors, they are committed to substituting for mother in all practical matters — and in a world where mother is so often away on the job, they are *very* much in demand.

Most women, at the beginning of the home-to-job exodus, saw the day care centre as an ideal solution to child care problems. "A good group for young children is a planned community that focuses specifically on what a young child is like and on what will help him function at his very best"; "Hundreds of children in centres seemed to be getting an exciting, happy start in life"; "The day nursery is home." This is a fair sampling of the 1973 climate.[58] Today, concerns about adverse effects of group rearing — in particular, health hazards — have stimulated a growing demand for in-home care. (This is partly, too, an effect of women's procuring better and better-paid jobs. Even an untrained nanny will cost more than most day care centres.) Ironically, rising demand has coincided with falling supply, virtually a cut-off. In the United States immigration laws have made foreigners' work permits so difficult to procure that most domestic agencies won't bother with the complicated sponsoring provisions. To bring in a foreign nursemaid, a family must prove that business responsibilities make live-in domestic help essential during evening hours. Applications for sponsoring involve submitting recent tax returns and providing evidence that every available source of native-born help has been exhausted. The procedure can take up to two years — at the end of which time, many "green card" candidates are refused. So it is not surprising that when Beth Smith, a British psychologist, set up Nanny, Inc. in 1982 to train and place child care professionals, her small Chicago operation rapidly expanded to a nation-wide franchise scheme. For a fee of $1,500 Nanny, Inc. offers a three-month course in the basics — child psychology, health, nutrition, safety. Since that time, nanny schools have sprung up all over the U.S. In 1985, the American Council of Nanny Schools was established to upgrade the status of the job by training an elite corps of nannies and setting national standards as in Britain. "This is no fad," says the director of a Columbus, Ohio school. "It's a new option in child care. We're talking about highly skilled professionals." U.S. programs, which range from 200 to 300 classroom hours in addition to supervised training in childcare facilities, are less comprehensive than the two-year British programs, and less concerned with housewifely skills. Some schools are licensed by state departments of education, and all claim to screen applicants for criminal histories, bad driving records, psychiatric problems, poor health and hygiene habits. The nanny who passes these tests, and the school's, will earn between $175 and $280 per week; that's in addition to board and room, health benefits and such perks as use of the family car. A good nanny can pretty much write her own ticket: most schools report 150 to 200 job offers for every graduate.[59]

In Canada the nanny situation is a lot more favourable. The government admits applicants for landed immigrant status on condition that they perform two years of domestic service in Canada — a ruling which makes available a large pool of Swedish, Dutch, British, Filipino and Caribbean nanny-candidates. Furthermore, Canada has two well-established training programs — at Oakville, Ontario's Sheridan College and Ottawa's Canadian Mothercraft — with the likelihood that more will follow. Sheridan has for over a decade offered a two-year program, Canadian Nanny. Recently cut to one year, to handle the traffic, the program provides unusually comprehensive instruction in everything from art to menu planning. Students (mostly but not exclusively female) study basic psychology, history and functions of the Canadian family, nutrition, health care, child development, personal relationships, infant stimulation, exercise. They learn how to choose and present toys, how to fit children's books to developmental stages, how to deal with special problems like hyperactivity or physical disability. Old-style nannies studied smocking, embroidery and knitting. How else could their little charges be assured of the proper bonnets, booties and leggings? New nannies learn how to make simple musical instruments. Old nannies *knew their place* — above mere servants, properly deferential to master and mistress. New nannies know all the latest techniques of active listening, behaviour modification, network-forming and burnout prevention. Old nannies concentrated on manners. (A British mother tells a lovely story of the children's birthday party in deepest Belgravia, where at tea time, behind each toddler guest stood a nanny on guard. Except, that is, for one child who, in the absence of her regular nursemaid, was being watched by a flustered mother. Eventually rescue appeared. "Oh, Nanny," wailed the young mother, "Thank heavens you've come. Which hand is Lavinia supposed to be eating her ice cream with?") And of course, of course, the old nanny's chief task was control. (Question on the Norland final exam: "What would you do if you were pushing a pram with a baby in it along a busy road with a small child beside you and the child ran away? Would you leave the pram and follow the child?" Answer: *The situation should never arise. A toddler is kept on reins.*)[60] The new nanny's task might be defined as setting the child free: developing, from toddlerhood, such strong internalized controls that by school starting time, the six-year-old can be trusted to venture and explore independently.

In addition to academic subjects, the Canadian nanny student is instructed in job hunting and contract writing and then, in her final semester, sent into the field — two days a week to work with a real family and real live children. If she passes this test in satisfactory style and gets at least a C rating on her courses, the nanny has her choice of jobs (an average of sixteen offers per candidate) at $200 to $250 a week. Since this is pretty steep for most households, families are encouraged to share a nanny where family style — and number of children — permits.

The advantages of a resident nanny are obvious. The baby or small child enjoys his own bed, toys, food and familiar surroundings, and his school age siblings can come home for lunch. He's not exposed to the infectious diseases which run like prairie fires through group facilities. If he's ill, he can be looked after with scarcely a missed beat (no frantic search for someone to nurse a feverish child sent home from the centre). Where parents work irregular hours, a nanny at home means flexibility and the assurance that a child is in good, familiar hands. Whereas in group care the child must adapt to caretakers, a nanny can be specially selected to match individual needs. Is this child shy? Vigorous and athletic? High-strung? Physically delicate? A search may turn up the perfect caretaker. A nanny can also balance parental temperaments. High-powered, hard-driving professional mothers and fathers will speak reverently and with amazement of their nanny's patience: "She can play the same game twenty times!" Often a nanny extends and enriches what might otherwise be a claustrophobic middle class experience: the offspring of undemonstrative parents may learn a natural loving acceptance from a warm caretaker. Because the nanny is constantly on hand, exchange of information with parents is easy and natural. "Miranda climbed on the chest today. . . She's begun to sway to the music box rhythm. . . She fell in the kitchen and got a little bruise. . . Oh, and look at this new tooth coming!" Above all, the child has the opportunity to form a close, affectionate, stable bond with one person other than parents. "Our nanny," says a professional parent, "means security for our child and comfort, psychological freedom for us."

Of course this rosy picture has another side. Precisely *because* the child has a single caretaker, the arrangement is subtly but continuously at risk. What if the nanny gets sick and there's no back-up? What if — as often happens with new-immigrant nursemaids — a change of legal status ends the agreement? Furthermore, the relationship with a single, live-in caretaker has, almost inevitably, a special intensity. If the nanny has problems — an unhappy love affair, a troubled home situation, chronic illness — then her problem becomes the family's too. "When an outsider lives and works in your house, you've got a situation not unlike a new marriage," says Leslie Corbet, co-ordinator of Sheridan College's nanny program. "There are all kinds of quirks and peculiarities you have to get used to. Most people aren't prepared for that, so small problems become big ones, and unless both parties are very tactful and reasonable, the pressure cooker explodes." There's a certain ambiguity in the parent-nanny relationship. Are they employer and employee? Friends? Somewhere in between, as a rule. Most nannies eat with the family unless guests are present. Some prefer not. There may be, if not actual confusion of roles, at least anxiety about possible confusion. Mothers are characteristically anxious that the child not see nanny as Mama — and a good nanny takes pains that this won't happen. One candid young mother confessed to jealousy in relation not to the baby but to the baby's father. "Our nanny is a gorgeous Swedish girl — healthy, intelligent, vital, with milk-and-honey skin and a sensational figure. Let me tell you when I was still out of shape from pregnancy and nursing, I didn't enjoy her easy relationship with my husband." As a kind of third parent, the nanny brings with her another set of standards (in relation to discipline, diet, whatever); that has to be negotiated, sometimes *can't* be worked out satisfactorily. A nanny whose impulse is to smack an unruly child cannot change by parental fiat. Since so many nannies are foreign-born, language may be a problem. Parents who can afford a nanny are, as a rule, precisely those most anxious that their children speak well, and if possible, elegantly. From this standpoint, the most loving newly arrived Portuguese nanny may not fill the bill. For both parents a nursemaid means some loss of control. After all, if the arrangement is to work, the nanny must be *in charge* when parents leave, and no nanny worth her salt (or her tea) would stay on in a situation where her authority was consistently undermined. Loss of privacy is an issue for almost everyone. A young couple with a new baby seldom wishes to share their lives with a stranger. "We don't feel really free to fight *or* make love," one mother-with-a-nanny confided. "It's not that our girl pries, but the house is small. If we want to discuss something confidential, we retreat to the bedroom and whisper."

Finally, the bottom line: nannies cost a lot — a wage not high for what they do, but high for most families to pay along with the added costs of food, room, electricity, heat, social and medical insurance. Nanny care has been called the Cadillac of day care and true it is. Wishes not being horses, no beggars may ride.

A rapidly accumulating body of new nanny lore features the expected complement of horror stories. There's the nanny who ran off with the silver and the one who ran off with the husband; the specially imported nanny who left one morning while parents were at work, abandoning a baby found screaming in his crib at day's end. There's the butter-wouldn't-melt-in-her-mouth nanny who had an abortion on her evening off and the one who was found to have syphilis. There's the nanny who invited friends in over the weekend, while the family was away, and celebrated with an orgy of drinking and drugs. And there are sad-terrible stories: a nanny pursued and beaten up by a rejected lover; a nanny, much beloved by the children, dying of cancer. Most of these nightmares could have been avoided by careful screening. Of course, parents who need child care may be in no state for careful anything: they need someone for the kids *right now* and jump for what's available. This is risky enough in any circumstances. In the case of a person who is to live with the family and to be left in full charge of children, it's sheer recklessness. Leslie Corbet suggests that parents begin their search some time before the nanny will actually be needed. (If a terrific prospect turns up before a baby's born, having her live with the family a month or so may be a wise investment.)

Portrait: A Nanny in the Family

Riva and Mark are a professional couple; he's a college professor, she holds a top-level government job. They live in an elegant house, cool-modern with original abstract paintings and some rather austere sculpture. Silk pillows. No nicknacks and no strewn toys. Until eighteen-month-old Peggy runs in for a good-night kiss, there's no sign on the first floor of child life.

Riva:
"Because my job involves women's issues, I'd thought a good deal about day care. The chief concerns for me were pretty much what they are for any parent: accessibility, affordability, quality. I never considered group care. Later on, maybe, when Peggy's old enough to need playmates. For now I didn't want the added pressure of taking a child to a centre, picking her up. I liked the idea of the baby's being here, in a

safe clean familiar environment. And I needed, besides child care, some help with the house. I guess you could say I wanted a wife to take care of me.

"First, I telephoned a local community college that runs a nanny-training program. Their fee range was too high for us — close to $800 a month. And in any case their graduates assumed responsibility for children only. No housework. So that was out.

"Then I called an agency and explained our requirements. We wanted someone reasonably mature and experienced, who enjoyed children and was willing to do light household tasks — laundry, daily cleaning, maybe a little cooking. Applicants came in streams, mostly new Canadians admitted under the two-years-of-domestic-service provision. Right off we discovered the complication of taking in another person. For instance, there was an appealing Polish woman, but she had a husband who beat her up regularly. I couldn't take on *her* problems. We interviewed a lot of young girls whose first question was "What do you pay?" or "Can I have friends over?" And then Victoria appeared and she was perfect. Filipino, 47, married, with four grown children. In fact, one of her daughters is nannying just down the street. We both liked her right off. She's solid, mature, responsible, has a happy disposition. When I asked why she wanted the job, she said, 'I love children and I love being a mother. It's what I do best.'

"She'd been a nanny before, in Italy. That was a plus. When we proposed a few possible trouble scenarios, her answers were reassuring. What would she do in case of a kitchen fire? She'd call the fire department, take the baby out right away. If the baby cried inconsolably? She'd check the diaper, burp her, look for rash or swelling, hold her, rock and sing. . . and if none of that helped, she'd call us or the doctor. We showed her the baby — Peggy was four months old — and it was instant love. We hired her on the spot. She agreed to sleep in, do basic housecleaning and baby-sit every second Saturday. For that, we'd pay $500 a month, plus room and board. Victoria moved in on a trial basis, but there was never a moment when we questioned the arrangement. She is very loving and has incredible initiative — scrubs the kid's room daily, fusses over baby clothes. If I encouraged, she'd put Peggy in ironed petticoats. As things have worked out, we've acquired a handyman too. Victoria's husband, Carlo, vacuums, does errands and odd jobs around the house. He even sews. He made a comforter cover with matching pillow cases. We pay him extra for things like that.

"At first, the understanding was that Victoria would sleep in but could go home nights when she wasn't needed. By degrees, this became a sleep-out routine which is okay with us. She leaves after supper, comes back at 7:30 A.M. in time to give Peggy her breakfast.

"Any problems? Such as they are, they're *my* problems. I've had some jealous moments. Peggy said 'Tor-ia' before 'Mama.' When she sees Victoria in the mornings she's ecstatic, positively squeals with joy. I feel a kind of pang when I miss a landmark — 'she took three steps today' — and when I realize Victoria knows my child better than I do. Not that she makes a point of that. It's just apparent. She'll say, 'You know how the baby loves chicken liver!' and I *don't* know, I've never offered it. She'll describe how Peggy flirts with male visitors, showing her new shoes, reaching up for a kiss, and I think, 'I wish I'd seen that.' It hurts me that my child makes strange with her own grandpa — she sees him so rarely — but is crazy about Carlo. There are little things that reflect a whole other way of life. Victoria gives Peggy marshmallows. *Marshmallows*, practically one hundred percent sugar. I've tried to keep her away from sweets entirely, but Victoria can't see apples or dry cereal bits as a treat. Victoria says, 'Want to make *caca*?' I hate that word. The baby might just as well learn the right adult word — but how can I ask another adult to speak in a way that's not natural to her? Victoria has set up an altar in her room — there's a cross, flowers and candles.

Peggy says 'Pre-tty' and obviously prefers it to our menorah.
This is fine now, but I want my child to grow up in our own,
Jewish tradition. As Peggy gets older, Victoria won't be —
what shall I say? — the right kind of influence, the right
model. She's essentially a childlike person: for her every day
is a brand new day, every event a new event. She's focused
on *now*.

"Well — these are not, for the moment, big problems. The
reality is that Peggy has a wonderful playmate and caretaker.
Victoria really *plays* — gets right down on the floor and
builds blocks. She never loses patience, never raises her
voice. She's sensitive to our primary position as parents;
when Mark and I come home, she slips away so we can have
the baby to ourselves. (Mind you, she keeps an eye on things.
One day — I was tired, not paying attention — Peggy fell on
the stairs and Victoria appeared from nowhere, snatched her
up.) She's created an orderly world for Peggy. They have a
routine, the two of them. Victoria comes in mornings and
does toast and eggs for the baby; we leave while she's eating.
Then they both watch 'Polka Dot Door.' Peggy recognizes the
music, skips to the living room. After that the baby plays in
her room, with the gate hooked, while Victoria cleans. Nap is
from eleven to one, lunch at one. Afternoons they go for a
walk, shop, visit friends, watch some more TV. (There's probably too much TV, but that's something I have to accept.)
Sometimes Peggy has a second nap while Victoria makes supper; they eat together, not with us (Victoria's choice). Peggy
cries when she leaves.

"Everything considered, it's an ideal arrangement. I'm free
to concentrate on my job, my child has a mother-substitute
who's absolutely conscientious and devoted. Let me tell you I
wake every morning and pray she won't leave us. Not that I
really worry. The young nannies from Jamaica or the British
Isles often don't take their jobs seriously; they meet a man, or
get a better job, often, and they're off. For Victoria, stability
is a central value. She regards this as her home."

One week after this interview, Victoria left without giving notice: her landed immigrant papers had come through. In the three months since then, Riva (pregnant again) has had one nanny who lasted two weeks and a series of makeshift arrangements. Now she and her husband are sponsoring a nanny from Hong Kong.

Chapter VI

The Effects of Day Care

Intellectual Development

All parents want the best for their children. The vision of what's best, however, is greatly affected by social climate. Fifty years ago, *best* frequently meant *best behaved*; today it's widely equated with *brightest*. In a 1980 poll of qualities parents most desired in their offspring, "intelligence" topped the list.[1] Harvard University's T. Berry Brazelton, who in his role as pediatrician has observed thousands of families, confirms the trend. "Everyone wants to raise the smartest kid in America rather than the best adjusted, happiest kid."[2]

It's not surprising, then, that day care investigation has so often concerned itself with cognitive development. Do children learn better at home or in surrogate care? In family groups or centres? What is surprising is the relative poverty of research findings. The mountain labours — hundreds of papers from universities across the land — to bring forth a very small mouse. What does research tell us? Send a child to day care or keep him home, provide him with sophisticated educational toys or kitchen tools, as far as intellectual development goes, it doesn't much matter. He will be what he will be, thanks to the genes he inherited and the social class into which he was born.[3]

That's an overstatement of course. In the earliest months, the human brain requires for optimal development certain kinds of environmental stimuli — the kind of stimuli, for example, that a mother (or constant caretaker) provides in a multitude of small daily interactions with her infant. Patting, rocking, smiling, feeding, babbling — all these instinctive responses, by stimulating alertness or pleasure, become part of infant learning. Where they don't occur, says child psychiatrist Humberto Nagera, the result is a permanent limitation of brain capacity and function. It follows that an infant in day care from 6:30 A.M. to 6:30 P.M., exposed to shifts of staff and multiple caretakers, will very likely suffer a lack of appropriate stimulation.[4] That's a distinct minus for some children in some day care situations. Conversely, take a child from what sociologists call a "high risk" environment — a chaotic home with depressed or angry parents and a generally low level of competence. Put him in a good day care centre, with a rich program and attentive caretaking, and he will show intellectual as well as social gains. That's a plus for some children in some day care situations.

In general, studies agree that day care of average quality has no apparent ill effects on children's intellectual development. Such positive effects as it produces, substantial gains for "disadvantaged" children, however promising initially, tend to wash out after the program ends. Children from relatively privileged backgrounds — homes with educated parents, books, music, conversation and a lively round of activities — are unaffected by even high-quality enriched programs. They don't lose anything intellectually, neither do they gain.[5]

Between day care and home care children some kinds of skill differences appear in the early years. Day care children outperform home care counterparts in those tasks which formal programs emphasize: stringing beads, doing puzzles, naming colours, remembering numbers, copying designs made with blocks, drawing circles, squares and triangles. (Presumably home care children might do better at sorting laundry and shopping from a grocery list.) Whether such accomplishment demonstrates "intellectual development" is debatable. Jay Belsky and Laurence Steinberg, in a review of day care effects, suggest that it's important to know "whether children in day care learn functional skills applicable in everyday life or whether they are simply being trained to take batteries of intelligence tests."[6] In any case, apparent gains are short-lived. When home care children get to kindergarten or first grade, they catch up very quickly. It appears that day care may affect the rate but not the ultimate range of intellectual growth.

Some of the most interesting material relating to intellectual development emerges incidentally from research. One study found that home care children tended to overestimate their cognitive skills, while those raised in day care were more realistic about their abilities — a consequence, probably, of being constantly in situations allowing comparison with age-mates.[7] Others have noted that day care children are less tolerant of frustration; they run about more, and given a choice, gravitate towards strenuous physical play. The home-reared group is attracted to areas for reading, making, pretending.[8] This inclination supports the theory, advanced by M.A. Pulaski, that the child on his own territory, in his own family, develops a fantasizing, imaginative life which reduces both aggression and the level of physical activity.[9]

A final consideration, central to intellectual development, is the relationship — it sounds sentimental but is demonstrably true — between love and learning. Children learn best from those to whom they have an emotional attachment, who make them feel cherished and secure enough to move out from home base — looking, feeling, testing, exploring. "A baby comes to know and turn to his or her special person, not only for the kiss that fixes up a hurt finger, but also for the help an adult can provide for learning how the world works and by arranging interesting experiences," writes Alice Honig of Syracuse University's College of Human Development. Test scores show a positive correlation between infant progress and the strength of attachment between baby and caregiver. Conversely, Honig says, "where the interaction of caregiver and baby is destructive or indifferent, early learning is often delayed."[10] In theory, there's no reason why a parent-surrogate cannot form with the young child a bond which enhances the child's security, joy and eagerness to learn. In actual fact, whether in centre or day care home, such bonds are rare. A Vanderbilt University study designed primarily to compare the differing effects of family day care homes and centres agreed, regretfully, with the conclusions of similar research conducted in England and in New York: "caregivers rarely engage in interaction with children which can be characterized as dialogue. Almost all of the communication between caregivers and children is neutral in affective tone. There is very little evidence of the kind of sensitive responsiveness we had hoped to find in child care environments. This situation exists despite the fact that the caregivers we observed were exceptional human beings dedicated to providing children with quality care."[11]

Social Development

Children accustomed to other-than-parent care, whether in a centre or a neighbour's home, achieve an earlier mastery of social skills: that seems incontrovertible. Watch a group of four-year-olds in a well-run day care facility, and you'll be struck by the highly organized behaviour. These children spontaneously put away their painting smocks and take out their pillows for circle time. They know how to gain entry into an ongoing game and how to stave off trouble by well-timed compromise or surrender. They remember to put the caps back on magic markers, return puzzles to the shelf. They approach and talk to strangers, are eager to show what they're doing. They sing unselfconsciously. "Children with a long experience of day care are notably independent," says Renee Edwards, Director of Toronto's Victoria Day Care Services. "They're skilled in looking after themselves, are fairly sophisticated socially, *competent*. They know how to cope with others, and have a better understanding of their own capacities."

If they've been in care any length of time, children under-

stand and adapt to the daily rhythm. (Now it's time for outside. . . for juice and crackers. . . for toileting. . . for story. . .
for Mommy and home.) Parents report with pleasure the day
care child's ease in the world, his capacity for mature and
complex relationships. "Our child is able to adjust to changes
and strangers very easily." "She's socially confident and loves
groups." "He has a social sense which seems much more
animated than what I've seen in children remaining at home."
These comments, from a Michigan survey of parental perceptions of their children's experience, are typical and typically
positive.[12] Other parents describe their day care children as
more competent, helpful and co-operative than stay-at-
homes. "Less timid" and "less fearful" are also often cited,
though here the research evidence is conflicting and con-
fused. Some investigators have found day care children more
apprehensive in situations involving strange adults — unless
they're in the comforting presence of peers. Very early day
care (before age two) seems to be associated with *increased*
fearfulness, and later day care with *diminished* fearfulness.[13]

A significant qualification: superior social competence and
co-operation tend to develop in centres but not in day care
homes. The most recent evaluations show family care
children as less compliant (less willing, for example, to pick
up and put away toys) and less developed in their capacities
for sympathy and empathy.[14] It would appear that structure
and adult guidance are crucial factors in social growth.

For most children day care seems to promote healthy
separation from parents, with an accompanying surge of
autonomy. Parents in the Michigan study comment with
pleasurable surprise on the independent spirit of even very
young children. And here is Pat Vandebelt Schulz, a pioneer
day care organizer in Toronto, describing the effect on her
daughter of very early day-long surrogate care. "Kathy is a
day care kid," Schulz writes, fortunate in having had caretakers who "enriched her life in a way I couldn't have done on
my own, and it's to them I give the credit for the strong, inde-

pendent and secure child who lives with me." A single working parent until her death (when Kathy was twelve), she credited day care with providing a range of experiences otherwise impossible in a life of isolation, tension and financial hardship. "Over the years, Kathy has become an autonomous person to me in a way that might not have been possible if she stayed at home with me."[15] This makes sense. Certainly a parent is less likely to live through her child, or to see the child as an extension of herself, if that child spends eight to ten hours a day in a stranger's care. One young mother, reflecting on her two-year-old's forays into an unknown world, puts it this way: "On weekdays, from nine to five, she goes to Irma's house, where she plays with other children, hears Spanish spoken, listens to Irma's husband, José, play songs on the guitar that I have never heard. The top of her head, that used to smell like me, smells like Irma's kitchen now. My daughter knows some secrets. We no longer own her, if we ever did."

Separateness, independence, social confidence and competence. . . so far, so good. The flip side of the coin, however, presents a less reassuring aspect. Bryna Siegel-Gorelick, a Stanford child psychologist, fears what she calls "a negative sense of separateness" in the child, who may feel cut off from the parent, and in the parent who, anticipating early surrogate care, may resist formation of a close bond.[16] (A suggestive analogy: many parents of premature infants experience attachment problems because, in the early critical days, they didn't *dare* love the child too much.) Dr Berry Brazelton has observed a similar phenomenon among expectant mothers planning to go back to work soon after giving birth. Such women, he says, seem to have "a lack of passionate commitment to the pregnancy. They don't have the dreams and fears and fantasies normal to most expectant mothers. It's as if they are guarding themselves from the turmoil of attachment. As if they are grieving already for what might be lost."[17]

If indeed the day care child feels more detached from parents than does the home care child, the often observed attachment to peers comes as no surprise. From toddlerhood on, children in group settings tend to be actively involved with their companions — playing, arguing, laughing, talking, scrapping. Sudden loss of a playmate becomes an occasion of true grief and mourning. As Otto Weininger says, "Peer group relationships of children who meet only in the special 'world for children' provided essentially as a service for their parents may indeed have an intensity which is peculiarly vulnerable to change and discontinuity."[18] The emotional reliance on other children appears to be accompanied by a corresponding thinness in adult-child relationships. Kindergarten teachers claim they can spot day care graduates by a certain jaunty indifference to adult opinion — and at least one study has found that the longer a child spends in day care, the better he gets along with his contemporaries and the more trouble he has with adults. Commenting on the presumed effectiveness of day care as a socializing agent, Weininger says, "We may well ask whether the goal of socialization is positive interaction with peers at the expense of adult relationships — a typical reaction for young adolescents perhaps, but not with four-year-olds."[19]

In general, day care children acquire superior social skills. The other side of this social confidence is often cockiness. Day care children tend to be less tractable, less polite, than children raised at home. They feel their oats, they're less impressed by punishment, less averse to dirt, more prone in the early years to tantrums and toilet lapses.[20] What adults want is not necessarily important to them. They will be loud and boisterous and quarrelsome if they choose. Yes, they enjoy groups, gravitate to groups; often this means that away from the group, they're at loose ends. Accustomed to companions and a highly structured life, children raised in day care may seek constant stimulation and suffer from an impaired capacity for entertaining themselves.[21]

The gravest social development problem presented by the day care child is increased aggressiveness. On this point all investigators agree: day care children are more inclined to get what they want by hitting, threatening, kicking, punching, insulting and taking possessions without permission. ("Day care may slow the acquisition of some cultural values," one observer says delicately.[22] Indeed.) A recent report found day care children performing *fifteen* times as many aggressive acts as home-reared age-mates.[23] Other studies say that these children enter school more hostile to both teachers and peers and that their aggressiveness is accompanied by (or is part of) much greater impulsivity and distractibility.[24] School performance may well be affected. A British study conducted by the Tavistock Institute, reporting the progressive acceleration of aggressiveness in day care children (the longer in care, the feistier), found that of eight day care graduates, all average or above average in intelligence, only one achieved average levels in reading, language and ability to concentrate.[25]

This is bad news, particularly in view of evidence that male aggressiveness, once developed early, is likely to persist.[26] Some early childhood specialists downplay gloomy reports, suggesting that *aggression* is "too global, too charged with meaning" for innocent playground mayhem. The "aggressive" child, they maintain, may well be the one "to initiate rich and sustained interactive play, to co-operate with his playmates and to offer comfort and reassurance."[27] From the standpoint of the child who has been punched or struck, comfort and reassurance may not altogether compensate for the richness of such interactive play. There is certainly much in a typical day care setting which invites aggression. Whenever a lot of children assemble, there will be noise and tension and shoving and assault, accidental or intended. If the adult-to-child ratio is low, caretakers will have difficulty policing the territory. And of course, where children are all more or less the same age, trouble develops more easily. A Yale study of thirty different day care centres found five- and six-year-old boys "substantially and significantly more troublesome" than home-reared contemporaries. The study's author suggests two explanations for their finding. One is that aggressive behaviour is reinforced in group care settings by the attention it receives from other children. The other is based on the psychoanalytic theory that children learn to control aggressive impulses by identification with a loved parent whom they hope to please. "If day care dilutes the intensity of children's identifications with their parents, then the motivation for boys to inhibit their aggressive feelings and actions might be considerably reduced."[28]

Some of these problems can be solved. Presumably, aggressiveness will decline if children are given plenty of space, no crowding; if groups contain a mixture of ages; if sufficient caretakers are provided — and the caretakers are alert to head off trouble; if day care staff concerns itself more with developing in their charges behaviour appropriate for school. (Jerome Kagan, commenting on the noise and wildness common in group care settings, observes that "many day care workers, trained in a philosophy of permissiveness toward aggressiveness and emotional spontaneity, are reluctant to punish every misdemeanor.")[29]

Assuming such possible changes, however, a question remains. Is there, in the very situation of the child-in-care, something which either stimulates aggression or inhibits its control? Selma Fraiberg, author of *The Magic Years* and a gifted child psychiatrist, thinks there is. She bases her argument on Freud's thesis that the conflict between love and aggression is central to all personality development. If the relationship with beloved parents is disturbed during the formative years, the child may have difficulty in controlling his aggressive impulses. This is likely to occur, Fraiberg says, with unstable and haphazard day care arrangements, when "a baby is stored like a package" with various caretakers, while his mother works. The day care arrangements available to most parents, she fears, work against the love, trust, joy and valuing which should flower between parents and child. So the child may learn that the world is indifferent or hostile, "that all adults are interchangeable, that love is capricious, that human attachment is a perilous investment, and that love should be hoarded for the self in the service of survival." He learns, in short, the aggressive stance.[30]

Or the child's aggression may go hand in hand with a kind of masked, thwarted love. In a brilliant portrait of Winston Churchill, psychiatrist Anthony Storr suggests that the British bulldog's extraordinary pugnacity originated in early emotional deprivation. Churchill's parents may have loved their child. But they were ambitious, preoccupied, intensely social; sometimes weeks passed when they barely saw young Winston. Storr observes that if a child's needs are not fulfilled, or only partially fulfilled, he feels frustrated. Frustration leads to feelings of hostility which cannot be expressed against those who have provoked it because the child needs the love they deny him. So he creates imaginary perfect parents. "A small child, being weak and defenceless, finds it unbearable to believe that there are no adults who love, support and guide him."[31] "My mother shone for me like the Evening Star," Churchill wrote in later life. "I loved her dearly — but at a distance." Meantime, what about the repressed hostility? It has to go somewhere. Frequently it turns itself against authority, crystallizing in a generalized aggressiveness. Storr hypothesizes that the master orator who roused England in an hour of crisis — "We shall go on till the end, we shall fight in France, we shall fight . . . we shall fight . . . *we shall fight*!" — succeeded precisely because his hostility, rage and aggressiveness had at last found a complete, legitimate outlet.

Well. Churchill in the House of Commons may seem far removed from the day care child pummelling a classmate on the playground. It is seldom lack of love or a demanding social schedule which impels parents to place a child in care. But what matters is the child's perception. A fifteen-month-old toddler cannot understand that both Mummy and Daddy need to work. Even a much older child has trouble understanding that. Otto Weininger describes a surely not untypical day care scene: a parting between mother and children — boy four, girl about three. "She obviously had a great deal of difficulty leaving them; they held on to her legs until she knelt down, talked to them, found materials for them to play with — and she kept postponing her leaving." The little boy finally wandered off to get a truck, but the little girl whimpered and clung. Eventually the mother hugged and kissed the child, offered her a book and left — "not rushed, but in a sensitive way." Soundlessly weeping, the little girl sought out her brother, shoved herself into his side, thumb in mouth, and said loudly, "Mommies are mean."[32] One can guess that for the child who feels inexplicably abandoned, hurt or angry or frightened, the temptation to strike out and bop somebody on the head must be very strong.

Portrait: A Day Care Mother

Celia has been active in the women's movement and the push for better day care since the early 1970s. She and her husband are both teachers; their sons attended two small day care centres from the age of three months until they entered school.

"A lot of families put their children in day care because both parents have to work; we both worked because we wanted our children to have the day care experience. At one point, when both boys were at the centre, our fees ran $125 a week — a lot of money for that time, 1978.

"Day care was already a familiar world to me by the time my first child was born: I'd been involved in the organization of a campus co-operative day care, worked there as a volunteer and ended up as a fulltime caregiver. Everything I saw at that centre convinced me that group care provided a healthy basis for young children's development. My first son,

Benjamin, started in day care at three months. Yes, it was hard to leave him. If unemployment insurance had been more generous, I'd have waited another three months. As it was — well, my work was close enough so I could bike over to the centre and breast feed him at lunch time . . . and I kept his picture with me. By the time John was born, five years later, I was more confident as a mother, more involved in my job and completely adjusted to the day care rhythm, so I took that separation more calmly.

"I have always had perfect confidence in the centres our children have attended. They're a community of friends, with a common appreciation of how children should be treated, a respect for the integrity and individuality of each person. One centre was a co-operative, with parents very much involved in decision-making. If anything troubled us, we had recourse. For instance, at one point we became unhappy with the meals served in Benjamin's infant centre. They were nutritious enough, but not attractively presented. The cook at that time had an everything-in-one-big-pot philosophy. We felt that texture and colour were important even to the babies, so we called a meeting and settled on a new system of menus and shopping lists that made for more attractive plates. You see, we didn't just turn our children over to the centre; we *were* the centre.

"What do I think are the advantages of day care? Actually, I don't think in terms of *advantages*. I simply believe that good group day care is a legitimate alternative for families who choose to use it. We made that choice because we wanted our children to have a broad range of experience, knowing other children and adults — and knowing that other adults would care for them. Our particular day care centres were free of the constraints you'd find even in an easygoing home (where you can't bring your pet rat into the living-room, say, or play ball in the kitchen). Benjamin thrived in that atmosphere; he loved the group and had loads of individual attention. He was *adored*. So when people tell me my

child missed out on being loved, feeling special, I don't buy
that. I also don't go along with those sympathetic murmurs
about what *I* missed, not being with my child all day. My
answer to that is always, 'You weren't there, you don't know.'
For every charming story people tell me about their baby's
first words or first step, I have a story about what happened
when I was in fact there.

"When we were paying out $500 a month for centre care,
some friends said, 'For that, you could have a nanny.' We
never considered that option. I think nannies tend to be either
fantastic or terrible. I've seen them walking along pushing
prams, staring into space, not saying a word to the kids. I
couldn't feel comfortable leaving my children alone in my
house with someone who after all is a stranger. In a day care
centre, you can visit, spend time, assess the situation. And
the fact that you've a staff of caretakers — in our case, four
helpers — means that there are built-in checks and balances.

"When it comes to social development, I'm not inclined to
say 'Day care makes a kid more this or more that.' Whether it
makes a child more outgoing, for instance, depends on individual temperament. I do believe that group care promotes a
certain tolerance. Children learn to share, to accommodate
other people's needs and desires (even when their own desires
are very different). I think day care kids are more likely to
stand up for their rights and assert themselves, if they think
they've been treated unfairly. You should hear the case our
kids make for their right to watch 'Night Rider' and 'Blue
Thunder' — which we *don't* allow. Our boys have attended a
pacifist, non-sexist centre, and by age five they had absorbed
those attitudes; they know that might is not necessarily right.
They know how to go about solving differences by thinking
and talking. Even the babies pick up the idea of co-operation;
I've seen groups of one- and two-year-olds getting together to
open the fire door — strictly forbidden. Posting a lookout,
too. Along with the co-operative spirit, I see in my children
and their day care friends a lack of *meanness*. The other day I

heard some little boys teasing a fat child with glasses, calling him a four-eyed freak. I honestly don't believe my children are capable of that; they couldn't *understand* such behaviour.

"Our day care centres are small — sixteen children — and organized into mixed-age groups, which I like. One nice thing is the way the older kids look out for the little ones. John, at five, loved the babies and played big brother to the little guys. If he got to the table first for snack, he'd save a place for Evan, who's two.

"Some of the research has raised questions about language development in day care children. I think that area needs to be looked at more carefully. There are so many influences on language development. Look at Benjamin. In grade four he chose to write an essay on the Stratford Festival, and he began with: 'Where do you go when you want to see the latest Shakespeare play?' "

Portrait: A Day Care Child

Benjamin is eleven. He doesn't remember starting day care, of course — "I was a baby!" — but he remembers vividly, and with some wistfulness, the leaving.

"When you get too old for day care, there's always a goodbye party, with a card and a present. They had great parties at day care. Tim — he was my special friend — would make pizza, and we'd play games and sing, like that crazy song about the elephant sitting on someone, and 'Here we are together.' *Of course* I liked going to day care. We had three big rooms to play in. A table room — that was for lunch and snacks and stuff. A dress-up room — that changed every month, like one month it'd be a hospital and the next month a house or a grocery store. And a climber room, with slides and big blocks, everything for adventure play. We'd get capes from the dress-up room and run around having sword fights. Sure the girls played too; they'd be Batman or Superman, you know, the major superheroes. There was lots of space for noisy stuff, and then there were quiet places, like a sort of linen closet in the table room, where you could sit and read.

"Sometimes we had real fights at day care, when we got mad — non-contact fights. The teachers would always come and break it up and tell us it wasn't right to fight with your friends and how we should make it up. If you did something really bad, like wrecking another kid's fort, you might have to sit on the bench for a while. That was the worst punishment, being sent to the bench in the hall.

"I learned lots of stuff at day care, like what a friend does. A friend is someone to have around to play with you and keep the fun going. I learned to draw real well, and I learned basic science and crafts — you know, like ornaments and paper chains at Christmas. Christmas was really neat at the centre. We had exchange of gifts, only they weren't store-bought; you were supposed to bring one of your own toys to give — good stuff, not junk.

"I had some friends who didn't go to day care. They really missed a lot of fun. At day care there's always friends to play with and talk to. There's more space to play in and more things to play with. I wouldn't have wanted to stay home. The grown-ups at day care were sort of like your mom. And there's stuff you don't have at home. We had a fireman's pole to slide down and a real trap door and a tree to climb and a rope bridge. Then across the road there was this park with really neat apparatus — tube slides, teeter-totters, logs to play on, a sandbox and a water fountain. . . . You know, just thinking about it, I really miss that place."

Emotional Attachments

The great fear of day care opponents has been that a child placed in surrogate care during the early years will suffer "maternal deprivation" — that, having failed to establish normal affectional bonds with his mother, he will fall prey to the various "diseases of non-attachment." Selma Fraiberg defined these as emotional impoverishment, inability to love and dangerous impulsivity. Others have foreseen consequences still more grave: delinquency, depression, mental retardation, dwarfism, acute distress and "affectionless psychopathy" — a callous indifference to others' feelings, inability to trust, inability to form lasting, mutually affectionate relationships.[33]

Most such concerns can be traced back to John Bowlby's landmark studies of attachment, separation and loss, conducted after World War II on displaced and orphaned children. Observing these casualties of war in institutional care, Bowlby concluded that lack of mothering and close emotional bonds during the early years had permanently impaired the capacity to make satisfying attachments later on. Rene Spitz reached similar, even grimmer conclusions on the basis of visits to South American orphanages, where neglected infants had regressed to a state of stuporous apathy. Spitz's and Bowlby's work — and that of the Robertsons, filming toddler reactions to hospitalization — has been tremendously influential; it can be largely credited with the phasing out of orphanages in favour of foster homes. As a critique of day care, however, it is only marginally relevant. The emotionally damaged children these studies describe had been traumatized by war and the death of parents. They had lost their homes, their familiar neighbourhoods and their comforting daily routines. Many were in poor health, suffering from malnutrition and the lack of any kind of exercise or educational program. Cared for by a small number of constantly changing attendants, without any source of warmth or personal interest, these little waifs suffered, not merely maternal deprivation, but deprivation of life.

The situation of day care children living at home with parents whom they see before and after the daily exodus is in no way comparable. Bowlby is surely right in emphasizing the effect of early life experiences on later development. He is right in insisting that "love in infancy and childhood is as important for mental health as are vitamins and proteins for physical health." What many child psychologists now question is the notion that this nourishing love must be, can only be, *mother* love. What about father love or grandparent love? The really essential condition for wholesome early development is love and attention from, not necessarily a single continuous caretaker, but from one or two — maybe three — *constant* love objects. If infants and toddlers experience a rapid turnover of attendants (in unstable day care arrangements), then confusion and anxiety are inevitable. But evidence suggests that small children can make more than one powerful emotional attachment. A pioneer Scottish study showed that by eighteen months, infants typically had about three "special people."[34] All investigators agree that though a child may be devoted to both his caregiver *and* his mother, he doesn't confuse the two roles and will, at moments of stress, reach for mother. In a striking demonstration of this preference, children from nine to twenty-three months old — all of them in day-long group care from their second or third month — were given a clear plastic box containing a tempting cookie. With caretaker and mother both present, the children settled in with their treasure next to the mother. Of those who sought aid in opening the box, all appealed to their mothers.[35]

"Most children develop bonds with several people," concludes Michael Rutter, who has conducted the most exhaustive studies of maternal deprivation, "and it appears likely that these bonds are basically similar." Furthermore, "the chief bond need not be with a biological parent, it need not be with the chief caretaker and it need not be with a female."[36] For the child, one person may be special because he or she does the feeding, another because he's the playmate and still another simply because this is the same-sexed parent. Father, mother, siblings, friends, teachers all influence development, more so at some times than at others. "Children do not suffer from having several mother-figures so long as stable relationships and good care are provided by each."

This is not to say that seeing more of a day care worker than of mother or father makes no difference. The time of entering surrogate care is important. Sally Provence and her Yale associates found that children entering the centre from the beginning of the second year, when attachment to parents had become strong, reacted to separation with anxiety, anger or apathy; some lost previously acquired skills. On the other hand, for infants placed very early in full day care, the process of attachment to parents suffered some delay or interference.[37] A study of infants in a low-income population found that out-of-home care initiated during the first year of life "greatly increases the likelihood of anxious-avoidant attachments." In other words, at reunion with the mother after separation, such babies are much more likely to avoid contact and resist affectionate overtures. This behaviour has troubling implications not only for the infant's future development, but for the parent's. The authors of this study report that mothers of infants who developed anxious attachments had more negative reactions to pregnancy, were more tense and irritable and more vulnerable to life stress than were the mothers of securely attached babies.[38] Some observers note less physical closeness between mother and day care children; the relationship may be loving but not intensely physical. Clearly there are imponderables here, mysteries not plumbed by the psychometrician's art. Both Rutter and Kagan, the chief researchers in maternal deprivation, conclude there is no firm evidence that daily separation from the mother weakens a child's attachment to parents. Yet both end on a hesitant minor note. "Any single evaluation procedure might be insufficiently sensitive to the subtlety of the attachment process," Kagan concedes. "If reasonable indexes do not reveal a difference between day care and home-reared children, one cannot conclude that there are none, but only that differences in attachment are at least not grossly obvious."[39] Rutter ends with a *but* and a *nevertheless*: "The evidence is inconclusive, but it seems that although most young children do not become overtly insecure and anxious as a result of day care, nevertheless it is possible that more subtle ill-effects occur in some children." And then, the familiar proviso: "The matter warrants further study."[40]

Portrait: A Father Who Stayed Home with His Child

"I came of age during the sixties, and for years my life view was pleasure-oriented, narcissistic. I would have procrastinated a long time about having a child, but Trisha was approaching thirty-five; she had a deadline. She used to say, 'I want you to want a baby,' and I maintained it was impossible for me to want what I didn't know. When I agreed, it was with the idea, in the back of my mind, that even if things didn't work out for me, the child would be fine because Trisha wanted one so much. Once she became pregnant, the doubts evaporated. There was an unexpected physical pride — *my child* — and the miracle of a life growing that was connected to us both.

"From the beginning, we agreed that I should stay home with the baby. Trisha had an absorbing job, costume designer for an opera company, and a good salary. I had my own contracting business, so I could move in and out without difficulty. Also I was a bit tired of what I'd been doing and wanted to try something new. I think I had some innocent notions of life with an infant as serene, quiet, with lots of time to read and think. I really wanted to live through the daily time with a child, to be the house person. Men of my generation are not insensitive to the whole women's movement dialogue about roles, the unfairness of women being defined in terms of their housekeeping skills. I'd done household jobs before, but mostly weekend binges of cooking and cleaning. I'd never been in charge. Certainly I had no idea of how different life would be when I was responsible for shopping, cooking, laundry — and a baby.

"I think the hardest thing for me, that year I spent at home with Robin, was adjusting to another life rhythm, a totally different experience of time. As a contractor I knew the way to get things done was to stick at a job, persevere without distraction. Baby-time is entirely fragmented; every day became a series of fifteen-minute bits, a jigsaw puzzle. Robin was from the first lively and demanding. He never slept for long; I couldn't put him down and go about my business. The minute he went down for his nap, I'd dash into action, try to get things done — and then he'd be calling again. Very frustrating. I juggled and juggled all day long, was endlessly busy — and at day's end I'd feel I hadn't accomplished anything.

"That's one side of the story. The other is that I was getting tremendous satisfaction out of watching Robin's development. When you're in a minimal situation, ordinary events and small things leap out. I registered the moment when Robin got control of his neck muscles, when he learned to grasp accurately. I could observe all the day to day changes, marvel at the practice that went into achieving little bits of control. The speed at which an infant acquires skills is humbling. I remember thinking, 'Here I am having a beer, watching a ball game on TV — and he's learning to talk.'

"Of course the arrival of a baby and the reversal of roles affected the relationship between Trisha and me. I discovered to what extent I'd defined myself in terms of accomplishment . . . and what was I accomplishing? I guess I felt less valued. So we had a lot of classic role-reversal stuff. Trisha would come home from work exhausted and bitchy. I'd push Robin at her — 'Here, take your son. I have to make dinner' — and she wanted a hot bath to relax. If she gave up the bath, because she felt guilty, then she wasn't in a good space. It took me a while to get over the feeling that my work day ended when she came through the door. We had the usual soap-opera confrontations, in reverse. She'd say, 'I had a really bad day,' and I'd flame. 'You think it's easy being home with a baby all day?' The whole sexual dimension changed, faded. Trisha went to bed early, worn out, and got up for night feedings. I got up early at 5:30 when Robin woke, she slept another hour and rushed off to work. When would you make love?

"Before Robin, we were a couple of mature adults with independent careers and lots of time to ourselves. We were both self sufficient emotionally and in other ways, so there wasn't much occasion for conflict. Having a child makes you mutual in ways you never could have imagined. Suddenly I couldn't go out for a drink without making the assumption that Trisha would look after the baby. Small ventures had to be arranged, negotiated. Also a shared child highlights differences in value systems. Trisha and I had very different notions about dealing with Robin's night-time crying. She wanted to reassure him every five minutes, I was for letting him cry it out. And so long as I was the home person, taking care of him, I felt I should be calling those shots. Little things created tension. Like Robin would be crawling towards something dangerous; Trisha's impulse was to sweep him up right away, mine was to let him explore: 'Relax. I've got my eye on him.' Suddenly we had different feelings about clean floors, which I now thought *very* important. Trisha's attitude to the floors seemed to me . . . a bit offhand. There were mutual recriminations over things we'd never thought about before.

"My househusbanding was hard on Trisha. She missed Robin terribly. Weekends were great, Monday and Tuesday OK. By Wednesday, she'd be anxious about not having enough time with the baby. Thursday was usually a *crise*. Then Friday was the weekend, relief — and the whole cycle began again. Though I was chief caretaker, Robin was always clingier with Trisha. In spite of what anyone says, I'm convinced that the physical-emotional connection with the woman is uniquely intense. It's one thing to weep with joy when you see your child pop out, another to give birth and to nurse. I used to watch Trisha nursing Robin and realize there was a dimension of feeling I couldn't experience — something profound, peaceful, oceanic. We were all glad when Trisha quit her job and took over at home.

"There's no question, my relationship with my son has been deeply, permanently affected by those early months together. Looking after a baby, there's an accumulation of daily detail, from the simplest physical thing — feeding, examining poops, tracking his digestion . . . and then, in time, seeing the growing competence, the joy, the sense of humour. Now that I see Robin briefly in the morning and again at night, I wonder about men who have that kind of relationship with a child from the beginning. You can't zoom in and out of a child's life and count on having wonderful special moments on demand. The special moments just happen, unbidden. Because Robin and I have had that accumulation of moments, I'm not to him just another person who parachutes in occasionally; I can tell that he experiences me as someone with whom he has a rich history. I come home, and he's full of talk — well, eighteen-month-old talk. 'Mummy park . . . Pee outside. . .' and always, 'Sip of boo?' That's his ritual sip of my beer. We have shared jokes. He'll fart loudly, point at me and say, 'Daddy fart!' If I disclaim responsibility, he turns to the cat: 'Kitty fart?'

"Because *I was there*, all those wonderful exhausting months, *I know my son*, with an awareness that begins at a physical level. Just from the way Robin moves, I can tell if he's overtired, a little out of control, teasing, mad. . . . I rejoice in his growing, and I'm growing with him."

Moral Development

Day care research focuses, understandably, on those aspects of child development which lend themselves to measurement.

A toddler's progress, for example, can be precisely rated on the Turalinski scale. Does he refer to himself by name? (Social skills.) Can he throw a ball? (Gross motor development.) Has he learned five colours? (Cognitive growth.) Moral development is a subtle, trickier matter — and one in which there may be no such general agreement about goals. In this most important life area, then, the relative absence of hard data compels a somewhat speculative approach. What do we actually know about the value systems of children who experience early long-term surrogate care? And what can we guesstimate, given the nature of children and the quality of average other-than-parent care?

The question "What kind of person will my child become?" always central, takes on in today's climate a new urgency. Consider the current scene. Adolescents have always found ways of distinguishing themselves from parents, cutting loose. But surely never before the post World War II generations has the shape and colour of rebellion assumed so dramatic — and threatening — a cast. The long hair, beads and ubiquitous jeans of the '60s, the aggressively ethnic costumes of the '70s (dashikis and Afros on the offspring of Daughters of the American Revolution or United Empire Loyalists), the punk savagery of the '80s (chains, black leather, neon-coloured Mohawk haircuts and "street makeup") — these signal profound change. The eighteen-year-old with shaved head, draped in Hiroshima-style tatters with safety pins through the ear lobes is not dressed for success, not concerned with making friends and influencing people. He or she is ostentatiously opting out of a scheme of values to which previous generations have paid at least lip service. Self-discipline and self-denial are OUT. Self-indulgence and self-centredness are IN.[41] The pursuit of happiness as traditionally defined has given way to the pursuit of immediate satisfaction, pleasure. Among the parents of rockers, or those banded together in the organization Toughlove to protect themselves against their own young, there must be considerable bewilderment. Among new parents there is certainly a new high level of anxiety (indicated by the proliferation and popularity of parenting courses). Battered by bad news — about juvenile crime, vandalism, drugs, drinking, teenage pregnancies and disease — most parents realize that a child's moral sense will not just happen like permanent teeth, as the result of normal developmental processes. Values are learned. Which values are learned, and how strongly, depends on early care.

Addressing the question of surrogate care for the very young children of working parents, Dr Annette Silbert, a Boston child psychologist, observes that each case is individual, no pat prescriptions apply. "Many people are unhappy when they hear that, but it is better to face this truth than to encourage the illusion that perfect, all-purpose prescriptions exist." The real question, she says, is not job or no job, day care or home care, but "What does it take to live in our society? If we want our children to become adults who can cooperate with one another, who have flexibility so they can adapt to changing situations, who can work, if we want people who are capable of affection, devotion, constancy and who will be wise parents when they are of age, then there are certain things we have to put into the care of these children when they are young." Only the family, Dr Silbert maintains, can provide children with some semblance of cohesion and harmony, with the basis for trust in other people and in themselves. What about the option of a mother-substitute? If the substitute is affectionate, responsive and loyal (in other words, stays on the job) the child may flourish, will love both caretaker and mother. But — "the values he will incorporate will most likely be those of the chief caretaker, the conscience he will develop will be influenced as much by the caretaker as the mother — and if the value systems of the principal characters in his little life's drama are not harmonious he has some ready-made conflicts."[42] Consider for example, the infant daughter of professional, academic parents who value intellectual distinction, industry, self-discipline and achievement. Put her for the first four years in the care of (a) a European nanny (b) a loving, aging matron (c) an active young *au pair*. The result, depending on care, may be a beautifully mannered social being, a relaxed carefree spirit, a wholesome skier or tennis player. . . Certainly her parents cannot count on genetic endowment and some judicious "quality time" to mould this child in accordance with their own value system.

Children learn what they live with. "If a child lives with hostility he learns to fight. If he lives with criticism he learns to condemn," Dorothy Law Nolte wrote in a well-known collection of aphorisms. "If a child lives with fairness he learns justice. If he lives with approval he learns to like himself. And if he lives with acceptance and friendship he learns to find love in the world." What of the child who lives in some form of surrogate care from infancy until school-starting age? "A day care centre that ministers to a child from his sixth month to his sixth year has more than 8,000 hours to teach him values, beliefs and behaviours and, potentially, is an enormously powerful influence over what that child will become," says Harvard's Jerome Kagan.[43] All day long, in care, the child is learning — and not just what's in the curriculum. When three-year-old Kelly draws faces on the fingers of her left hand — "Look, puppets!" — a teacher snatches the felt marker with a reproving, "We draw on paper, not fingers!" (Lesson: *Do what you're told. Experiments get you into trouble.*) Jason wants to finish his block tower but is propelled into the circle for "Show and Tell." (*Your own work is not important. Fitting into the group is important.*) Charlie — whose mother is in hospital with a new baby — is having a bad day and the caretaker, suddenly tired of his whining, says, "That's enough now. I want to see a smile on your face." (*It's not safe to show your feelings.*) After juice the children are given collage materials to make greeting cards. "Let's see who can finish first!" the caretaker says. (*Speed matters more than quality. Get ahead of the next guy.*) Both Margie and

Steve are having difficulty with their Easter basket handles. The day care worker briskly attaches a handle to Margie's basket — "There, isn't that pretty?" — and tells Steve, "You're a big boy. Put more paste on the handle and try again." (*Girls need a lot of help. Boys can manage on their own.*) Ellen interrupts the story with an earnest question, "Why can't boys have babies?" and is silenced with "This isn't talking time, it's listening time." A particularly horrifying example of unintentional values-teaching appears in *Children and Day Nurseries*. A group of four-year-olds is being taught numbers and colours and days of the week as part of their school preparation. Mention of school triggers in one small boy a passionate outburst: "My Daddy's dead, but I've got a grand-father and he's going to take me to school!" "Is he?" says the teacher. "Now, everyone, after me: It-is-Wednesday-the-30th-of-June."[44]

But surely parents have the last word in value-teaching? In theory, yes. Working parents may fantasize delightful quiet times at day's end when they hold a little one close and share their thoughts about life. Reality is somewhat less idyllic. Reality is tired parents collecting a tired child (who has been away from home as much as ten hours). Child is cross, also angry at mother in the sheer nervous excitement of seeing her again; mother, all set up for tenderness, feels a surge of guilt and anger too. ("I work hard all day and this is what I get.") There's dry cleaning to collect, a stop for milk and coffee, supper to prepare, bath and bedtime still to come. . . Who wants to talk (or hear) about Beauty, Truth and Goodness?

And of course, values — like sex education, like any kind of complicated learning — are not taught in orderly segments at selected times. (Today, honesty. Tomorrow, fair play.) Values emerge continuously in the course of daily life. "It's rude and unkind to stare at a child who has trouble walking. That girl has cerebral palsy, and it's hard for her to get around. Why don't you hold the door open for her?" "No, you can't keep the Smurf you found on the school steps. Give it to your teacher and she'll try to find out whose it is." "Yes, I know you'd like to go to McDonald's with the kids. But you promised to go to Grandma's this afternoon. You mustn't break a promise." Value issues are raised constantly in a child's questions — about war, about people who are different, about sex and divorce and the TV commercials. "Children do not make notes about their questions to bring up at a more convenient time," Rita Kramer writes in *In Defense of the Family*. "They wonder about things according to the rhythm of their inner life, and ask whoever is there at the moment. Being there more often than not when they're constructing their view of reality, their outlook on life, is a value to be seriously weighed against the reasons any mother may have for not being there."[45]

This is perhaps the time to talk about quality time. A recent, much overworked addition to the language of working parents, quality time is invoked as a good equal if not superior to mere quantity. Two hours of concentrated attention, the theory goes, is better than a day-long diffuse relationship in which mother and child, together at home, go about their separate business. It's an elegant theory. One catch is that you have to have a certain amount of *quantity* before quality is possible. The other is that true quality time can't be programmed. It happens — when parent and child are emptying the dishwasher or making cookies or planting petunias. It may be called for when a child falls off a swing or has a fight with her best friend. Past infancy a healthy child neither wants nor needs mother's continuous presence. What he *does* want is the assurance that she's there when needed.

The question of moral values comes down to this: who will interpret the world for the growing child, who will teach him about right and wrong — parents or substitute caretakers, who may or may not share the parents' value system? If a child is cared for in a large day care centre, the question is further complicated by the adult/child ratio — so few adults (very busy, often unavailable) and so many children. In that case the values a child learns may well be those of other three- or four-year olds, what psychiatrist Selma Fraiberg called the "survival values" of the peer group: *Get yours.*

The pre-school child, Jerome Kagan reminds us, "is in the process of establishing a set of beliefs about how the world is and he, like all of us, is tempted to conclude that *what is, ought to be.*" If he is to believe that other people are kind, fair, honest, trustworthy, good, and that persistence in the face of difficulty is worthwhile, then he must be provided with an environment which supports such beliefs. If he is to feel in charge of his own life but watched over by responsible adults who care about him, provisions for care must support that conclusion. None of these beliefs develops automatically.

Consider now the child in a large fairly typical day care centre — not wonderful, not terrible. There are eighty children here, mostly ages two to four, with eight caretaking adults whose job at times may be simply to prevent mayhem or co-ordinate boots with boot-owners. Noise level is high; activity constant. A shy child or an unhappy one goes virtually unnoticed. If he requires attention — somebody hits him on the head with a block — there's time for a bandage but not, probably, for close holding, a gentle explanation of *why* Mike hit him ("You knocked over his space station. I know, you didn't mean to.") and reintroduction to the scene ("Let's go over and see if you can help."). As for feeling in charge of his own life — the freedom of a day care centre is illusory. At home, maybe, he can have a snack or go outdoors when he pleases. Here, of necessity, the schedule decides. At home he inhabits an adult environment where he must learn what can and cannot be done. The stove is hot, knives dangerous, the china vase fragile, the garage and the baby's room off limits. So he practices the art which is at the core of moral behaviour, making choices. If he has been well parented, he becomes, in Milton's grand phrase, "sufficient to have stood, though free to fall." The child in a day care centre, an artificial child-centred environment, is in a sense not free to fall — at least he can't fall very far. His choices are all trivial: puzzles or paints? Apple juice or orange?

The child in a centre is also poorly provided with adult models. Remember the ratio: one adult to eight, ten, sometimes fifteen children. Albert Bandura and his colleagues have shown that children learn moral standards (as well as general coping skills) by observing others in a wide range of situations. Research also demonstrates what most of us know from experience: that we admire and strive to emulate adults whom we love and who love us. Separated from parents for almost all of his playing-working day, tended by adults who may be kind, devoted, conscientious but cannot be expected to *love* all their charges, the child in day care chooses models from the most plentiful source of supply — other children. In the generally neglected area of moral development, fraught as it is with imponderables, research agrees on one crucial, alarming point: day care children tend to acquire values and standards from their peers.

Peer group ascendency develops early. A Boston study of emotional development in middle class children compared those placed in day care around age one with those cared for at home, primarily by mothers. At twelve to eighteen months, day care children in the presence of their mothers are more likely to look at and become involved with peers than are matched home-reared infants.[46] By age four, differences are marked. Four-year-olds who had grown up in day care were less responsive to adult expectations and control, more prone to temper tantrums and revolt. They also showed more fearfulness in situations where no age-mates were present; the study's authors conclude that "for day care children, peers become a daily source of comfort and gratification; day care toddlers learn how to use peer contact to reduce anxiety or distress."[47] Over time, this alliance of children with children, a "substitute bonding to peers,"[48] strengthens. Other studies have found that day care veterans were drawn to other children rather than to adults — and to rowdier forms of play,[49] also that they were likelier, in games like marbles, to opt for competition rather than "the winning strategy of taking turns."[50]

To date, the only research tracking the effects of substitute care beyond the pre-school years is an eleven-year English study conducted in London.[51] T. Moore compared development in two groups of children from pre-school up through age fifteen. One group consisted of children who had experienced early substitute care (beginning at an average age of three and continuing for two years). The other group, up to age five, had apart from occasional baby-sitting been in full time mother-care. Both children and mothers were observed and interrogated at regular intervals (child ages, six, seven, nine, eleven, fifteen), and the first-hand assessments supplemented by school evaluations.

In the first assessment (1964), when the children were six years old, those who had experienced substitute care were judged significantly more self-assertive with both other children and their parents, less conforming and less impressed by punishment, less averse to dirt and more prone to toilet lapses than their home-reared counterparts. The differences by mode of care were far more pronounced for boys than for girls and became increasingly marked as the children grew older. Moore calls this a "sleeper effect."

Compared with home-reared boys, teenage males with a history of substantial substitute care were more likely to be described by the mother on a behaviour checklist as telling lies to get out of trouble, differing with parents about choice of friends, using parents' possessions without permission and taking "things they knew they should not have." As a group, Moore concluded, these boys are characterized by "fearless, aggressive nonconformity."

Boys raised primarily in their own families were described on the checklist by items like the following: "Can be trusted not to do things they should not do," "Slow to mix" with other children. Compared with their counterparts who had experienced substitute care, the boys themselves expressed a stronger interest in academic subjects, "making or repairing things," and "creative skills." The boys also read significantly better at age seven and were more likely to remain in school and pass their final examinations.

The differences among girls were similar but much less marked. The girls experiencing substitute care before the age of five "revealed more aggression and ambivalent feelings." They showed more confidence in the standardized task situations but revealed considerable unease about their adult sexual roles. Girls raised exclusively at home described themselves as "active" and expressed a positive attitude towards sex.

At study's end, Moore reached these conclusions:

1) Where a mother keeps her child in her own care full time to the age of five (to the exclusion of nursery school as well as of other substitute care) the child tends early to internalize adult standards of behaviour, notably self-control and intellectual achievement, relative to other children of equivalent intelligence and social class.

2) For boys, this effect tends to persist into adolescence and involves anxiety for adult approval, with consequent inhibition of assertive behaviour, fear of physical hurt and timidity with peers.

3) Where mothering is diffused by substitute care of any kind for most of the day starting before the fourth birthday, boys come to care less for the approval of adults and more for that of their peers; their behaviour tends to become active, aggressive, independent and relatively free from fear despite some adolescent worries, and they are less likely to stay on at school and study for examinations.

4) In girls, the effect of regime as such is less clear. Exclusive mothering seems to involve for them less anxious inhibition than for boys. In adolescence it is the exclusively mothered group that appears more outwardly, and the diffusely mothered group more domestically oriented.

Reviewing Moore's work in relation to their own much smaller study, a research group at Syracuse University reached the tentative conclusion that "Early day care experience may not adversely affect adjustment with peers, but it may slow acquisition of some adult cultural values."[52]

Why are day care children less influenced by adult standards than children reared at home? A Swedish study suggests that the answer lies in the frequency and duration, the *realness* of encounters between adult and child. At home the child has, in the course of a day, dozens of conversations and experiences involving the parent. He inhabits an essentially adult world where neighbours visit and adult possessions must be respected. He can play (carefully) with things not designed to be played with — pots and pans, mother's lipstick, dustpan and broom. "He has access to the dishwashing detergent, the back stairs and the cat," and must learn the adult rules which govern that access. Opportunities for exploration are more numerous in the homes than in the centres, where the single role of the adult is child care and the setting is single purpose in design." A natural result of this difference is that at home, "the child is constantly reminded of the saliency of the adult, while the centre child's attention is drawn . . . to the importance of appropriate peer relations."[53]

Social psychologist Urie Bronfenbrenner, a student of cross-cultural child-rearing, adds a melancholy speculation as to why the young choose other young over parents. It is not necessarily the attractiveness of the peer group, he suggests, which produces a peer-oriented child. In general, peer-oriented children hold rather negative views of themselves *and* the peer group. They gravitate to age-mates to fill a "vacuum left by the withdrawal of parents and adults from the lives of children."[54] Seen from this perspective, group day care may be experienced as one more life area where youth sets the standards and tone.

At this point some readers, those perhaps who once saluted the greening of America as the dawn of a new day, may ask, What's bad about that? Is peer-oriented by definition a less admirable, less moral stance than adult-oriented? It all depends upon the peers. In the Soviet Union every educational agency, from nurseries to universities, embodies the ideals of obedience, self discipline, co-operation, industry, sharing, loyalty to the state, and it is to these ideals that the peer-oriented young Russian conforms. In Israel the peer-oriented young kibbutzniks embrace similar values but with a higher priority given to initiative, independence and physical daring. Both in Israel and in the Soviet Union, the peer group is heavily influenced by adult society. In North America and in Britain the peer group is relatively autonomous, cut off from the adult world and in fact defining itself by opposition and difference. Writing in 1970, Bronfenbrenner described peer-oriented young Americans as defiantly antisocial, off-hand about playing hookey, lying, teasing and "doing something illegal."[55] He found young Americans *more* likely to break a rule or law if they thought their peers would know about it. His gloomy prediction: If parents are removed from active participation in the lives of children, and the resulting vacuum is filled by the age-segregated peer group, "we can anticipate increased alienation, indifference, antagonism and violence on the part of the younger generation in all segments of our society — middle class children as well as the disadvantaged."

Portrait: A Home Care Child

Anya is nine. Apart from occasional baby-sitting, she has been cared for exclusively by her mother, a secretary-translator who stopped working when she was born, and her father, an English teacher. Because she has friends with working mothers — and strong opinions on the subject — Anya was eager to talk about the advantages of Life with Mother (even more eager when she discovered that the interview was to take place in an ice cream parlour).

When we arrived at Krazy Kone, the tip left by a previous customer lay on the table. Deliberately provocative, I said, "There's fifty cents you could have." Anya was shocked. "That would be stealing. It's obvious that money wasn't meant for us. It would be stealing from the waitress and stealing from the person who left the tip. That's two stealings."

Has she never stolen anything? "I took a marble once. It was so pretty, blue and shiny. My parents didn't know, but I felt . . . embarrassed."

What does she think are the worst things a kid can do?

"Well, stealing for sure. Saying mean things to somebody. If I get really mad, I try to turn my back and walk away." As for the worst things *she* has done: "Sometimes I show off — like what a good reader I am. And sometimes when Mom asks me to pick up my room, I just keep putting it off and putting it off. I like to do things my own way. Mom says I'm headstrong." Though she hasn't often been punished, she's emphatic about what hurts most: "Knowing I made Mom unhappy. That's worse than losing privileges."

Anya has never gotten into trouble at school. "Lots of kids copy other people's work. I'd never do that. It wouldn't be showing the teacher that I know anything, only that I know how to copy." She worries when she sees friends "sneaking a look" during tests. "Maybe I should report that because it's a bad thing to do, but I wouldn't want to get them into trouble."

Her great pleasures are playing with friends, reading, bike riding, talking to Mom. ("Dad and I go for walks with our dog. I don't talk to him as much as I do to Mom.") When she gets home from school, there's usually a special treat in the oven — a doughnut, a grilled cheese sandwich. "Mom and I sit and talk things over. Like if somebody was mean to me, she helps me see why the person behaves that way, and maybe I'll feel a little bit sorry for the mean person instead of mad. Mom and I read to each other. Right now, we're doing *A Time Trilogy*. We discuss why so and so did what he did — and what *we'd* do in his shoes. I think when kids don't have a mother at home they miss out on a lot, because mothers have a special way of teaching. My mom shows me things. I'm learning to knit now. When I practise my piano pieces, she listens and makes suggestions. I think I'd be angry if my mom couldn't be here when I get home, because I'd be missing the fun."

Blissfully polishing off her pistachio ice cream, Anya considers one final question: What's a good person? "A good person is someone who doesn't steal or lie (except maybe little fibs) or hurt people. She has a good sense of humour, she's interesting to talk to, somebody you can have fun with. She's not a bore to be around."

"*She*?" I ask.

"Or he. There are lots of good boys."

Portrait: A Home Care Mother

"I did not grow up dreaming of playing house and having children. I really had never thought much about children until I became pregnant, but with the first rounding and kicking, I found myself charmed by this new living creature. Then Anya was born — and how could I not love her? When she nursed, she would look at me with big unblinking clear eyes; there was a kind of pure inquisitiveness, a wish to look and see — none of the scheming, grown-up emotions. Some of my friends put their babies in day care at six months. I couldn't have done that. I needed to know at all times exactly what was going on with her. She was always a sturdy, independent person, even as an infant, but of course vulnerable too. Imagine if anything hurtful were done to her and she couldn't tell me. . . . I felt that way until she was past three.

"Being with Anya almost constantly the first year, I could rejoice in every landmark: the first time she turned over on her back; the first time she gurgled at her mobile; the first time she woke without yelling. When she sat and crawled and walked, *I was there*. At twelve months she produced her first word: *Moah!* (More!) That's absolutely typical; she has such a sense of life — *more* rather than *less*. I've always talked and read to her, even when she couldn't possibly understand the words. As soon as she could crawl, she would scuttle across the floor for a book and bring it to me. And I sang, remembering all the old songs my mother sang to me. At around eighteen months, Anya began humming with pure pleasure while she ate.

"Once Anya could walk, friends started asking when I'd be going back to work — and suggesting, often, that she needed to be with other kids. For myself, I couldn't bear to be separated from her at that point: she was so much fun. That's the only time in my life I was glad I didn't have a profession to rush back to. I loved taking Anya for walks in the stroller and showing her the world. She'd blow dandelions, smell flowers, laugh at the way our dog Sarah switched her tail. In stores she'd wave and call to shoppers; she reached for colourful boxes, and I'd let her choose a few. Being with a child brought back my own childhood; I found myself remembering hand plays (Two little blackbirds sitting on a hill, one named Jack, the other named Jill . . .), rediscovering the pleasures of Christmas and Easter. I shared her joys — and I was there when she needed me. One day at the playground she tackled the big slide, caught her sneaker on the way down and got a terrible gash. I was there to carry her into the emergency room and make a little party with popcorn and candles when we came home. I'm grateful for that. Anya is bold, fearless really — but she has always felt looked after, protected.

"Being with a young child, you can *see* the growing. At

eighteen months Anya got one of those little mailboxes with different-shaped slots — triangles, circles, squares — for mailing blocks. She'd work and work and just not get the hang of it. Then we went to Germany for four weeks. When we came home, Anya headed straight for her mailbox and mailed all the pieces, swiftly and surely. It was like an announcement that established her coming home as a bigger girl. *Here I am, this is my toy, I can do this.* She's always developed that way, in sudden leaps. At eighteen months her speech was still babyish: 'Mamma help you.' Three weeks later, in Germany, she said, 'Will we ever see Daddy again?'

"Anya likes to say I'm her best teacher and maybe I am, but there's nothing deliberate about the teaching. Of course I pass on skills. I've taught her to crochet rugs for her doll house; right now, she's learning to cook. But mostly what I do is interpret the world for her. We used to watch Mr Rogers together and talk about that; now, she sometimes watches the news with us, and we try to explain, on her level of understanding, about wars and nuclear dangers, evil in the world, but also to encourage her hopefulness about what good people can accomplish. We try to shield her from ugliness — and at the same time, to be truthful. Even as a toddler, she *expected* the truth from adults. When she was about two, we took her for shots, and the nurse said, 'This won't hurt at all, dear.' On the way home Anya was terribly upset, not so much by the painful jab as by the fact that the nurse had lied. For days after that, she played hospital, saying very firmly to the dolls before every shot, 'This is going to hurt *a lot.*'

"I am very clear about what I want for my child, and frankly, I couldn't have trusted any stranger to take charge of her life those first years. For instance, I want Anya to be confident of women's unlimited potential, not to be exposed to any sort of sexist treatment. I want her to feel good about who she is, to be able to attract and keep friends, to find a life work that will give her a sense of competence and usefulness.

I want her to be resilient, so that when things don't work out, she finds another way. These are life skills we practise together. When she gets frustrated with an art project, I suggest alternate ways of approaching the assignment. And I remind her that she must be patient with herself; she still has growing to do. Sometimes all that's needed is to set the work aside for a while, come back to it later. I encourage persistence — and rejoice when she comes shining through. I try to teach her to lose with some grace, in card games or anything else. Often I have to remind her that manners are a way of showing consideration for other people. (When she put up a sign on her room, DO NOT DISTURB. DON'T EVEN KNOCK, I told her that was needlessly abrupt and she changed it to PLEASE COME IN. KNOCK FIRST.

"I have never felt martyred about staying home three years with Anya and working part time after that. How could I? I have gone on doing the things I love — reading, walking, going to concerts and museums — and taking Anya with me. She didn't always enjoy these things. Symphony concerts were a struggle at first — she said, bor-ing! — but I always insisted she stay for one number. After that, we'd go home if she wanted. Now she sits happily through an evening. When the big Egyptian show came to Boston, she was only two; I carried her through the rooms, pointing out objects that I loved and she could relate to, like the cat statues and the bust of Nefertiti. By and large, I've found that a child will try to please parents and take an interest in what pleases them. Already at nine, Anya's tastes, her standards and values, are pretty much ours. She has become an ideal companion, a friend as well as a dearly beloved daughter. Would that have happened if she had spent the first years of her life, from 8 A.M. to 6 P.M., in someone else's care?"

Creativity

As a life skill and life enhancement, creativity would seem a prime goal of child-rearing. Yet in the vast day care literature — studies which tell us how day care affects attachment, exploratory behaviour, intellectual competence, dependency, aggression, health — almost nothing is said about creativity.[56] For some notion as to how day care is *likely* to affect children in the western world, we can study the sketchy reports of group care and creativity in other societies — and consider what is known in general, about the kind of environment which nourishes the creative impulse.

First, those other societies.[57] In Russia, China and Israel — all three, countries which have embraced communal child-rearing in their rejection of a troubled past — emphasis on community has meant a corresponding de-emphasis of individuality. In a *yasli*, a Russian day nursery, children perform assigned tasks exactly as prescribed (one red flower, two green leaves, bed of grass and sun in sky). Everyone's effort is displayed, no one's work is signed. In China three-year-olds take daily classes in Officially Approved Thought, learn to help each other and do most things quietly, either sitting with folded hands or marching two by two. On the Israeli kibbutz the young are socialized to peers, not parents; group needs and group standards dominate. It is not surprising that outside observers have found, in all three countries, a general dampening of the creative impulse. A psychologist visiting a Moscow *yasli* comments on "a tendency to work toward conformity rather than to encourage the creativity and diversity that American educators work for in the belief that a changing world requires individuals with ingenuity and flexibility."[58] Kibbutz-raised young people, widely praised for their courage, co-operativeness and loyalty, have also been described as somewhat "flat," with a diminished capacity for intensity, whether expressed in personal relationships or individual work. As for the Chinese: though foreigners seem unanimous in their enchantment with Chinese children — their friendliness, courtesy and sturdy faith — one of the most perspicacious and admiring observers raises the troubling question, "Doesn't the lack of individuality stifle creativity?" Ruth Sidel, conceding that yes, it's likely the Chinese way will produce uniform prescribed thinking and stifle unusual ability or insight, proceeds with scrupulous fairness to point out that modern Chinese "regard as creativity whatever furthers their cause in an innovative way."[59]

Between three such different societies and North America or Britain no easy comparisons are possible: on the one hand, socialist countries which exhibit a remarkable homogeneity in goals — what Bruno Bettelheim calls "a community of consensus" — and on the other, highly individualistic societies with a plurality of goals. Still, some characteristics of early group-rearing emerge. Margaret Mead long ago, studying the Hutterite communities, suggested that here, as on the kibbutz, children "raised with age-peers, with changing and overburdened nurses, who see parents . . . for short intervals every day," suffer impaired mobility, flexibility and individual venturesomeness — in other words, impaired creativity.[60]

Comparisons apart, it's fruitful to consider the day care experience in terms of what we know about the creative impulse. Creativity with a small "c" (as distinguished from the Creativity which produces novels, operas, scientific discoveries) is a quality of mind — lively, inventive, flexible and free. Every child is born creative, in the sense that he's an absolute original who sees things in his own unique way. Whether he retains what poets call "the innocent eye" depends very largely on early environment — on whether he's encouraged, *allowed* to be himself or urged towards conformity.

What is the most hopeful foundation for creative life? When psychologist Donald E. MacKinnon tested a group of architects nominated as the most creative in their field, he found a very wide range of intelligence. Some highly creative people had unimpressive IQs. Others, on tests, broke the bank, made all the bells ring. The common factor turned out to be not unusual intellect but high self-acceptance and confidence, sheer energy and whole-hearted commitment to a chosen task.[61]

Of course this result begs the question, What produces such individuals? MacKinnon found that his creative subjects had parents who showed "an extraordinary respect for the child and confidence in his ability to do what was appropriate. They did not hesitate to grant him rather unusual freedom in exploring his universe." Anyone who has grown up in a relatively safe, open world — a small town, a quiet suburb, a farm — recognizes the principle at work here. Riding a bike down a country road, building a tree house, organizing a backyard carnival, picking daisies and blackberries. . . Such experiences, freely chosen and pursued without adult involvement, contribute to venturesomeness and a sense of mastery. They are totally unlike any experience possible in the necessarily structured supervised day care world.

The institutional organization of centres may affect the child's development in ways not always obvious. Otto Weininger suggests that the day's division into "times" for doing this or that regardless of real desire, the unchanging environment of the playground (same tires, ladders and sandpit, same neatly laid out tricycle path) — all this acts as "a subtle yet controlling device which makes for a kind of enforced conformity to an essentially abstract pattern of sameness." This is probably not what the child most wants or needs for growth as a free, independent spirit. We have to ask, Weininger says, "how the learned dependence on structure and sameness affects children's ability to follow out the implications of their play, to use unplanned time creatively, and to begin to learn by themselves."[62]

As important to creativity as independence is privacy and quiet, lots of it. What child does not rejoice in the discovery of a secret hidden adult-proof place — an attic crawl space, a draped spot under the dining room table — to sit and dream? "Children need lots of free quiet time to get used to all that's developing within them," says television's Mr Rogers.[63] This need goes directly counter to the North American bias against anything that looks like idleness. Where Eastern cultures have always valued the art of silent contemplation, what the Japanese call *shikan-taza*, the West has, since the days of the *New England Primer*, emphasized the importance of keeping busy lest the devil find work for idle hands to do. To develop their creative potential, however, children need to waste time, to fool around, to try things out, to read junk and watch television in a half-conscious way.

All these apparently pointless non-activities provide a basis for fantasy, which is one kind of quintessentially creative activity. Jerome L. Singer, a clinical psychologist at Yale University, says that daydreaming and make-believe promote not only creativity and problem-solving, but also the capacity to postpone immediate gratification in the interest of future aims. Singer's tests have shown, for instance, that children with a highly developed fantasy life can sit still for much longer than low fantasizers, that they have a longer attention span and greater powers of concentration.[64] Fantasizing strengthens a child's language ability, is associated with original thought and richer imaginative powers. Children who fantasize a lot tolerate frustration better; their imaginations take flight from stubborn reality to happier possibilities. Low fantasizers tend to be more active physically, more impatient with difficulty — and considerably more aggressive. Singer and other researchers in the field are convinced that creative fantasizing is a skill which can be developed by encouragement and some kinds of adult modelling (telling stories, stimulating make-believe play). But here, as elsewhere, the early years are crucial. A child's predisposition to fantasy appears to be pretty well formed by the age of five.[65]

How do these discoveries bear on the day care scene? First and obviously, it's hard for a child in day care to be alone. It's virtually impossible for him, in a centre, to do nothing.

Caretakers in group settings show an overwhelming bias for visibly fruitful activity: completing a puzzle, making a picture which can be taken home to show parents. In *The Erosion of Childhood*, an investigation of American day care, Valerie Suransky comments sadly on the intrusiveness of caretakers: "Children who did not play busily were considered to be problematical and in need of help."[66] During periods of free play, children were not truly free to play since well-meaning teachers interfered constantly. (To a child swooshing down a slide, "What colour is the slide?") They were also not free *not to play*. Dreaming youngsters were either urged "Go and play" or firmly provided with instructive play materials. "Engagement and task involvement were constantly reinforced by the staff"; any kind of free-flowing, spontaneous activity was likely to be "organized" by a helpful adult concerned with products or results. Jerome Bruner notes the same tendency in British nurseries. "Being occupied was felt to be better than being idle"; adults promoted structured activities and ignored or discouraged spontaneously generated play: "Come and be busy," "Make something with the bricks" and even a judgmental "Sit down and make something — you never do anything, do you?" "There are times to let children be," Bruner concludes, "however zealous one might be about helping them."[67]

Language Development

"Society's principal sorting system, formal education, rewards one kind of intellectual ability almost exclusively — language. Other abilities rarely count."[68] That's Theodore Sizer, Dean of Harvard University, writing in 1973. The arrival of the computer age has not fundamentally altered this reality — or the fact that, as Sizer noted, "a home where a mother helps a child to learn and use rich and varied language advances him materially towards more sophisticated skills of communication and reading." Language is power. It is also the beginning of thought. As the Russian poet Kornei Chukovsky observes, "To teach a child to speak well means also to teach him to think well. One is inseparable from the other."[69] Through language the child comes to understand himself and the world around him, and to reach out to others. If his language is impoverished, his range of thought and feeling, his whole development is circumscribed.

Now that *communication* has become a magic word in relationships both personal and professional, few would dispute the critical importance of a child's acquiring rich and varied language. What's perhaps disputable — or what needs to be shown — is that advancement in this skill is best achieved by parents, *at home*. Might a good day care environment not do as well, or better? Obviously, much depends on the kind of home we're talking about. There are depressed mothers who rarely speak to their children; those children would learn better in surrogate care. And many mothers speak badly, by conventional standards — though it should be noted that the "incorrect" speech of some ethnic groups is in fact exceptionally colourful and expressive (black English, Chicano English).[70] When home and day care environments have been studied in relation to children's language development, it turns out that there is indeed no place like home. The findings of Barbara Tizard are typical: children were more talkative at home, and so became more often involved in conversations which enlarged their vocabulary and their understanding. Adult-child conversations averaged twenty-seven per hour, as compared with ten per hour in group care; while group care exchanges tended to be brief (eight turns), with the teacher moving from child to child, home exchanges were elaborate and extended (sixteen turns).[71]

No group care environment and no caretaker, however devoted and competent, possesses the mother's special advantage as a facilitator of language: the mother has been present from the beginning. Language does not arise *de novo*.

It emerges rather, crystallizes, out of those rich, varied, complex communications which begin the first time a newborn moves rhythmically in response to his mother's voice.[72] What Rudolph Schaffer calls the "rudimentary dialogue" between mother and child consists of multiple harmonies: baby gazes at mother, she gazes back; he looks away, she shakes her head; she croons, he makes a small responsive noise. Even nursing becomes a dialogue, as the mother adjusts to alternate rhythms of sucking and ceasing to suck. Three-month-old infants and their mothers, gazing at each other, will move their heads in perfect time. (Dr Daniel Stern of Cornell University Medical Center, who has filmed such encounters, compares the pattern to a waltz, where both know the steps but cues are given now by one partner, now another.)[73]

"Linguistic competence is preceded by communicative competence," Schaffer says. "The dialogue begins long before the first word is heard."[74] Early dialogues are initiated by the infant. A frequent pattern, filmed by Stern, shows the infant smiling, widening his eyes, opening his mouth and thrusting out his tongue; adults instinctively join the game, repeating, elaborating, modifying.[75] Action games prefigure the language game which is to come, when the child finds a word — "Kitty!" — and the mother repeats with verbal embroidery. "Yes, *nice* kitty. Baby pat the kitty. Pat, pat. Oh, nice. See what *soft* fur kitty has." Long before children have the resources for consecutive speech, they will surround a real word with a rise and fall of rhythmical sound, a varied babbling, that clearly represents their version of what adults do.

No one need *teach* a child how to talk. The child learns by being spoken to — and the more he's spoken to, the better he learns. "From the very beginning, a mother bathes her baby in language," Schaffer observes.[76] Though a very few mothers feel self-conscious talking to an infant, most quite naturally accompany the day's routines with affectionate patter. "You're wet *again*. I don't believe it. Didn't I just change you?

Okay, don't cry. Up we go. Upsadaisy. Diaper off, cycle the little legs, up with bottom. . . *There* you are. Doesn't that feel good? Nice and dry, dry and nice." (The baby here hasn't a clue as to the meaning of words, but the *tone* is unmistakable — teasing, playful, affectionate, delighted, ending in a nuzzle. From hundreds of such conversations, the child acquires the varied intonations which compose adult speech (question, exclamation, instruction, reproof. . .). Gradually he learns the words to the tune. Mothers the world over adopt with very young children a language the social scientists call *motherese*.[77] Statements are brief, words simple; sentence structure is direct subject-verb (with verb in the present tense). Intonation and emphasis are exaggerated, often reinforced by pointing to objects named. Important words and phrases are repeated. Children evidently need individualized, one-to-one language experiences; research reports the case of a normal, hearing child of deaf parents who remained speechless for some time, even though his parents turned on the TV and radio for him.[78]

So hearing language is not in itself sufficient. Children must be *spoken to*. Another bizarre instance of retarded speech comes from British educator P.M. Pickard: a five-year-old brought to a Child Guidance Clinic because she had not begun to speak. Pickard discovered that the mother, an educated woman living alone with her child, had never talked to the little girl because she "felt like a fool" addressing someone who couldn't understand. This is an extreme instance and freakish; but many children talk late and badly — for this simple reason, that nobody talked *to them*.[79]

In talking to their children, parents enjoy an advantage not available to out-of-home caretakers: they share the same world and can use that as a basis for expanding language power. Caretakers generally don't know enough about the child's family to pick up cues and ask the questions which will trigger a conversational flow. So asking, "Did you have a good time at the circus yesterday?" may produce a flat "Yeah" (no details), while a parent's "Why do you want Charlie [two-year-old brother] to sleep in your room?" elicits a true conversation:

> Audrey: I want him to protect me.
> Mother: I don't think he'd be much protection.
> Audrey: Well, he's not afraid. He doesn't know 'bout being afraid. If a dragon came, he'd maybe be afraid, but if it was a robber, he'd prob'ly say, "Want a kiss?"

Family members naturally encourage speech by their understanding and concentrated attention. Here's a four-year-old talking with her grandmother:

> Grandmother: Did you see Charlie the minute he was born?
> Audrey: Well, I was sleeping. But next morning I tiptoed into Mom's room and I saw this little blackness, like hair. And that was my baby brother.
> Grandmother: I'll bet you were happy.
> Audrey: I *like* Charlie because he's heavy and when I carry him that makes my bones strong.
> Grandmother: He'll be fun to play with when he's a bit older.
> Audrey: I play with him now.
> Grandmother: How can you play with a tiny baby?
> Audrey: (grinning, a good joke) I play guitar with him. (Miming) *Charlie* is the guitar. When he's big I'm going to teach him to like McDonald's. I think he's the type. Mom doesn't like McDonald's. It's not her cup of tea.

It's worth noting, at this point, that past babyhood, children don't respond well to test-like questions of the sort asked in a semi-educational setting: "What colour is your sweater?" They're challenged by real questions, most likely to be posed by intimates. British educator Ruth Clark tells a lovely story about the four-year-old emerging from an interview with the headmaster of a school in which his parents hoped to enrol him. To the mother's reproof — why didn't he reply to questions whose answers he well knew? — the child responded indignantly: "If that man didn't know, I wasn't going to tell him."[80]

At age six, the little girl who played guitar with Charlie has become curious about the figure of speech so jauntily introduced two years before. In a conversation about the newest baby brother, Willie, she suddenly wonders, "Why do we say *cup of tea*?"

> Grandmother: It's a way of talking. It doesn't have anything to do with tea. Like, I could say, "You're driving me up the wall" and of course I'm not driving up the wall. I just mean, you're getting me all nervous and excited, frantic. If something gave me the shivers, I could say "That gives me the willies."
> Audrey: (ecstatic) So I could say to Willie, you give me the willies. But if Willie got the shivers, he'd have to say, "That gives me the *mes*."

These exchanges illustrate another feature of child language in the home: its playfulness. Ruth Clark, in a study of pre-school language development, concludes that "children produce their most elaborate speech in familiar surroundings among people with whom they are completely relaxed. . . . If the complexity of a child's language is in any way related to the complexity of his thinking, then we ought to expect his language to be at its richest when he is thoroughly at home, unstressed by unfamiliar objects, surroundings and people, and therefore free to elaborate his thoughts and express them."[81] Children at home, with adults, learn to play with words as they play with toys.[82] Here's four-year-old Susannah, a chatty child with a chatty mother, happily discovering the excitement of language:

> Susannah: Mommy, does Santa Claus get dead?
> Mother: No, he's a wonderful elf who lives always.
> Susannah: But God gets born all the time, doesn't he? All those Christmases he gets born. Christmas after Christmas after Christmas, he is every time a newborn king.

> Susannah, getting up after sitting in a cramped position: "My toes are sparkling!"

Susannah's imaginary companion is named Isabel — "because she's *invisabel*." Of herself, she says, "I should really be Honey. Because I'm sweet as sugar. I'm a sugar-burger."

This kind of rich inventiveness requires for its encouragement a one-to-one relationship of adult and child. Children playing with age-mates often hit on a small language discovery, like the five-year-old who, having protested "That's not *fair*" was suddenly struck by the word and mystified his playmates with "Nyah, nyah, fair hair." It would require the presence of an adult to unravel the complexities of *fair/fare* as just, light-coloured, fee for travel. . . A good deal of research indicates that children who spend most of their time with peers speak and comprehend less well than children accustomed to the company of adults.[83] A suggestive corroboration is the fact that twins and children born close together tend to speak poorly, because they talk mostly to one another and so lack a mature adult model.[84]

In addition to providing a good model, a caring adult — one who has time and not too many children to care for — can encourage elaboration, expanding and explaining in what is really a sophisticated version of The Game.

As well as sensitively tuned, stimulating talk, children need for language development the special excitement provided by the written word. Long before they know the meaning of in-

dividual words, children respond to the music of Mother
Goose. By three they want stories, loving best those that
vividly reproduce the sights, sounds and feel of the real
world. ("He *huffed* and he *puffed* and he *blew* the house
down." "Oh please, Mr. Tiger, don't eat me and I'll give you
my beautiful little blue coat." "Mirror, mirror on the wall,
who is fairest of us all?") Of course children will be read to in
most day care situations, but there's an important difference
between what's possible in reading to a group and reading to
a single enthralled listener. The day care provider, choosing a
book for her four-year-olds, tries for one which all the
children can enjoy without too much interruption and explanation. Inevitably, some listeners will be left behind and
some, those advanced in development, will be bored. A
parent reading to her child can adapt book to listener, often
choosing a story whose language and ideas are at the outer,
growing edge of the child's capacity. For example, Audrey at
four loved William Steig's *Tiffky Doofky*, a book whose
language and subtle tone (frequently ironic or mock-heroic)
put it beyond the range of an unassisted pre-schooler.

> Crows were rummaging in the debris for dainty
> tidbits. . . . They were sitting in a field of daisies caress-
> ing one another. Her embrace was gentle, sinuous. . . .
> The breath of life was being pressed out of him. He
> decided to face death with dignity. The sun was now on
> the rim of the earth, about to leave this gruesome
> scene.[85]

To sum up: reflection on the very different language environments of home and day care supports research findings
that parents talk more often, more easily and freely with
children than do professional caregivers and that the quality
of talk is richer, more various, more wide-ranging and more
original (i.e. less stereotyped, routine).[86] The relatively con-
straining effect of day care can to some extent be modified by

organizational factors. Barbara and Jack Tizard have shown that adult-child ratio is not the only definitive influence on language development. A stable staff, a small proportion of children under three and greater staff autonomy are all positive influences. With many under-threes, caretakers become preoccupied, quite literally, with caretaking. With all those little noses and bottoms to wipe, all those reckless adventurers to be supervised, there's little time for talk. When staff turnover is high, caretakers often don't know a child well enough to understand and improve imperfect speech. And where staff autonomy is low, the caretaker views her job largely as minding the children under the eye of her supervisor.[87]

Even with the most favourable day care organization, however, some elements of the caretaking situation work against what experts like to call an "optimal" environment. The caretaker responsible for no more than six children will still be constantly on the go, settling a dispute, locating a missing boot, helping out with a puzzle, wiping up a mess. . . How can she tune in to an individual child long enough to sense what he's thinking and feeling — and to provide words for the inner need? In his Oxford pre-school study Jerome Bruner notes that there's certainly no absence of *talk* in playgrounds and nursery schools. Quite the contrary. The sheer social distraction of the group setting, however, works against the possibility of *connected* conversation. "Richer dialogue seems to require more intimate and continuous settings. . . . If connected discourse is the forge in which conversational skill is fashioned — and the evidence overwhelmingly points that way, then the interruptions and good-hearted din of the pre-school is surely not ideal."[88] In a typical pre-school group, a child averages three minutes per hour of talk with an adult. Taped recordings show that eighty percent of the talk flow contains no sustained conversation.[89]

Sometimes a harried caretaker, eye on the clock or the next

job to be done, actually cuts off a language opportunity. Here, for instance, are two four-year-olds in a day care centre.

> First boy: My daddy's better than your daddy.
> Second boy: Is not, is not.
> First boy: My daddy can lift a car.
> Second boy: My daddy drives a truck, and he can fly a airplane too.
> First boy: That's nothing. My daddy went on a submarine. . . .
> Caretaker, interrupting: Boys, stop that. You both have good daddies.

It is alas, not unusual to hear "This is not *talking* time, this is clean-up time" or whatever, as though the two activities were mutually exclusive. Sally Provence, of the Yale Child Study Center, observes that "even naturally talkative adults, taking care of several children not their own in the day care setting, may find it hard to remember to talk with them."[90] Job pressure, fatigue and boredom take their toll. A day care observer reports that in one and a half hours she counted thirty-eight commands of "Put your work away!" Prohibitions, commands and instruction combine to produce no response or minimal response. The number of monosyllabic replies one hears in a day care centre (as contrasted with a home) is striking. Commenting on the language-restrictive effect of day care environments, Courtney Cazden laments the tendency of caretakers to ask pointless questions or, worse still, preachy ones. Here's a bleak dialogue between caretaker and child.

> Caretaker: Do you see all that paper in the street?
> Child: Yeah.
> Caretaker: How do you think it got there?
> Child: It blew there.

Caretaker: Do you think that children could do anything to help keep the street clean?
Child: Nah.

One's sympathy here is with the child. What tedious nonsense. What *ill-conceived* nonsense. Cazden comments that "The tendency to act as an agent of social improvement is difficult to resist even in the midst of an exploration of the child's verbal skill."[91] In contrast to these high-flown aims, most parents are in the position of Molière's hero, amazed to discover that all his life he'd been speaking *prose*. Parents quite naturally *talk* — explaining, asking, narrating, responding — without any self-conscious awareness of providing what psychiatrist Michael Rutter calls "the single most crucial factor for the development of verbal intelligence,"[92] a rich natural conversational exchange.

A last reflection on children and language. How often, how sensitively and how freely children are involved in conversation with adults affects, obviously, the quality of children's speech. But the ultimate effect goes beyond words. One of the most interesting findings of the Bermuda day care study (see p. 274) was a clear correlation between emotional adjustment and the quality of the language environment. Where physical setting was judged to be poor, but the exchange of talk rich and lively, children were better adjusted emotionally than children in "high-quality, low-verbal" centres. In centres with good overall quality but impoverished language life, children were found to be more anxious, hyperactive and aggressive.[93] So one of the really big questions for parents of young children turns out to be, not just "Will my child be physically safe here?" or "What are the nutritional standards?" but "What about conversation?"

Health

Of all concerns surrounding early surrogate care, none is

more troubling than possible health risks. Parents who *must* use day care are torn by suggestions that in doing so, they may endanger their children. So the tendency is, understandably, to dismiss as unduly alarmist the growing evidence about day care disease. In this attempt to put the best possible face on things — to make necessity, if not a virtue, at least acceptable — parents are joined by day care advocates of unquestionable idealism and integrity. Columnist Ellen Goodman, dismissing a *Journal of the American Medical Association* editorial on day care epidemics, insisted that the increased risk of such diseases as dysentery and hepatitis is "real but small." Instead of focusing on "the relatively minor problems" of those who (fortunately) have access to day care, Goodman insists, we should concentrate on the problems of those who need day care and can't get it.[94] Dr Mary Howell, a distinguished pediatrician and child psychologist, responded to the JAMA charge with assurances that young children get sick a lot, whether at home or at centre, that increased illness may build up resistance, and that scrupulous hygiene practices can virtually eliminate day care related infections.[95] This debate, which sets doctor against doctor and one child advocate against another, highlights a true dilemma. Working parents with young children must have day care, and should have access to the best care possible. If, however, it appears that even good group care carries health risks, then that knowledge provides ammunition to policy-makers and politicians who don't want to increase day care funding. These are troubling matters. All an objective observer can do is present the evidence.

The questions which need answering are these: Does the day care environment (centre or family home) facilitate the spread of disease? If the answer is *yes* or *sometimes*, is that disease "relatively minor" or serious? If the answer is *yes*, can we take comfort from the possibility that each disease episode strengthens the child's immunity? Is it perhaps true that the presence at home of older siblings, particularly those who attend school, poses just as great a health risk as day care attendance?[96] Would regular handwashing and stricter standards of admission for slightly unwell children (coughs, runny noses) help? What about immunization against day care diseases? And finally, could the hazards of day care infection be virtually eliminated by scrupulous attention to sanitary procedures in every aspect of group life? These questions have been regularly considered since 1974, when "Day Care Centre Diseases" first appeared as a special category in the *Index Medicus*. But it was not until the first international symposium on infectious diseases in day care (June 1984) that the accumulated evidence was systematically presented.

Low key and unsensational, symposium papers on the whole support the claim made by Dr Stanley Schuman of the Medical University of South Carolina that "communities large and small are experiencing outbreaks of enteric [intestinal] illness — diarrheas, dysentery, giardasis and epidemic jaundice — reminiscent of the presanitation days of the 17th century."[97] This is not, to be sure, a modern bubonic plague with corpses piling up in the streets. Some of the illnesses, like giardasis, a diarrhea accompanied by bloating and cramping, are relatively benign. Some, like hepatitis A, carried by children and spread in day care centres, affect principally adults. (Child carriers may have no symptoms and no obvious ill effects. But infected adults develop jaundice and may be severely ill with nausea, fever, diarrhea, vomiting and abdominal pain.) And some "day care diseases," to use a term increasingly common, are life-threatening. *Haemophilus influenzae* type B (HIB), the major cause of bacterial meningitis and other serious infections of the bloodstream, is particularly dangerous to infants. About five percent of child victims will die of the disease; about fifteen percent of the survivors are left with some neurological handicap.[98] Other infections commonly spread in day care are shigellosis, a serious diarrhea often necessitating hospitalization; conjunctivitis, a highly contagious inflammation of the eye; impetigo, a bacterial skin infection; streptococcal infections (including scarlet fever and strep sore throat); *otitis media*, a middle-ear inflammation caused usually by *streptococcus pneumoniae* and *Haemophilus influenzae*; and cytomegalovirus, a member of the herpes virus family, fatal during the first weeks of life. In addition there are the minor afflictions: ringworm, head lice, pinworms and Coxsackievirus (otherwise known as hand, foot and mouth disease), characterized by sudden fever and an abundance of small, painful sores on affected parts of the body.

Just how common are these diseases — and how connected to group care? The figures on hepatitis are suggestive and troubling. In a 1980 study of a viral hepatitis outbreak in Arizona, forty percent of reported cases occurred in "persons closely associated with day care centers."[99] In most cases, these "closely associated persons" were parents of children younger than age six. (Children between the ages of one and two show the highest attack rates for hepatitis A, five times higher than that of any other age group.) Or they were day care workers, generally those whose charges were still in diapers. "Hepatitis would appear to be an occupational risk of day care," observes Dr Stephen Hadler, the study's author. As for the hepatitis A risk in day care generally, Dr Hadler, Chief of Hepatitis Epidemiology at the U.S. Centers for Disease Control (CDC), Atlanta, Georgia, calculates that a *minimum* of thirty percent of all cases originate in day care centres, the actual figure being considerably higher. "Outbreaks of hepatitis A, shigellosis, giardasis, and presumed viral gastro-enteritis in day care centers have been reported increasingly in recent years. In these outbreaks, infection characteristically has spread not only among children, but also to the adults who take care of them, both within the center and at home. The spread of infection beyond the day-care center into families and then into the general community represents a major potential problem in public health."[100]

Other infectious childhood diseases present a similar pattern of day care origin and spread. A ten-year review of shigellosis in the United States (1964-1973, a period preceding the major expansion in day care facilities) identified group centres as "special high-risk settings" for transmission of the disease.[101] A CDC investigation of shigellosis outbreaks in Lexington, Kentucky and Cleveland, Ohio concluded that "children aged 1 to 5 who left the home to mingle with other children in day care settings were significantly more likely to introduce shigellosis into their households than were children who stayed at home."[102] A notable feature of this study is evidence that the disease is not, as sometimes assumed, an inner-city ghetto problem. The major outbreak in Lexington, where one infant died, occurred at a licensed private centre patronized by upper-income families.

The dismal catalogue of disease risks in day care settings continues.

GIARDASIS. At least one child with giardasis was found in sixty-six percent and eighty-five percent of day care centres in two recent surveys. It takes just *one* child to infect the group. Tests repeated after five months showed three-quarters of the children still infected, presumably either chronically ill or re-infected. Of twenty-five day care centres surveyed, only three proved disease-free.[103]

In addition to diarrhea identified as caused by giardia and shigella, "non-specific" diarrhea is rampant. During his first five weeks in a group setting, a child experiences an average diarrheal attack rate of twenty-five percent. This declines to ten percent in the following weeks if he remains in the centre. However, if he enters a new one, the risk rises again to twenty-five percent.[104]

HAEMOPHILUS INFLUENZAE TYPE B. Of 333 cases in a Minneapolis epidemic, forty-one percent were day care related; in Dallas, that rate rose to sixty-two percent of 224 cases. Dr Dan M. Granoff estimates that roughly fifty percent of all patients hospitalized with HIB show a history of recent day care attendance. The risk is highest for children eighteen months or older; day care attendees in this age group are ten times as vulnerable as home-reared children. (Under eleven months, there's no significant difference in risk between home and centre.)[105] HIB vaccine exists but is not always effective; some infants vaccinated during an epidemic develop meningitis none the less.[106]

OTITIS MEDIA. A common result of upper respiratory infection, this is a middle ear inflammation with accumulation of fluid which temporarily impairs hearing. As any parent who has dealt with earache knows, it is one of the most painful diseases of early childhood. It is also demonstrably more likely to occur in group centres than at home. In a typical finding, thirty-seven percent of children in centres had at least one episode of *otitis media*, as compared with twenty-three percent of home-reared children.[107] Dr Frederick Henderson, who has studied OM at the Frank Porter Child Development Center (University of North Carolina), estimates that children in group care during the early years are from two to four times as susceptible to middle ear problems.[108]

CYTOMEGALOVIRUS. In a recent study investigators found a high rate of infection — fifty-nine percent — in a day care centre, a result surprising in that the children here came from well educated middle and upper income families.[109] (The disease has generally been associated with either primitive cultures or low income groups.)

The accumulated weight of evidence unquestionably points to day care as an increased health risk for young children. This is not hard to understand. A group centre brings together in one place large or relatively large numbers of children at an age of high susceptibility to infection. When some of these children are in diapers — as one researcher elegantly puts it, "too young to have learned personal hygiene practices, and often guilty of indiscriminate defecation" — the risks are greatly increased. Fastidious handling of diapers does nothing to counteract a main route of disease transmission — hand to diaper to toy to mouth. Infants drool over rattles and rubber ducks as soon as they can grasp; toddlers have been observed to mouth a hand or an object every three minutes.[110] As Dr Schuman says, day care is "a labor-intensive, loosely regulated custodial-educational business." Attendants may serve more meals and snacks than a local restaurant, but without training in food handling. (It's not uncommon for the same individual to handle diapers and sandwiches.) Financial constraints, a low adult-child ratio and high staff turnover produce, in many centres, a rushed and casual attitude towards sanitary practices. Meantime, the child population fluctuates along with the staff; children enter and leave the centre, "ensuring maximum mixing of infected and susceptible subjects."[111] Since many infections confer no immunity or are chronic, cycles of re-infection move through the centre population. As Dr Klein notes, children are social beings. When they touch or hug or share toys, a "pooling of secretions" occurs. A child just recovered from giardasis gets it again from the caretaker who got it from him. The physical facility itself presents problems: "a closed community, sometimes crowded, sometimes inadequately ventilated, becomes an excellent incubator for transmission of infectious agents."[112] Intestinal bacteria (shigella, salmonella, parasites) spread by the fecal-oral route — hands, toys or food contaminated by the stool of infected individuals. Other infections, like impetigo and scabies, spread by direct contact with discharges from the affected area. And still others are air-borne. With each sneeze or cough, thousands of infected particles are released into the atmosphere.

Clearly, this situation bears no resemblance to a home, even when that home contains older siblings. Dr Mary Howell, attempting to minimize day care dangers, says that "spending time with other children — even as few as three other children — has certain expectable effects on the well-being of young children; it does not matter whether the youngsters come together in a family day care home, a child care center, or Sunday school." Most epidemiologists say it matters. Physical setting, child population, attendants, play materials and food service in a day care centre all carry risks not present at home or in Sunday school. Day care centres which bring together large groups of pre-school children for eight to ten hours a day, says the CDC's Dr Stephen Hadler, "represent a fertile environment for the spread of communicable diseases."[113]

What about the argument that early exposure to day care infections builds up resistance or helps develop immunity? Even if this were true, one would wish to protect infants, in the first vulnerable months of life, from the stress of illness. Young infants have a less efficient mode of responding to infectious challenges; they are, for example, much more severely affected by meningitis and middle ear problems. Far from building up immunity, repeated early episodes of *otitis media*, each one involving a period of hearing loss, have been shown to impair speech development, language and other cognitive skills.[114] Numerous investigators have concluded that severe or recurrent middle ear infections in early childhood are connected with the later development of learning disabilities, the result of impaired reception of speech after infections.[115] As for diarrhea — a case of diarrhea does not make an infant immune to later attacks; it does, however, pose the threat of serious dehydration. The psychological effects of even brief illnesses are difficult to assess. A recent study of infant-toddler day care disease cautions that "pain and discomfort can be psychologically threatening to [young] children who have so little perspective on change with time."[116]

What can be done to protect children from day care infections? Rigorous handwashing — with every diaper change,

every trip to the bathroom (child or caretaker), every meal —
reduces or controls some diseases. Diarrhea under such a
regimen can be cut by fifty percent. Emphasis on sanitary
procedures has also reduced community cases of hepatitis by
as much as seventy-five percent. It will not, however,
eliminate risks. Dr Hadler explains that when transmission of
disease is from child to child — and those children are involved in continuous hand-to-mouth activity — it's impossible to interrupt the passage of infection. "You'd be washing
hands till they're raw." Under normal conditions of
temperature and humidity, the virus can survive a month on
toys, doorknobs and other surfaces. Some hepatitis A outbreaks have occurred in day care centres with model sanitary
arrangements.[117] The ultimate risk factor is not hygienic practices but the age of centre children (the presence of children
under two greatly increases risk), the size of the centre and
the number of hours it stays open. In a large centre with a
long day, which means children moving in and out on different schedules, there will always be risk. The same is true of
Haemophilus influenzae. So far, vaccines have not proved an
answer to day care disease. With *Haemophilus influenzae*,
vaccines have proved ineffective in the very group most at
risk for life-threatening disease — infants. (Older children
develop antibodies which make invasive HIB less likely.) The
drug Rifampin is being used prophylactically, to prevent HIB
in groups at risk; it is described as "promising" but not proven
effective.[118] Immunoglobulin can prevent hepatitis A if given
within two weeks of exposure; it is effective for several
months. There is no preventive vaccine available. For the
various diarrheas, there is no specific preventative — and no
immunity acquired by episodes of disease.

As for the hope that stricter admission controls can cut day
care disease, most physicians say this is not a promising approach. For one thing, when a sick child is turned away,
desperate working parents often take him to another centre
whose standards are less exacting. In this way, disease

spreads from one centre to another. Futhermore, children in the carrier state may have no symptoms whatsoever. So a rosy-cheeked youngster with a well-developed case of hepatitis, a lively infant whose nasal secretions are loaded with *Haemophilus influenzae* organisms, could pass any visual inspection, while the child with an innocent runny nose might be dismissed (again and again, in view of the average run of noses). By the time hepatitis A appears in caretakers or parents, the child carrier has passed the communicable stage.

What can parents do to protect a child's health? For infants, home is unquestionably the safest place. The American Academy of Pediatrics (northern California branch) recommends that under the age of two, a child be cared for only with siblings. If this is not possible, next best is a small group: six children or fewer, from no more than three families. Group turnover should be minimal. If the baby must go out to care, then a small family day care home offers advantages from the standpoint of exposure to infection. *Usually*. In a rare but alarming instance, two children developed tuberculosis carried by the husband of a family day care provider.[119] Edward Zigler, who has been active in day care development over the past decade, cautions that though exposure to infection is less of a problem in family care, in other respects unlicensed home care poses a broad health risk to infants. With no other adults around, the infant has less protection against negligence or abuse; the attitude to immunizations may be dangerously casual.[120] Where parents have good reason to trust a family caregiver, however, a home setting seems safer at this stage than all but the very best centres.

If a young child is to be put in a group centre, the safest situation, from an infectious disease standpoint, would be a small centre with small groups, one which does not admit infants. A child no longer in diapers should be cared for with others who have also graduated to dry pants and potties. (Dr Hadler's study of hepatitis A patterns, for example, shows that of centres caring for children under one year, seventy percent had outbreaks; in centres with a minimum age of one, the rate was cut in half; for centres with no children under two, the rate dropped to ten percent. Centres with a minimum age of three had no cases.) The bigger the centre, the bigger the risk. The more hours open, the more risk. Centres open twelve hours a day, six days a week, are high risk by virtue of sheer numbers cared for. Ideally, a child should be cared for by one person. Ideally too, diapering and toileting are not performed by helpers who handle food.

The 1984 symposium on infectious disease and day care offered the following guidelines for sanitary procedures. When you visit a centre or day care home, check to see how it measures up to these standards:[121]

Caretakers wash their hands every time they change a diaper or wipe a runny nose.

There is a clean water supply. If there is no running water next to the changing area, a supply is kept near by in a covered container.

Handwashing procedures are posted next to the water supply. Caretakers avoid recontaminating their clean hands, using a paper towel to turn off the faucet.

The diapering table is cleaned after each use, either by replacing disposable paper covering or by disinfecting after each change. Diapers are changed only in this area, never on the floor or any other location. Children are washed and dried with individual toilet articles at each change.

Diapers are dropped into a covered pail before handwashing. Disposable diapers are preferred.

Children are taught to wash their hands promptly if they have wiped their noses or put hand to mouth during a coughing spell. Toilet trained children use flush toilets, washing their hands afterwards.

Children and staff wash hands before meals. Tables are washed before meals.

Cribs and cots are two feet apart. Children have their own rest equipment, clearly marked and regularly cleaned. Children have individual towels (or disposable ones) and soap.

Toys that infants put in their mouths are washable and are not frequently passed from one infant to another.

In group centres food preparation, storage and handling areas are separated from rooms used by children — and not used as a passageway.

All solid waste is stored in flytight, watertight, rodent-proof containers which are easily cleanable and inaccessible to children. Garbage and trash are not stored next to the outdoor play area.

Dirty linen storage is separate from clean linen, food and other supplies. Soiled and clean laundry areas are kept separate and clearly marked.

Turtles, hamsters and birds have been examined and certified free of disease by a veterinarian. Dogs should have a current vaccination for rabies.

All caretakers should have tuberculin tests or chest X-rays and annual physical examinations, with a certificate of good health on file in the facility.

Even perfect sanitation won't guarantee a well child, January to December. Dr Klein says philosophically, "Infections should be expected in day care. There will be many infections." But home care children get sick too. With luck and extreme diligence, parents can reduce the day care odds.

Part 3

How to Choose and Where to Find Help

Chapter VII

Choosing Day Care

What Kind of Care?

Whether to put a child in surrogate care is in itself a huge decision. After that comes a choice equally momentous and much more complicated, because the range of possibilities is wide. Will you keep the child in your own home? In that case the options are nanny, sitter (or sitters), *au pair* girl from a foreign country, relative — including the child's father. Have you decided on out-of-home care? Then the options are family day care; a friend, sitter or relative; commercial centre (private or chain), non-profit centre (and in this category, workplace care, co-operative, church or charitable organization).

Here are the considerations which should guide your choice.

Age and Stage of Child

Child development experts and day care directors agree: babies do best at home, nurtured by one or two loving individuals. Advocates of early day care — or those who, without exactly advocating, are obliged to use it — point to reassuring studies demonstrating "that babies felt comforted when they were around other babies."[1] This may well be true — but one is moved to ask why they need comfort. A baby in his mother's or father's arms does not look about for friends.

Where circumstances permit, a baby needs at very least six months of parent care. Pediatrician Berry Brazelton, a humane man sensitive to both sides of the equation (mother needs, child needs) sets four months as an absolute minimum. After that — well, the infant can survive surrogate care, may gain weight and develop according to established norms . . . But "so little research has been done to help us know where we stand about this kind of early separation that so far we are on pretty shaky ground."[2] Premature separation is not just the baby's loss, it's the mother's too: she loses, inevitably, the sense of closeness and the gratification which come from coping and surviving through the turbulent first months. "The relationship may not actually be endangered, but it may never be as rich as it might have been."[3]

For the baby in surrogate care, the whole delicate process of mother-child adaptation is short-circuited. He may be left in his crib for hours at a time, except for feeds and changing; he may be bombarded with miscellaneous noise. James and Joyce Robertson, passionate advocates of children's rights (and opponents of day care) worry particularly about infants. "If mothers absolutely must leave the child in alternative care, then make it as late as they possibly can. Even an extra couple of months in these early years can have such significance for the child's security and eventual development."[4]

Suppose now the infant, six months or more, is to be placed in surrogate care: what's the best option? Home, in familiar surroundings, with a constantly available familiar caretaker. If mother must go out and work, perhaps father can take over. Of all possible substitutes, fathers are most likely to provide generous care, love and attention — and to stay on the job. This is a happy solution where mother has the better job, earns more, is more ambitious professionally and is less naturally attuned to children and their needs. (The motherhood mythology notwithstanding, many men are more patient and tender than many women.) If father is not available, what about a relative? This possibility, initially attractive, should be approached cautiously. In some respects a grandmother, say, appears ideal. She is bound to this child by ties of love and loyalty; she will presumably not watch the clock; she will be reliable; she will cost little (or nothing). All to the good. One the other hand, precisely because she *is* family, she doesn't take orders and may need kid-glove treatment. If a hired caretaker hits your child or feeds him marshmallow fluff instead of cottage cheese, you can protest and if necessary end the arrangement. If grandmother violates your values and standards, that's trouble. Given the enormous changes in attitudes towards child care over the past two or three decades, the potential for grandmother conflict over toilet training or "spoiling," say, is considerable. Not to mention that a member of the older generation, with a touch of arthritis and impaired hearing, is not the ideal companion for a growing child.

Relying on other relatively inexpensive home care possibilities — *au pair* girls, miscellaneous sitters — is carrying water in a sieve. *Au pair* girls, who come from Europe in order to learn the language and experience the American way of life, are at best a short term arrangement (one year is usual). They are young; they get homesick; they fall in and out of love. You may be lucky, come up with an absolute jewel who adores the baby and cleans house besides. Or you may find yourself with a second child on your hands. As for miscellaneous sitters — students, married women making a little extra — this is a precarious source of help for anyone who must get to work every day. The most reliable in-home caregiver (reliable but not infallible) is the nanny. She will cost a lot. If you can't swing a nanny salary, the next best bet is some form of family care. A group centre (hard to find in any case for this age) is the least desirable form of infant care.

The toddler needs actually *more* attention than the baby. He needs a vigilant caretaker to keep him out of trouble, a patient one to cope with his wildly fluctuating moods, a wise one to guide his learning about the world. Under favourable conditions, language acquisition proceeds rapidly at this age; the toddler benefits from lots of one-to-one conversations with an adult who sensitively encourages his talking. Ideally, a single caretaker fulfils all these needs. Between eleven and eighteen months, a period of high separation anxiety, the toddler should be able to rely on the comforting presence of a familiar face and lap. If toilet training is to begin at this time, the child should be cared for by someone who shares the parents' attitude towards this important task. Here again, home care is best. A family day care mother will have her own system of toilet training and cannot reasonably be expected to change with each new set of parents. In most respects, however, family care works well for toddlers: not too many people and an atmosphere which one child development expert has characterized as "soft."[5] The typical centre is "harder" in its physical aspect and certainly harder for a two-year-old who is feeling his oats and resists structure.

The well-developed three-year-old is ready for centre life. Home alone with a caretaker, he may be restless and bored and will certainly be missing opportunities for social and intellectual development. Now he can handle himself physically on swings and jungle gym, keep up with other kids. If early experience has provided a secure foundation, he has the confidence to meet new people, try new things. He'll enjoy the rich range of "stuff" a good centre provides: books, building blocks, clay, sand, paints, puzzles, dress-up materials, musical instruments, dolls and trucks and tricycles. The cluster of age-mates which a year ago would have seemed daunting is now an invitation to play. So he learns valuable, necessary life lessons: to share, to take turns, to wait, to control unruly impulses, to care for and comfort other children. Provided that he's not away from home *too* long, centre care is a positive experience for most three-year-olds.

A special caution, having to do not with age and stage but with happenings in the child's life. Because all other-than-parent care involves some stress, a child's entry into day care should not coincide with other severe stresses. Sometimes, to be sure, parents have no choice. Father leaves, mother moves from a house with yard to a small apartment and is obliged to take a job — and the three-year-old suddenly spends his days in a strange place with strangers. How can he adjust to so many alarming changes at one time? Whether he falls apart or brazens it out, the emotional cost will be high. Ideally, a child should not begin day care soon after the birth of a sibling (he'll feel ousted), or when there's a death in the family (he'll feel frightened, left out) or when separation, moving or parental illness has already shaken his world.

The Child's Temperament, Health and Capacities

In the heyday of behaviourism, psychologists confidently announced that environment was all. The baby was, in effect, a *tabula rasa* awaiting imprint, clay to be formed. John B. Watson, chief prophet of the movement, insisted that he could take any child and, by controlling early experiences, produce a doctor, lawyer, Indian chief . . . whatever he wished.

This notion may never have persuaded observant parents who know that some babies are *born* Indian chiefs; no kind of environmental tinkering will turn them into lawyers. Research support for this conviction comes from the pioneer work of Drs Stella Chess and Alexander Thomas in a long-term study which concluded that temperament and constitution are inborn.[6] Some children are natural cuddlers, others "slow to warm up," some are easily upset; some — the "mother killers" — begin life tense and given to tantrums. So we can't speak glibly of "appropriate" care without defining: appropriate *for whom*? The sunny cherub who eats and sleeps well, has a smile for everyone and cheerfully shares his cookie — this kid can go almost anywhere and be loved. (Love produces happiness produces more love.) But some children are not — let's face it — conventionally attractive. They cry a lot. They seem always to have rashes, diarrhea and a runny nose. They sleep irregularly, protest against baths and new people and new foods. In a group situation, a child of this sort will not be Mr Popularity. Neglect or inattention will then exacerbate his problems. He does best with a single caretaker or in a small family group. What Chess and Thomas call the "slow to warm" child can't be swiftly consigned to any kind of surrogate care. He needs to dabble his toes in the water before he takes a swim, be accustomed very gradually to a day care situation (an hour or so at a time to start with). Energy level, attention span, fearfulness, willingness to try new things, excitability, usual disposition — all these should be considered and discussed with potential caretakers.

With some children health is a factor. The parents of a sturdy resilient youngster may cheerfully accept the infection risks of group care — "We might as well get all the kiddie diseases over now." When a child is allergic or asthmatic, or has been diagnosed as having any chronic health problem, then a centre full of small germ-bearers may pose too great a risk. Children with physical handicaps need a situation as homelike as possible. For a child who can't hear or can't get about easily, a roomful of active age-mates can be terrifying.

Your Own Situation: Job, Home, Money
If working parents hold jobs involving irregular hours, changing shifts or occasional travel, then centre care is out. Centres open and close at regular hours (few stay open after 6 P.M.), and late pickup is expensive. In this situation, home care by a live-in relative or nanny is ideal. If that is not possible, next best is a flexible warm-hearted day care mother who will accept the last-minute delivery of a still-sleepered guest at 5:30 A.M. or provide supper and bed when parents are delayed at work.

The possibility of live-in care hinges always on available space. Obviously, you can't expect a caretaker to sleep on the living-room couch — and you probably don't want to share small quarters with any helper, related or otherwise. Though it would be nice, at the end of a long day's work, to find that Aunt Gertrude has fed and bathed the children, the prospect of a whole evening with Aunt Gertrude may not delight.

Privacy, the freedom to unbend and relax with a book or whatever, may be worth the effort of daily chauffeuring.

Money, of course, is the bottom line. If you have only one child, then paid live-in help can eat up an alarming proportion of your salary. With two or more children the picture changes. In Toronto — but not in New York — the nanny who cares for two children will cost less than centre care for two. If you can involve a neighbour in your arrangement — pay the nanny a little more for accepting an extra child — live-in help may turn out to be not a luxury but, incredibly, an economy.

And then there's shift work. Figures on the numbers of couples who solve their child care problems by alternation are hard to come by. One recent American study (limited to non-farm families in which both parents worked fulltime) found 1.1 million families living the upside-down life of shift employees. In about one-third of these, husbands worked nights and wives days, with no overlapping hours.[7] This situation produces arrangements like that of two airline employees — wife a reservations agent, husband a mechanic — who met daily at a point midway between home and the job for the changing of the guard. He would hand her the baby and drive off.

Sometimes couples accept a shift existence as part of the job (police officer, nurse, waiter, telephone operator, newspaper reporter). In most cases, however, it appears to be freely chosen as a solution to the day care dilemma. When *The New York Times* interviewed these families, couples explained that they wished as far as possible to avoid using sitters and centres. Virtually all professed to believe that the child was better off with a parent, even a sleeping parent.[8]

Whether children really benefit from this arrangement seems questionable. Often a child must tiptoe about the house to avoid waking a parent. ("She's a real good kid, keeps quiet most of the time," a graveyard shift mechanic says of his ten-year-old.) When they're old enough — and maybe a bit before — children of shift workers are likely to be assigned an unusual share of household tasks. This may or may not be healthy. What is certainly not healthy is the child's vision of family life as ships that pass in the night. In effect, these children acquire a single-parent perspective; they seldom see mother and father talking, laughing or arguing either together or with them. While some mental health professionals look determinedly at the bright side — "It's a way of adjusting to the closeness-distance dimension that is comfortable for the parents," says a California psychologist — common sense inclines to the view of Luciano L'Abate, a psychologist at a counselling service for blue collar and shift workers: "It's essentially no good. They're always tired. The night shift changes all their natural cycles — sleeping, eating. Five days a week they're zombies. They sleep all week-end. With the children, what you get is a degree of depression. Sometimes they have only television for company."[9]

Location

If a child is to be taken out to a sitter, centre or day care home, it is important that delivery and pick-up be convenient. Workplace care, when available, seems ideal from this standpoint, but apparent convenience has to be balanced against the difficulties of transporting baby, stroller and baby-gear to a downtown job. A basic early decision will be the choice between having the child near you, at a centre, or with a day care mother in your own neighbourhood, where there may be familiar companions and a playground or park. Older siblings needing after-school care can be included in such an arrangement. With infants particularly, some mothers need the security of knowing the child is close by in case of emergency. Whatever you decide, bear in mind that a workable arrangement should add no more than half an hour's travel time (both ways) to your working day.

Attitude of the Other Parent

The best laid plans can go awry unless, in a two-parent household, there's firm agreement about the child care arrangement and the responsibilities it entails for both parties. A young mother who thought hiring a nanny was *her* business ("I'm paying") precipitated a marital battle and frantic last-minute changes because she hadn't taken into account her husband's feelings. ("I do not want to find the nanny on the sofa reading *Cosmopolitan* when I come home from work. I will *not* share a bathroom.") Into each life some crisis must fall; when the day care mother phones to say your child's running a fever, when the sitter must be driven to her night class, when one parent can't get to the centre in time for pick-up, then the other parent's support is crucial.

Making a Judgment: Is This the Right Place for My Child?

The central considerations in choosing a group care arrangement — physical safety, affectionate attention, play provisions, nutrition, behaviour management, cleanliness — are the same for both family and centre care. Because the situations are so different, however, it seems wise to provide separate guidelines.

The Family Day Care Home

Preliminary screening should be by telephone: a brief conversation will eliminate unlikely candidates. The first contact answers practical questions: how many children the caregiver looks after at a time, how many children she has (at home or school), how long she has been doing this work, what hours she keeps, what she charges. Ask for references — at least two families who have used her services — and follow these up. If the referents were satisfied with the care their children received, make an appointment. Allow enough time to observe typical activities and to talk privately with the provider. Take your child along. His reaction to the day care home may not tell you much (few pre-schoolers respond enthusiastically to the prospect of another mother), but the caretaker's response to your child will help you decide.

Things to look at:

The Home and Yard
Does the home appear well cared-for, reasonably clean, reasonably orderly? (A spick-and-span house means strictly controlled children.)

What evidence do you note of safety precautions? (Electric outlets covered, carpeted or blocked-off stairs, safety locks on cabinets, radiators protected, a non-slippery non-splintery floor, no peeling paint, no dangling extension cords.) Ask to see where cleaning supplies and medicines are kept. Are they absolutely out of children's reach? Are first aid supplies available?

What's the condition of toys and playground equipment? Again the point is not shiny but functional and safe. Books with torn pages are frustrating, so are puzzles with missing pieces. Keep an eye out for broken equipment with sharp edges. Is there potentially dangerous debris (tools, bottles, rocks, bricks) in the yard? Is the yard fenced? Is there a soft surface area for play and another, hard, for riding toys?

What rooms of the house are open to the children? Does there seem to be enough space for the numbers present? Check the kitchen (clean? pot handles turned to the rear of the stove?) and the bathroom. If this home takes children in diapers, are changing provisions sanitary? Are heavy pieces of furniture securely anchored, safe from tipping or pulling over? Is there plenty of natural light? ventilation? Is the indoor temperature comfortable?

Is the nap area conducive to sleep (room-darkening shades, uncrowded)? Are there shelves or cubbies for personal

belongings and private comfortable corners where a child can
sit and be quiet?

Is there a television — and is it on?

The Caregiver

The quality of the person in charge should be your prime
consideration. Intelligence and education are of course desirable, but genuine feeling for children matters more than
either. A high school graduate of average intelligence who
reaches out warmly and sensitively to her charges may do
better than a business-like Early Childhood Education
graduate.

First impressions: is she *attractive*? (Not conventionally
good looking. Attractive, pleasant to look at.) Is she relaxed
and friendly? Has she an agreeable voice? Does she speak to
children in a special intimate way? Does she smile a lot? Do
her language and speaking style provide a good model? (You
may have to compromise on this. A loving foreign-born
mother can have qualities which more than compensate for
deficiencies in English. But good speech is a plus.) Has she a
sense of humour, is she playful? *Do you like her?*

Ideally, the initial interview has the quality of a visit, not a
cross-examination. In the course of informal chat over coffee,
however, you should be able to discover whether this person
is right for your family.

Things to find out:

> Has the day care mother held other jobs? What moved
> her to take up this work — and how long does she plan
> to continue? Has she had any special training, such as
> courses in child care and development, given by local
> service agencies? (Like licensing, courses don't guarantee
> the important things. But they give some indication of
> interest and preparation.)

> Ask what she likes best about working with pre-
> schoolers and what she finds difficult. This last subject

leads quite naturally to a tactful exploration of child-raising attitudes. In a mother-to-mother spirit, ask how she copes with temper tantrums, with kids who bite or hit. Does she find boys harder to handle than girls? How early were her own children weaned and toilet trained? (If she has passionate views about dry pants, that tells you a lot.) How would she cope with a fussy eater, an aggressive child, a shy one? How does she comfort children who cry for mama at the beginning or end of a day care day? Since the point of this conversation is to discover her views, not convert her to yours (what a hope!), questions should be phrased in an open way. If you announce that under no circumstances is your child to be spanked, a spanker may hold her tongue. Ask, instead, "What would you do if a three-year-old repeatedly hit and kicked other children and grabbed their toys?" If she says, "I'd give him a licking he'd remember," you've found out what you wanted to know.

Besides getting a sense of the caregiver as a person, you'll want practical information. Can she take your child earlier than usual, or keep him later, if necessary? What does she charge for overtime? Does she provide meals, and if so, can she make any allowance for individual situations (allergies, foods you don't want your child to have)? What happens on holidays? Does she have back-up arrangements for times when she goes on vacation, has a sick child or is sick herself? What if your child has a bad cold? Has she a room where a not-up-to-snuff child can rest or play, isolated but supervised? What are her criteria for deciding that a child is not well enough to attend?

Watch the caregiver with the children. Does she move easily from household chores to a crying child or a frustrated one? Is she upset by messes — spilled milk, boisterous water play? Does she exercise good judgment in knowing when children can settle their own squabbles and when they need help? Do the children's needs come ahead of housework? What effect has the presence of her own children? Of her husband? Do the children get along well together, and do they seem fond of the care-giver?

The Program

Ask the day care mother to describe what happens on a typical day. Her response may be offhand, general. "Well, you know — they play inside, and they go out some. If I have errands, they come along. We have snack, lunch, nap, a story . . . the usual things." In that case, try particular questions. Do you have a sand and water table indoors? Is there a place for clay-work? Have you easels for painting? What about finger-painting? What kind of building toys do the children like best? What are the children's favourite books? Do you allow television? Which programs, for how long? Do you have a music time? Can children choose what they want to do, or have you a set program? Do the children have a chance to do simple cooking? When you take children out, do you go on foot or by car? Is the car equipped with seat belts? Have you a helper for excursions? Do you ever take the children to special places — the library, the fire station, the zoo?

What do you most want children to gain from their experience in your home?

Nutrition

If there's no posted menu (in most homes, there won't be), ask what was served yesterday for snack and lunch, what she's planning for today. Find out — tactfully — whether she cooks fresh vegetables and soups or opens cans. Ask, as one homemaker to another, about food preferences. What breads does she like — whole wheat or fluffy-puff white? Does she served tinned spaghetti, packaged macaroni and cheese? Do the children get real fruit juice or sweetened concentrates?

Does she use cookies as reward or bribe?

The Other Children
Do the children appear to be happily involved in play, or is there a lot of aimless wandering? Is the general spirit sharing-cooperative, or do you see too many hitting, scratching incidents? Is there a good mix of sexes and ages? (A mixed age group leads to more harmony and affection between children.)

The Day Care Centre
Most of the suggestions for evaluating family day care apply to centre care as well. For considerations applicable to centre care only, you'll want to check:

Building and grounds
You can reasonably expect from a centre more play equipment than the average home provides. Are there opportunities for climbing (jungle gym), crawling (pipe or tunnel), swinging, riding (tricycles, child-size cars, wagons), balancing, building (big blocks), digging? Is the outdoor play area some distance from streets with the noise and fumes of heavy traffic? Is the playground well supervised, and do the children appear to have been schooled in safety precautions (for example, not running in front of swings)? Are there both sunny places and shade for hot days? Is there a covered area for rainy days? Is the yard — and any street exits for it — securely fenced?

The Director
A centre director, unlike a day care mother, is presumably a person specially trained, someone who by education and experience has developed a coherent philosophy of child care and development. So it's appropriate to ask her questions you wouldn't pose to a home caregiver. Ask what her goals are for children in her care. Does the program have a heavy

educational component (phonics, beginning reading and number-work), or is she more concerned with social-emotional development? What kinds of children does the centre serve? Is there a good ethnic and socio-economic mix? What qualities does she most value in caretakers? Do most of the staff have some early childhood training? If not, does the centre provide for workshops, courses, conferences, in-service training? Are there men on the staff? (A rare but distinct plus.) What is the adult/child ratio here? If your child is under one year, an acceptable ratio is one adult to three babies — at very most, four. Since some regional authorities permit six, seven, eight infants per caregiver, parents should confront Dr Edward Zigler's question: "How could one adult carry eight babies out of a burning building, much less provide the finer aspects of quality care?"

What is the average group size? (Remember that it's not only the total number of children which affects quality care; it's the size of groups. Small is beautiful.) Is there more than one shift of caretakers? Will your child be the special responsibility of one person or be cared for by whoever is handy? (This question matters enormously if your child is under eighteen months.) What is the total number of caretakers? How many left last year? (According to some experts, a turnover rate of more than fifteen percent should give you pause.)

Is the centre licensed? This question seems appropriate, but is less helpful than one might suppose. An unlicensed centre may be very good, a licensed one terrible. Licensing practices vary widely; few states or provinces meet the standards for safe day care set, but never enacted, by the U.S. Department of Health, Education and Welfare in 1980. In 1981, for example, only four Canadian provinces and *one* state required one caretaker for every three infants. Some states prohibit propped-up bottles for babies and insist that infant positions be changed every thirty minutes. One state stipulated that babies be held "at appropriate times" and encouraged to manage finger foods; this apparently exemplary regulation, however, came from a state which permitted a single eighteen-year-old with a high school diploma to care for eight infants under one year. And of course, regulations on paper are only as good as the enactment provisions. Licensing procedures are notably hasty and sporadic, largely because bureaus haven't sufficient staff to visit facilities even once a year. So the possession of a license doesn't guarantee that a centre lives up to official requirements.

Does the director talk plain English, or do you sense an attempt to snow you with educational jargon about cognitive enrichment and ego-enhancing exercises? Does she ask about your child and seem genuinely interested in finding out what kind of a person he is?

Does she show an awareness that not all families consist of mother, father and the children of that couple? If yours is a non-traditional family, you want to be sure your child will feel comfortable, included.

The Program
Do toys and equipment indicate a broad range of activities? Ideally there should be: programmed learning materials (puzzles, take-apart toys, abacus, magnets, magnifying glasses, prisms); materials for imaginative play (dolls, dress-up clothes, housekeeping equipment, puppets); art and craft materials (lots of coloured paper of various kinds, crayons, markers, scotch tape, paint, interesting junk); playthings to develop strength and co-ordination (pounding toys, work-bench, big blocks); natural materials to mess with (clay, water, sand); growing things and small animals to care for; music-making equipment (triangles, cymbals, xylophones, bells, drums); lots and lots of books.

Ask about the program for a typical day. Do children have some choice as to activities, or does everyone do the same thing at the same time? How does staff deal with the child who, for instance, resists "messy" play, or doesn't want to nap?

The Home-Day Care Connection
What provisions does the centre make for integrating the child's home and centre experiences? Some superior centres require parents to fill out each morning a daily information sheet covering not only practical matters (Who's picking up the child today, at what time) but also a report on the previous night (Did he sleep well? For how long?) and a general estimate of mood (happy, sad, playful, upset. . .). There's a place to record significant physical events (a new tooth, diarrhea) and any family happenings which may affect the child's behaviour. Where the centre doesn't routinely collect such information, are there provisions for parents and caregivers to share concerns? Good centres may post on the bulletin board a summary of the day's activities; this provides a natural basis for talk at home. With infants, a daily report on what baby ate, how much he slept, is a great help.

Is parent involvement expected — and welcomed?

Health, Sanitation and Safety
Because of the ease with which infection spreads in a group setting, you should pay particular attention to sanitary arrangements. Fastidious handwashing is critically important. Watch to see that caretakers scrub with soap *every* time food is served, every time they change a diaper or take a child to the toilet. Look at the changing area. Is the change table covered with disposable cloths or scrubbed down between changes? Are soiled diapers promptly placed in a covered container? Does every child have his own face cloth, and are disposable wipes used for bottoms? Are baby toys washed frequently?

What provisions are made for a child who becomes ill while at the centre? Is there an isolation area where the patient can comfortably await pick-up? Does the staff keep medical records and emergency phone numbers for each child? If your child comes home with a cut, bruise or bite, will the circumstances be explained by note or telephone call?

Will you be informed if your child has been exposed to a contagious disease? (Well-run centres send out letters promptly telling parents the date of exposure and the germination period.)

Have building and furniture been checked for lead paint? Does the fire department check regularly, and has it approved plans for evacuation in case of fire? How would babies be moved out safely in an emergency?

The most important information about a centre will come not from answers to questions, not from promotional brochures (Totland for Happy Tots and Merry Mothers) but from observing. There are three ways to watch what goes on. You can do "event-sampling": that is, keep your eye out for those typical child-hassles whose handling will tell you a lot about caretakers. A child falls from the jungle gym and howls; two little girls are fighting over the same dress-up cape ("It's mine!" "I got it first!"); a baby weeps with frustration because he can't quite reach the rolling ball; a toddler bites a playmate. How swiftly — and wisely — caretakers react to small tragedies will help you decide how you'd feel about entrusting *your* child to their care.

Another technique is to watch one or two children only, follow them through the day. Do they seem involved, or listless and detached? Are caretakers sensitive to their need for help, comfort or stimulation? Do they engage in a variety of activities, play with other children? Do they appear to find satisfaction, joy, in what they do?

Then pick out one caregiver and watch him or her. Does she manage to complete each encounter with a child (conversation or play), or does she appear to move about distractedly, keeping order but not really *engaging*? Does she seem to be enjoying herself — or counting hours to the changing of the guard? What impressions do you have of her as disciplinarian, as teacher, as comforter?

Though there's no way to evaluate care precisely on a zero

to one hundred scale, a caregiver observation form developed by Dr Richard Fiene of Pennsylvania's Office of Children, Youth and Families will provide a useful check of your impressions. Here's how to use the form which follows. Choose one or two centre caregivers to observe for a short period, say five minutes. (In a family care situation, you'll need considerably more time to get a sense of the provider's interaction with children.) Record in each box behaviours which did or did not occur during the observation period.

Caregiver Observation Form and Scale (COFAS)

During your observation, did the caregiver:		Weight
Speak unsolicited to a child	Any adult-initiated conversation	+2
Use the child's dialect	Adapting normal language to the child's level, with sensitivity to cultural differences (e.g., black English)	+1
Respond verbally to a child's speech	Cooing or babbling in response to infant murmurs, picking up and expanding a toddler's or pre-schooler's talk	+2
Read or identify pictures to a child	Taking time to help child pick out and identify pictures of familiar objects	+1
Sing or play music with a child	Playing an instrument, singing, using rhythm band instruments	+1

LANGUAGE

Speak slowly and clearly to a child at all times	Enunciating clearly, making sure child understands what is said	+1
Interrupt or cut off a child's verbalization	Not allowing child to finish what he has to say	−3
Scream or yell at children	Raising the voice to unpleasant levels, either to get the group's attention or to reprimand a child	−30
Allow noise level to become so high it is hard for observer to understand children	Permitting a degree of noise which disturbs and distracts everyone in the room	−1
Give affectionate physical contact to child	Picking a child up, patting a child's head, rocking an infant, holding a child in the lap, hugging or putting an arm around a child	+3
Make activity suggestion to a child	Demonstrating or guiding the child to another activity, giving suggestions or proposing alternatives	+1
Physically punish a child	Hitting, pushing, shaking or pulling violently	−100
Use food as reinforcement	"If you don't do this, you won't get dessert" − or withholding dessert when a child doesn't finish the main meal	−3

SOCIO-EMOTIONAL

Make fun of or ridicule a child	Publicly embarrassing the child by drawing attention to idiosyncracies or handicaps, lowering the child's self-image and making him feel there's something wrong with him	−30
Let other children make fun of or ridicule a child	Making no attempt to redirect children who make fun of another child or to get at the underlying problem	−30
Verbally scold, criticize or threaten a child	Open, direct, demeaning threats or criticism	−30
Isolate a child physically	Removing an acting-up child from the room, making him sit in a chair by himself or otherwise cutting him off from group activity	−1
Ignore a child's request	Failing to acknowledge in any way a verbal or non-verbal appeal (e.g., toddler tugging at caretaker)	−5
Interrupt a child's activity and prevent its completion	Ignoring individual skills and rhythms, requiring all children to complete the same activity at the same time	−5
Leave the child alone	Leaving children unattended, for any reason	−40

SOCIO-EMOTIONAL

MOTOR	Foster development of child's gross motor skills	With infants, encouraging any activity which involves rolling, sitting up, pulling up, walking, crawling, etc. With pre-schoolers, any activity which involves running, jumping, climbing, etc.	+1
COGNITIVE	Show impatience or annoyance with child's questions	Giving quick thoughtless answers to dispose of a child's question — or showing annoyance at the question's being asked	−2
	Use terms which are above the child's reasoning ability	Expecting children to grasp and retain, after brief exposure, information about numbers, colours, letters, shapes, etc.	−3
	Deal in abstract concepts without concrete examples	Counting without actual physical objects present, talking about shapes without offering an object for children to see, touch, manipulate	−3
	Show intolerance with a child's mistakes and not accepting faulty thinking	Placing too much emphasis on the one right answer, failing to make allowances for developmental differences in children's thinking	−2

Prepare or serve food for a child	For infants, preparing baby food, setting up high chair, warming bottle, feeding by bottle or spoon. For older children, setting table, serving or helping child serve food	0
Prepare activities or arrange the room	Organizing materials, placing tables and chairs, in preparation for an upcoming activity	0
Do nothing	Though not on a break, detaching from children; unresponsive, staring into space	−15
Talk with other adults	Directing attention and conversation to staff and not to children	−5

CAREGIVING

To arrive at a final score, proceed as follows:

Every check counts as, plus or minus, the "weight" given in the last column. For example, if you see a caregiver hug or pat a child, that's +3. If a caretaker ridicules a child, that's −30.

Add up the individual scores. Multiply by 10. Should you observe two different caretakers, add the two scores and multiply by 5. For three caretakers, multiply the three-caretaker total by 3.3. (There is no need to feel apologetic or embarrassed by the fact that you're attempting an assessment of this day care situation. A good provider will welcome your interest. If you en-counter opposition to prolonged observation or note-taking, that's a bad sign — as is refusal to permit parental visits without appointment.)

Now interpret your final score by using Dr Fiene's rating system. (The cautious official "non-optimal" label for a score in the −1560 to −100 range probably translates as *Run, do not walk, to the nearest exit.*)

How Good Is This Caregiving Facility?

RATING	LEVEL	RANGE IN SCORES
Good	I	+30 to +130
Fair	II	−10 to +29
Poor	III	−99 to −11
Non-optimal	IV	−1560 to −100

Few centres will score a perfect 130. This house is not a home. Combining the COFAS results with your own impressions should tell you, however, whether your child can be reasonably happy here, and whether you can feel comfortable about his joining the group.

The Nanny

How do you find a nanny? Your best bet — and most difficult — will be a training school, either a community college which offers a special course as adjunct to its Early Childhood Education offerings or one of the new short-term institutions designed to train nannies for the North American market. The great advantage here is that the staff really knows its students; anyone who has taught your candidate will have information and judgments not elsewhere available. Next best would be grapevine, a personal recommendation from someone who knows a good nanny. And next, obviously, an agency, which will charge roughly one month's salary as finder's fee. And finally there are the ads — either yours, or the would-be helper's.

However you locate your candidate, the interview is crucial. Ideally both parents are present, with the child or children to be cared for. Since the children may not want to sit out the entire interview, use the first part of the time to observe how the nanny relates to children. Does she pick up the baby, get down on the floor with a toddler? Does she have a swift instinctive sense of the child's level of talk and play? Is she tactful in her approach — for example, not swooping down on a shy or stranger-anxious child? A young woman who can't get something going with a child in the first half hour — a game, a conversation, some cheerful silliness — is probably not going to do much better given a day, a week, a month. Take time to ask the candidate about herself, and not just the obvious what-is-your-work-experience gambit. When the candidate is a recent immigrant, you'll save yourself time and trouble by finding out right off her legal status. If she's in the country illegally, you'd be wise to end the interview.

Try to get a sense of the whole person. Does the nanny come from a big family? Is she an only child? What sort of upbringing did she have (strict, permissive, in-between) and how does she feel about that now? Why has she chosen to work with young children? What does she think are the most important qualities to nourish in children — and how would she propose to achieve these goals? (This is not intended as a drillmaster quiz — just suggestions for things to talk about as you chat or show her the house.) Ask what makes her happy, what distresses her. How does she cope with boredom and loneliness? (Depending on your situation, she may have to come to terms with that.) What are her favourite leisure activities? Does she watch much television? What are her favourite programs? What does she ultimately hope for in her life? How long — realistically, honestly — would she expect to hold your job? You'll find this sort of conversation goes more easily if you share some of your own feelings and experience.

On a more practical level, you'd want to know if she smokes, if she can drive a car and would feel comfortable chauffeuring the children. Does she know basic first aid? Can she cook? Can she swim? Does she enjoy brisk walks? How does she feel about household shopping? If, after these preliminaries, the nanny seems a serious prospect for you, define very precisely what her responsibilities would be. For example: she might be expected to make a child's breakfast and lunch, but not the family dinner unless she chooses. She might do the baby's laundry, but not the family's. She would be expected to clear up the kitchen after breakfast and lunch and take charge of a child's room, but not do household chores. (Washing windows is not a nanny activity. Neither is mowing the lawn.) If you want a *lot* of housework done, you need a maid, not a nanny.

At this point you'll want to find out the nanny's attitude towards some child care fundamentals. What sort of discipline does she use? What are her feelings about messy play (mud, sand, water, finger-paint)? Does she think manners are important? How would she help the child understand the difference between nanny and parents? The most fruitful approach in determining attitudes is to ask questions about concrete situations. What would she do if a two-year-old refused to eat? If she came upon four-year-olds with pants down, playing doctor? If two pre-schoolers were fighting over a tricycle? If one hit the other on the head? If a child touched a hot iron and got a bad burn? If a two-year-old staged a tantrum in the supermarket? If she found him with an open aspirin bottle and didn't know whether he'd taken any? Ask her to describe a good day's routine for your child, a good lunch, an appropriate treat.

Ultimately, the deciding question is: do you like this person? Does she seem to like you and your family? Would you enjoy having her in your house?

If the candidate passes these tests with flying colours, you're ready to discuss a contract. A good contract protects both parties to the agreement, spelling out both rights and responsibilities. Use of the telephone, entertaining visitors, playing music — these need to be considered in the contract arrangements, as well as the obvious questions of pay, hours, vacations, medical insurance. Generally a nanny contract is for one year, with a preliminary trial period, say one month, before it becomes binding.

A caution: however attractive the nanny, ask for references and *follow them up.* It is, alas, perfectly possible that someone who's impressive at an interview has problems or weaknesses that could appear only on the long haul. If you talk to someone who has known the candidate over a long period, you may be spared experiences like that of parents who hired a charming, intelligent, lively nanny — and discovered, a few months later, that she was subject to manic-depressive episodes. It is always important to know how long a nanny stayed at her last job, what her strong and weak points appeared to be, and why she left. To this last question, one would-be employer following up references got an answer that no doubt saved her a lot of grief. "She didn't exactly *leave.* The police took her away."

Making Day Care Work

The first step in making day care work is choosing carefully. Many otherwise conscientious parents don't, for obvious reasons: a job comes up suddenly, a previous arrangement collapses, a centre with a good reputation reports a vacancy. . . People who wouldn't buy a car without checking all makes in their price range will sign up for the first or second day care place they see. Yet day care, over a three-year period, will cost more than a Volkswagen, and what's involved here may be the whole family's happiness. Deferring return to work or taking a few days off from the job in order to check out possibilities is time well invested.

Also at this time, make provision for back-up arrangements should your child be ill, or the caregiver unable to provide her usual service. Having a fulltime job and a child in care is always to some degree a stress situation; without the confidence of alternate provisions, the stress may be intolerable. In some cities a locating service can direct frantic parents to day care providers offering emergency in-home care for sick children. For example: in Toronto Victoria Day Care runs a Home Helpers Child Care Service. If a child is sick and must remain home; if the usual caregiver is ill or unavailable; if a child needs to convalesce at home after an illness; if the child cannot attend school because of a professional development day; if the parent is sick and needs competent child care — Victoria will send carefully selected and bonded Home Helpers trained in children's health care, child development and first aid. Families wishing to use this service pay a $10 registration fee; this entitles them to same day service for short term care, providing they call before 8:30 A.M. The fee is a $27 minimum for five hours or less, then $4 per hour for each additional hour up to ten. (After ten hours, the charge is $6 per hour.) In Norfolk, Virginia, The Planning Council, a non-profit agency licensed by the state as a family day care system operator, runs a Child Care Assurance Plan which locates carefully screened emergency helpers who will come to the child's home. In San Jose, California, a special Sick Care Unit accepts up to twenty mildly ill or convalescing children, provided there's no contagious disease. Such emergency help services are becoming more common. But generally speaking, parents faced with a sick child or a sick caretaker must find their own solutions. If you've a family member available for such crises, you're very fortunate. Otherwise, when you make your regular day care arrangement you must also compile a list of sitters or practical nurses who will come to your home on short notice.

Once you've made your decision, begin preparing your child if he's old enough to understand even vaguely what's about to happen. Ideally, a pre-schooler should be introduced to the idea of a new caretaker as gradually as to the idea of a new brother or sister; the change in his life will be no less momentous. If you've chosen live-in help, try to arrange for the caretaker to spend some days with you before you leave the child alone with her. If the child will be going to family or centre care, talk about the coming change, play it out. "You'll be going to a house where there are kids to play with and somebody nice to look after you. There's a sand box and jungle gym . . . blocks and books and puzzles. . . . You'll have lunch there — they make the kind of vegetable soup you like. And you'll have a little nap, with your own bear and blanket, and then, Mum will be coming to take you home. . ." Do not expect your child to respond rapturously to this prospect — and don't oversell. Children who've been promised wonderful friends and a cornucopia of toys may find the actual situation a letdown. Be brisk and clear and matter-of-fact. This is not something you can negotiate. The child is going, you'll be dropping him off and picking him up, *of course* he'll have supper at home, *of course* he'll sleep in his own bed at night. (Remember that anxiety and uncertainty are catching. Your attitude has a lot to do with your child's acceptance.) Use the dolls or stuffed animals to practise Going to Day Care. "This morning Cabbage Patch is going to her new day care. What do you think she should wear? Not a party dress, because she'll be sliding and swinging. . . . Oh, those shorts are perfect. Let's put some stuff in her tote bag. Would she like a hat, do you think? Let's take a towel. . . ." You put Cabbage Patch in the back of a truck, zoom her across the room and play out a version of the daily ritual. Once your toddler or three-year-old is familiar with the idea of day care, take him for a brief visit. Play a game with him there, show him the toys and play equipment, try to involve him with other children (but don't push if he's reluctant).

Give the caretaker a chance to get to know him. Then home again, with a cheerful, "Tomorrow you can stay a little longer." Next time, detach yourself as much as possible, stay for two hours and take the child home, explaining that the following day he's really going to school (or day care), whatever you're calling the new arrangement. Count on an upper limit of one hour's stay daily for the first week, during orientation period. With luck, love and patience, your child may release you early. Some little extroverts abandon parents for playmates so blithely that you may feel a small pang. Congratulate yourself and say "Bye-bye." If, after a week, your child still clings and cries, you'll have to be firm. "Mummy's going to the office now. I'm coming back to get you after nap." A kiss, a hug, goodbye. Any mother who has left a weeping child in strange hands knows how awful that feels. Any experienced caregiver can assure you that the lament will not long outlast your departure.

Some suggestions for easing the moment of parting:

> Ask the child to make you something while you're gone. "Will you do me a picture? Draw Sally on the swing so Daddy can see you high in the sky at day care."

> Offer a repeated daily assurance. "Mommy loves you *very* much. You have a good time playing and I'll be back to get you after nap."

> Devise an affectionate good-bye ritual which helps the child recognize the moment and adjust. Here's one that worked well for a three-year-old:
>> One, two, Mommy loves you.
>> Three, four, Take me to the door.
>> Five, six, Karen's doing tricks.
>> Seven, eight, Mommy can't be late.
>> Nine, ten, *I'll soon be back again!*
> (Chanted to the rhythm of hugs, pats, claps — whatever feels right.)

Keep the actual *good-bye* brief. Long explanations or reassurances exacerbate an anxious child's anxiety.

For your own peace of mind: consider the attitude of the father who said, "When we left Robin weeping and screaming at the centre, Trisha suffered because she heard the cries as misery. I heard them as outraged protest — a healthy response to being left."

Reunion with a child at the end of a day care day is a complex experience, easily misread. If your child bursts into tears at the sight of you, that's probably relief, not distress. If he pointedly ignores you, goes on with his play as if you were a not-very-interesting stranger, don't imagine that you matter less to him now. On the contrary, this kind of off-handedness may be the child's way of expressing anger at your betrayal. (You *left* him. For hours.) Sometimes the expression of anger is direct and open, a blow or a furious "Bad mommy!" Don't take such attacks to heart. Again, they demonstrate attachment rather than detachment. It is hard for a young child to understand why Mommy or Daddy left him — and why they didn't appear the minute he wanted *home*.

Don't let fear of a parking ticket or rush hour traffic push you into hurrying the reunion and departure. A child who has been separated from parents all day needs a big hug — "Oh, I'm glad to see you!" — and perhaps attention to his latest creations, the macaroni necklace or collage. Though there probably won't, in the chaos of pick-ups, be time for talk with the caretaker, it's important to manage a greeting and proper farewell so that the child has a sense of rapport between the important people in his life.

Everything you can do to connect home and day care will ease your child's path. Give him, by all means, his special security possessions to take along: the grubby dishtowel or frayed felt mouse. You might want to add objects which will remind him of home — a scarf with your perfume on it, a mobile (for his cubby or to hang above a baby's crib), a family photo in plastic cover. The mother of an insecure three-year-old, informed that her daughter spent a lot of time sitting in her "lion cubby," bought an identical lion decal and pasted it in the child's closet at home. For a few days, the little girl tried sitting in *both* closets; then she gave up cubby-sitting.

Because you want your caretaker to feel appreciated and your child to see that appreciation, keep an eye out for ways in which you can reasonably contribute. A fulltime working parent can't help out on group excursions. But perhaps you could bring cookies for a valentine party. You might visit one day to show your collection of shells or to demonstrate a skill the children might learn (making paper, forming coil pots from clay). Could the centre, or the home, use your old toys, books, records? The practice of inviting teachers home for a family meal seems to have died out, and that's a pity. It's good for the teacher — in this context, *caretaker* — to see the child at home, and for the child to feel that his day care person is part of the family. Can you invite the caretaker for a simple supper? Another possibility is asking her to join a family picnic or attend the child's birthday party.

An ongoing sharing of information between parents and caregivers is both important and hard to manage. Delivery and pick-up times are too rushed for more than brief exchanges — though if something really significant has just happened (a bad nightmare, family illness), you'll want to let the caretaker know. Day care centres generally arrange consultation times; with a family care mother, you may all have to do a bit of juggling in order to manage a quiet talk. At the beginning of an arrangement, you'll want to tell caregivers about any special fears or nervous mannerisms indicating anxiety; as time goes by, you should pass on word of major developments likely to affect a child's behaviour (death of a grandparent, imminent moving, pregnancy, separation).

Be *very* business-like in the matter of arrangements: prompt pick-up and delivery (or a telephone call to explain

necessary delays), payment at agreed-upon times. Never try
to pressure a caretaker into taking a feverish or sniffly child
because you've *got* to get to work; that's unfair to her, and to
the other children. If your child has been exposed to a contagious disease, let the centre know.

What if, after a few months of day care, you have reason
to believe that your child is unhappy? To begin with: don't
jump to conclusions. A talkative child's complaints about
mean teachers or mean kids may be exaggerations or sheer
fantasy. A sudden resistance to the regular morning departure doesn't necessarily indicate an unsatisfactory day care
situation. Children who have placidly accepted surrogate
care from infancy often, around nine or ten months, protest
passionately. This is part of normal developmental change.
They know the difference now between mother and others.
They want mother. Another period of stranger anxiety typically occurs between twelve and eighteen months. In both
instances, the crisis will pass with reassurances and patient
support.

Sometimes, though, a child's behaviour, his whole de-
meanour, signals trouble. A child who has been dry night and
day begins having accidents. He has nightmares or new persisting fears (of dogs, the dark, robbers). He picks at his food,
cries easily. A normally sweet-natured youngster becomes
hostile, aggressive and destructive or, equally serious, listless
and apathetic. This *may* be a passing phase, but the appalling
day care scandals of 1984 — large scale child abuse and sexual assault in New York and California centres — serve as a
grim reminder that a child's evident anxiety must be investigated. If your child says anything to arouse the suspicion
of actual abuse, take him out of the day care facility immediately and consult with the police or a children's welfare
agency. If you encounter merely a generalized unhappiness,
try questioning. ("Does Miss X get mad at the kids? Does she
ever hit them? Does anybody make fun of you?") Few pre-
schoolers, however, possess the verbal fluency to explain

how they feel. (And of course, when there has been physical abuse, the child may have been terrorized into silence.) If your child seems deeply troubled, make an appointment with the caretaker. Has she noticed changes? Has she found your child recently less co-operative and happy — and has she any ideas as to the cause? You may begin to suspect, in the course of this conversation, that the problem lies with the caretaker. Perhaps she's exhausted, feels put down, is newly irritated by the kinds of ordinary childishness that might once have amused her. She may feel unappreciated. If you can't boost her morale, or don't have reason to believe she'll come out of this trough, you may indeed have to make other arrangements. When a family day care mother has come to the end of her rope, is sick and tired of looking after other people's kids for low pay (or late pay or no pay), you can't change her feelings with an encouraging word. On the other hand, you may sense, from the caregiver's report, that your child has simply entered a new, more restless and demanding phase. Perhaps you can supplement the routine day care activities with a course in karate or backyard science. Changing a day care arrangement is so stressful for the child that you should explore all possibilities for improvement before deciding that this one won't work. It may be that a large, busy centre is wrong for your child — that he'd do better in a family day care home, with a few playmates and at least facsimile mother-attention. Or he may be bored by the day care home and be revived by the livelier group pace and structured life of a group centre. Assess the risk-benefit ratio carefully. If the potential advantage of change clearly outweighs the advantages of averting major upheaval, begin your search, give the caretaker reasonable notice . . . and back to square one.

Chapter VIII

Staying at Home:
How to Keep from Climbing the Walls

The Drop-in Centre

Drop-ins are proliferating in churches, schools, libraries and public rooms all across North America — the newest and perhaps strongest support for mothers at home with young children. A drop-in is a club, a play space, a forum, a *kaffee-klatsch*, a challenge, a haven, an information centre and, when it works really well, a new family. It may function as an informal baby-sitting service. It may serve as headquarters for the local La Leche League. Always — and this is perhaps its ultimate function — it's *a place to go to*. "At a time when she's physically under par, a new mother confronts a stagger-ing number of problems,"-says the director of a Boston drop-in. "Suddenly she has 24-hour responsibility for a small demanding stranger — an ungrateful one at that. She doubts her own competence. She's tired all the time. When she looks in the mirror, she hardly recognizes that lumpy figure in the bathrobe with baby-drool on the shoulder. Her sex life is shot, her freedom gone. If she's used to holding a paid job, she misses both financial independence and the satisfaction of visible achievement. But the worst of all, for most women, is isolation: being home alone with the baby all day. That's where the drop-in can make a critical difference. Our centre's open from 9 A.M. to 5 P.M. A parent can come here any time. She doesn't have to rush a feeding for fear she'll be late. And whenever she gets here, there'll be other mothers who under-stand how she feels."

Companionship, sympathetic listening, is a sanity-saver to women marooned in an urban setting, far from families and friends. The drop-in provides, in addition, reassurance. Colic *won't* last forever, the baby *will* eventually sleep through the night. Most centres have at least one trained staff person on hand — someone who can give professional advice on child development norms, say, or make referrals in the case of children with severe emotional or physical problems. But it's other parents who make a steady, ongoing contribution in the area of survival skills. Does your child bite other kids? Are you having a struggle over toilet training? Does your oldest beat up on younger siblings? Has your child been labelled hyperactive? Someone at the centre has dealt with the problem or knows someone else who has done so. The network function of a good drop-in is considerable. Through connections made over coffee or block-building, parents share apartments, help each other in emergencies, organize co-operative ventures for baby-sitting and shopping.

Some drop-in centres offer formal programs: lectures on various aspects of child care, or panel discussions ranging from breastfeeding to child abuse. These programs may work well for mothers of older children, women whose lives are sufficiently ordered to allow for precise time commitments (Tuesday at 2 P.M., a workshop on music for children). Most young mothers find such appointments an additional pressure in an already high-pressure existence. "If I've been up half the night and my three-year-old suddenly insists on tying her own shoelaces and the baby's napping at last . . . I'm really not equal to getting everybody to the church on time." A mother of four under six years says, "I've been to super-organized drop-ins — all those structured tot-and-mom affairs with twenty minutes singing, twenty minutes snack and now it's time to go home, kiddies . . . I like a free-flowing situation where I can meet other parents while my children play with other children."

The combination of parents *and* their children is part of the drop-in's appeal. Most family support programs — nursery schools, day care, parent groups — serve parents or children separately. A good drop-in brings the two groups together in a warm, free, lively, supportive environment. Mothers isolated in high-rise apartments often don't know another soul with young children; here they find friends who appreciate the importance of a new tooth or a reading breakthrough. Children learn from playmates about sharing, taking turns, helping and being helped. And — a special advantage — a drop-in is one of the few public places where under-threes are always welcome.

Besides offering a general talk forum, the drop-in functions as a trouble-shooter and trouble-prevention agent. A mother confronts the director with a panicky "What constitutes child abuse?" Gentle questioning — "Why did you hit Emily?" — may elicit reassuring information; this is not a pattern of abuse but an outburst triggered by fatigue. The director has suggestions for this first-time mother. "You need more sleep. Nap whenever the baby naps. Lie down to nurse. Don't worry, you won't roll over on the baby. And you need to get out more. Arrange baby-sitting trades. Go to a movie. Take a walk with your husband." If hitting — or emotional abuse — appears to be a developing problem, the director knows where to get help from a child guidance clinic or a special parent support group. Sometimes it's the director who identifies potential trouble. "You say Alec's hard to handle, doesn't come when you call. I'm wondering if there's a hearing problem. Would you like me to set up an appointment with an audiologist; just check it out?" The drop-in serves as an informal guide to community services. Legal aid, allergy clinics, day care, play groups, distress centres, emergency home nursing, housing offices, family planning. . . The director knows where to go, will often help with the initial contact. This sort of personal support is particularly important to parents who might hesitate to approach a social service agency. A teenage mother who is afraid her baby may be taken from her is not likely to call on Children's Aid; neither is a recent immigrant with little or no English. "We're multi-purpose

— by happenstance," says the director of the Children's Storefront in Toronto. "This place began as a toy lending centre and grew by responding to the community. We don't ask ourselves whether we're to be a social service, a recreation service, an educational centre or a mental health program. We're here for whatever families need."

That need may be as simple as a place to leave the baby while a mother goes to her dental appointment. (Though drop-ins are not baby-sitting services, there will usually be someone to help out at such moments.) Or the need may be considerable, as when a father finds himself suddenly in charge of three children, the youngest barely a month old. The father in that (actual) instance gives some idea of how vital the drop-in can be. "They located a reliable sitter — an Italian grandmother who didn't speak a word of English but was wonderful with the kids. They helped me organize my life. But the really big thing was emotional. I started out feeling completely at sea. How was I going to look after three little girls? The people here were totally affirming; they helped me find my own strength. The first day I came, I carried my baby like a fragile piece of china, I was so afraid she might break. Two months later, I was packing her under my arm like a football — totally secure."

Support Groups

The new mothers enrolled in a post-partum class given by the Oxford County Board of Health (Ontario) seemed notably reluctant to end their get-back-in-shape meetings; months after delivery, they continued to attend. Sister Carolyn, the public health nurse in charge, realized that the program had stretched beyond its original design and was meeting special needs. The same questions recurred again and again: questions about stress, about women's bodies, about family frustrations and anxieties. For these women, mostly farmers' wives, there were no clubs, no community college courses.

So the post-partum mothers reorganized as a support group, a place where members could make friends, develop a steadier self-esteem, learn about health. Monthly meetings (with baby-sitting provided by local high school students) now deal with topics ranging from assertiveness to pre-menstrual tension; Sister Carolyn describes the dynamics as "very exciting," with women bringing to the group problems they couldn't discuss with husbands or even close friends.

Oxford County's Health Clinic is one of thousands of support groups which have sprung up, over the past few decades, to fill the gap left by the absence, for most families, of uncles, aunts, grandmothers and long-time neighbours living within easy reach. Many of these groups are designed to help new mothers over the first months of a life different from anything they've known — or expected. Women who sailed through pregnancy buoyed by visions of rosy, dimpled babes find themselves weary, disappointed — and often frightened by their own indifference or hostility to the longed-for child. An organization like Aid for New Mothers, a Toronto group, offers emotional, social and practical support. Meeting in small informal groups all over the city, members learn about nutrition, child development, discipline, intellectual stimulation. They use ANM's motherhood-and-related-issues library, they have access to a 24-hour hot line for desperate moments. Above all, they find friends in similar situations, with similar concerns and a willingness both to listen and give advice. With names like MAGIC (Mothers Against Going Incredibly Crazy), TAB (Talk About Babies), and Meet-a-Mum (Britain), such groups are springing up in Canada, the United States and Britain. Then there are the groups focusing on special parenthood problems: mothers of twins; mothers of children suffering from diabetes, learning disabilities, sight and hearing impairment. Other groups are multi-purpose, defining themselves in terms of the community they serve. In Toronto's Jane-Finch area, for instance, a project initiated by the local university and subsequently taken over by the neighbourhood calls itself the Child Care Network but in fact deals with all aspects of family life. Volunteer workers locate baby-sitters, arrange for passing on of children's clothing, toys and furniture and keep parents informed about local activities. They have started a co-op nursery, run low-cost recreation programs, offer fitness classes for mothers (children welcome). They are available to help new residents find friends or to act as mediators in conflicts between residents. When appropriate, they put parents in touch with mental health professionals or legal aid. Always the attempt is to empower individuals rather than act for them. "We lay out the choices, explain what's available," a worker says. "For instance, with a really serious behaviour problem, we'd talk to the parents about the various child guidance clinics and treatment centres. We'd accompany families if they wish. But the actual decision — what to do — is left to the parents themselves."

The proliferation of self-help groups is a striking new social phenomenon. Until recently, the most widely known of such groups were those dealing with alcoholism and overweight; now, there are organizations to help parents with problems ranging from autism to schizophrenia, from mental retardation to exceptional ability. Family breakdown accounts in part for the surprising growth of groups. So does mobility; how many young couples can rely on help from the family of origin? Most potent has been the erosion of faith in traditional supports — the church, the physician and even the psychotherapist. "When my baby was stillborn," says a member of Parents Experiencing Perinatal Death, "my minister said, 'God wanted her. She's in heaven now.' My doctor said, 'Forget it. Go home and get pregnant again.' The first real help came from another woman who'd lost a baby. She said, 'Of course you don't forget. You're a *mother*. You lost part of yourself. You have to cry and rage and scream.' I needed that permission to grieve, so I could begin to heal."

Self-help groups are not directed by professionals (though

they often invite professional counsel). They listen. They realize that a distracted new mother needs to share her fears and anxieties with other women who know how she feels. Volunteers on the hot line of Parents Anonymous, for example, an organization concerned to prevent child abuse, will encourage a distracted parent to describe just how a child-battering episode came about; they reflect the mother's feelings and her perception of the child, knowing that she must feel *understood* before she can change.

The next stage of self-help, generally, is information and advice based on first hand experience. A La Leche volunteer listens to the frantic report of a new mother. "The doctor says my milk gives the baby diarrhea — and anyway he's not getting enough." Herself a breast-feeder, the volunteer can explain that what looks like diarrhea is the normal stool of a nursing baby — and that breast-feeding follows the law of supply and demand. (The more you nurse, the more milk you produce.) A volunteer with Voice (an organization to help hearing impaired children) shows the mother of a deaf toddler how to make high-set patch pockets on overalls, to hold the body hearing aids he must wear. A Parents of Twins volunteer shares her secrets for keeping Baby A quiet while Baby B is fed.

Support groups serve as surrogate families, bonded not by blood but by common concerns and sharing. The Parents Auxiliary of the Canadian Diabetes Association holds parties and picnics where only permitted treats are served. The One Parent Families Association organizes circuses, bowling and skating excursions with enough mothers and fathers to go round. Some special interest groups work to promote public interest and understanding — presenting briefs to legislators, producing films, organizing conferences.

One of the subtlest benefits of support groups is suggested by this comment from a club for parents of children with asthma: "Getting involved with other parents' problems helps with your own. And when you can give others hope, your own faith is strengthened." As they say in Alcoholics Anonymous, "In order to keep it, you've got to give it away."

How do you find a support group that fits your need? Look at the listings under "Social Service Organizations" in the yellow pages of the telephone directory. Ask the local YWCA, Childbirth Education Association or Family Service Association. If the group you want doesn't exist, *organize one yourself*. Extend-A-Family, an imaginative exchange program linking families of handicapped children with host families who provide relief care and new social experiences, publishes a useful booklet that tells parents how to start their own support group. (Write to P.O. Box 122, Station K, Toronto, Ontario M4P 2E0.) Or attend the meeting of *any* local group and ask how it got off the ground.

Baby-sitting, No Money Down: Co-ops and Other Swaps

The Baby-sitting Co-operative
Every mother needs time away from her baby, whether for a visit with friends, a quiet dinner with the baby's father or a lovely solitary walk. If that time costs upward of $2.00 per hour, though, many mothers will feel they can't afford it, except for "real reasons" like a doctor's appointment. One way out of this trap is the baby-sitting co-operative, a friendly arrangement by which payment is made in mother-time — one hour of mine for one hour of yours. At its simplest, the co-op is a loose swapping agreement between half a dozen good friends. The most flexible scheme is a larger, more formally organized group of parents involving from ten to as many as seventy-five families. Experienced co-opers say that fifty is just about perfect.

A baby-sitting co-op of any size needs two (unpaid) officers: a chairperson or president, and a secretary. The chairperson maintains the membership list which records for each family: names of the mother and father, names and birth dates of each child, home and workplace addresses and telephone numbers, name and telephone number of family doctor. In some co-ops the chairperson visits each prospective member in order to explain the group's operation and to discreetly determine whether both parent and home are right for the organization. Open stairwells or an unsafe play area, for example, might constitute grounds for judging a home unsuitable. If the co-op holds regular meetings, the chairperson looks after time, place and agenda.

The secretary keeps accounts in one of two ways:

a. She acts as intermediary for all arrangements. When a member needing a sitter calls with her request — Jane Jones; Monday, April 8; 3:30 to 5:30 P.M. — the secretary finds a member willing to provide service. The sitter reports to the secretary her actual caretaking time. Two hours of baby-sitting gives her two hours of credit on her account — to be applied against time owing or for future use. And the secretary records that Jane Jones owes two hours.

b. The secretary issues fifty tickets to each member, each ticket good for half an hour of sitting time. For daytime services the members make their own arrangements using tickets as payment. For evening baby-sitting the secretary makes the arrangements, provided that she has at least 24 hours' notice. When a member leaves the group, she is required to turn in fifty tickets. Members may sell tickets to other members at an agreed-upon rate.

In return for her services, the secretary is credited with as many sitting hours per month as there are members. The job of secretary may rotate monthly or be held for longer intervals.

To survive and flourish, a baby-sitting co-op needs clear

ground rules. Here, based on the experiences of many groups, are principles which promote harmony and efficiency:

> Daytime sitting takes place at the sitter's house. Evenings, the sitter goes to the children.
>
> Rate of payment is the same, regardless of the number of children in a family. If, however, children of other families are present, then *each* family pays by the hour.
>
> Time is counted to the next half hour. For example, from 6 P.M. to 9:40 P.M. is four hours. For an evening assignment, the minimum charge is two hours. Sitting past midnight costs time and a half.
>
> Preparing meals, feeding infants, picking up or delivering children adds an extra half hour's charge for each such service.
>
> All members complete a release form authorizing the sitter to arrange any necessary medical attention.
>
> Parent and sitter must agree as to whether children may be allowed to play outside or to be driven anywhere by the sitter.
>
> Both sitter and secretary should be given 24-hour notice if an arrangement must be cancelled. Parents who cancel with less notice owe the sitter a two-hour penalty. Sitters who cancel with less than 24 hours' notice must find a co-op substitute or pay for a regular sitter.

To organize a baby-sitting co-op, invite likely families — friends and friends of friends, mothers from childbirth education classes, families you've spoken to in the park or laundromat — to a first meeting at which ground rules will be worked out.

On what basis will members be accepted? By sponsorship, personal application, interview with chairperson?

How many members will be accepted? How many children can be cared for at one time? (Five is a reasonable limit.) May non-members' children be included in an arrangement, and if so, how will they be paid for?

What about overnight and weekend sittings? At what rate will they be charged? (Usual: overnight counts as eight hours, weekend rates to be arrived at by mutual agreement.)

How many hours can a member owe before being refused another sitter? (A member who owes more than thirty hours can be asked to work off some of this debt before using another co-op sitter.)

During what hours, on what days, may telephone calls be placed to the secretary about sitting arrangements? (As a rule, before 10 P.M. and never on Sunday, except in emergencies.)

The baby-sitting co-op saves money and increases the freedom of couples on a tight budget. But economy isn't its only advantage. With a co-op, parents enjoy the confidence that comes with a vouched-for, experienced caregiver: their sitter is a mother or father, someone who presumably knows how to cope with temper tantrums or sudden fever. Often good friendships develop between members who exchange sits regularly — and between their children.

The Two-Family Exchange
Some parents find the idea of a baby-sitting co-operative either complicated or restricting. "I don't want to be even theoretically on call for fifty other families" and "I'm not leaving my home nights to look after someone else's children" are

typical responses. For such parents, the most workable no-money-down system is a two-family exchange arrangement. With luck, you find another family with children roughly the ages of yours. Consider the Woods and the Garfields, who started trading with their first children. Now both families have: an eight-year-old, a six-year-old and a toddler. The two eight-year-olds are boys, the six-year-olds girls; the Garfields have a two-year-old girl and the Woods a twenty-month-old boy. The older children all attend the same school, enjoy many of the same sports (swimming, skating, skiing); they get along well together and the parents are friends. Rita Garfield says the best part of the arrangement has been freedom to leave for a week's vacation with her husband, knowing that the children are well cared for in a familiar setting. ("Helen Wood's not going to be upset by a six-year-old's finicky eating or a two-year-old's *no*s. I don't have to explain about homework or the Saturday morning ballet class. Helen knows the routines.") The visiting toddler goes to a household that's already set up for two-year-olds. For the older children, the experience is a special treat, "like sleeping over at a friend's for a week of Saturday nights." Problems that may crop up — one boy likes a night light, but it keeps the other awake — are worked out by good-natured compromise. All the children learn to share — their rooms, their toys, their privacy and their parents' attention. The six- and eight-year-olds are learning how to be good guests. Both sets of parents find that visiting children tend to be on their best behaviour, eating foods they might reject at home, accepting the host family's rules without complaint. "At home the kids bicker a lot," Rita says. "Our son teases his sister mercilessly. But Helen says that at her house he plays big brother, all protectiveness and reassurance, helping out with the baby and persuading Ellen to try the funny-looking green soup." For the host family the exchange period is fairly hectic; six children are certainly more work than three. But both families feel that the shared times add an extra dimension to their lives. "My children have no grandparents or cousins living near by," Helen Wood says. "But they have two extra part-time parents and three semi-siblings. It's a special sort of extended family."

The Goods-for-Services Exchange

When my children were small, we lived in a college town. Often, when out walking with my daughters — one in the carriage, one helping to push — I'd look at the fresh-faced, energetic young students and wish I could afford such helpers in my family. Paid baby-sitting was out, but it occurred to me that many students, weary of institutional food, might give time in return for home-cooked meals. I posted a sign in the Student Union: "I'll trade a delicious family dinner and a packed lunch for two hours of help daily with two pre-schoolers. Good cook, pleasant home, lovable and reasonably well-behaved children." For the next five years I had devoted student help. Our girl would come at arsenic hour (4 P.M.) and take over the children. Weather permitting, she'd go out with them — or I'd leave. We had dinner together, she cleaned the kitchen and packed herself a lunch. Often, because she knew and enjoyed the household, our student would move in for a weekend while my husband and I took a short vacation. One girl proved so ideally harmonious that we fixed up a room for her in our basement, and she lived with us until graduation.

An exchange of this sort would work in any community with a college near by, with payment taking the form of whatever a family can readily offer: piano lessons (or use of a piano to practice), dental work (where one parent is a dentist), use of a garage, etc.

The Library: It Isn't Just for Reading Any More

The public library used to be a sacred preserve — hush-hush territory where small children were barely tolerated on their way to Margaret Wise Brown and A.A. Milne. Today's library has flung wide the doors, embracing with particular enthusiasm the mother-and-toddler pair. In small towns, as well as cities, libraries now frequently include a drop-in centre (juice and cookies) as part of their community offering. They hold story hours for all ages, stage puppet plays and craft workshops adapted to the season. They show films. They lend records and patterns for Halloween costumes and — wonder of wonders — *toys*. This is not the place to go for a Cabbage Patch doll, or a 1,000-piece Lego set. But parents who want to introduce a young child to a busy board — pull, push, turn, ring — or a hammer and pegs table will find one here, along with a good assortment of sturdy, clean playthings designed to stimulate both physical and imaginative activity. There are play farms and simple musical instruments and puzzles and shape sorters (though generally speaking, libraries go light on games involving many small parts). Libraries which lend toys will also offer age and stage advice: what kinds of playthings stimulate small-muscle coordination, for example, or when a child is ready for puzzles. They can make available consumer reports on recommended toys (safety, durability, potential for stimulating play); they offer guidance in both choosing toys and making simple playthings. Using the toy library, parents can try out a marble shoot or a big wooden dump truck before making purchases — or give their children an opportunity to play with toys too expensive to buy.

In the toy-lending department young parents meet other parents and often move off with them to another library program like Toddler Sing-along or Books for Babies. A typical Books for Babies session is attended by pre-readers ranging from nine months to two and a half years. Each small guest gets a picture name tag and a chance to pat the group mascot, a plush bunny puppet who emerges from his bag to chat. Then there's a ritual greeting song — "Good morning, good morning and how do you do, I hope you are well today" —

followed by action games. For book time — the serious stuff — the new-breed librarian embarks on a picture book story, plentifully illustrated with sound effects and things-to-touch, as babies creep, clamber and stagger about (some chewing thoughtfully on books). These children are all too young to follow a narrative, but some study intently the pictured objects, and all appear to sense that there is something interesting going on here. Sessions are short — half an hour at most — and a happy mixture of book-looking, finger plays and action songs. Parents learn new ways to play here. And the babies learn . . . well, the babies have a good time and perhaps, who knows, begin to get a good feeling about libraries and books.

What else does the library offer mothers and children? Even small town libraries now reach out to the community. The library in Concord, New Hampshire lends out marvels of the taxidermist's art; a young nature enthusiast can take home for study a great horned owl or a snarling bobcat. The public libraries of any big city system regularly publish a calendar of happenings. In the month of November, for instance, a mother living in one large Canadian city could take her pre-schooler to any or all of the following: puppet show (Three Billy Goats Gruff, The Ugly Duckling); craft sessions (clay, seed mosaics, pine cone constructions); films (Mickey Mouse and Goofy, Alice the Chimpanzee); story hour (for various age groups); children's concert (with demonstrations of pan pipes and maracas); babytime (songs and fun for babies six to eighteen months); playtime for tots (stories and games for children from eighteen months to two years). Or a special session on dollhouse making or a folk dance event or an assortment of parent programs (You and Your Child, Strategies for Single Support Mothers), all providing refreshments and child care. That's in addition to programs for school children, teenagers, senior citizens, etc.

If your library doesn't offer anything for mothers and pre-schoolers, talk to the librarian. Tell her what kind of programs you'd find useful. Collect brochures from library systems which offer a wide range of services. Talk to other mothers and solicit their support. Write to the local newspaper. Keep talking and writing and prodding until you have the kind of library you and your family want.

Play Groups

The play group is a hybrid growth — not baby-sitting or a mother's group or a co-op or family day care, though with elements of all these arrangements. It *does* offer child care and child diversion. It does often, though incidentally, bring mothers together in a pleasant social context. It does involve a *quid pro quo*. And it does place the child periodically in the care of a family not his own — with the expectation that the mother in charge will be actively involved and not, as in family day care, a background presence. While baby-sitting co-ops work best with lots of members, the play group must be restricted to the number of pre-schoolers one parent can comfortably manage. Four is just right — big enough for companionship, small enough to allow for group outings and gaiety without pandemonium.

The play group requires a minimum of organization: it consists of four mothers (assuming one child per mother), each of whom agrees to take charge of members' children one morning or afternoon a week, in her own house. Ideally, all the children are walking age. A caregiver with one lap would be hard put to entertain four babies, and babies derive no special benefit from group life. The usual system gives a group mother responsibility for care on the same day each week; she'll switch or cancel only in case of illness or emergency. Parents deliver their children to the designated home at an agreed-upon time — say 10 A.M. — and return for pick-up two or two and a half hours later. (For a toddler, two hours away from parents is plenty.) Schedules are loose and flexible: a period of free play to start, with materials (paint, clay, whatever) set out and ready; a mid-morning snack; an active interval, out of doors if possible, or singing and marching indoors; then clean-up and a simple lunch (after which many of the children will be ready for a nap).

That's it. No officers, no fees, no special equipment and no long-term commitments. Members join or leave as their needs change. The first step in forming a group is choosing compatible parents who can be relied upon to meet their obligations. (The people one might choose for friends, to talk and laugh with and confide in, are not necessarily the ones you'd want as fellow play-groupers. But certainly members should hold similar views on discipline.) A good play group mother is well-organized, reasonably even-tempered, flexible, patient, energetic, a person who can take charge and command respect. If she's also imaginative and energetic, a good gymnast or dancer or musician, that's wonderful. But the main thing is that she enjoys being with young children, and that she's *reliable*.

Since the idea of a play group is to simplify life, not complicate it, a single organization meeting should take care of basic rules and arrangements. Each member supplies an emergency list of telephone numbers (home, office, physician). It's helpful, also, to discuss and record each child's particular concerns and needs. (Jason shouldn't have sugar. Margo's afraid of the flush toilet.) Mothers will want to set general guidelines about food (gum? sweets?), about suitable clothing, about bringing toys from home, about policy governing coughs and colds. Though every household has its own set of prohibitions, it's essential that play group mothers reach an agreement about the kind of behaviour that's not allowed. If, as occasionally happens, one child turns out to be hopelessly disruptive, his mother will have to be asked to withdraw him from the group.

Membership in a play group gives three free mornings a week in return for one morning's strenuous activity. Another advantage: by caring for other people's children, a new mother gains in both confidence and understanding. She gets a sense of the normal developmental process and also of individual departures from the norm. Seeing her own child in a new context, she may well arrive at fresh insights — that she's been helping too much (look how competent the kid is on his own!) or that she needs to introduce more activities requiring patient concentration on a task.

For a child, the meaning of play group varies according to age. A toddler may or may not respond vividly to the presence of other children. What he will unquestionably get is a valuable, gentle experience in first separation: saying goodbye to Mummy or Daddy, surviving without them for a little while and finding that they infallibly return. Because every mother's interests and personal style are different, the child extends his range of activities. At home he may play mostly with blocks, paint and clay; here he climbs and swings. Children benefit from the realization that other adults, besides parents, will care for them. In the presence of other children, they progress towards sharing and taking turns. (The toddler's progress in this area will be negligible.) In the presence of other children, the small child's egocentric view of the universe is subtly altered. Other kids have rights. Other kids have parents who think they're the greatest. And — other kids can be fun. A good play group offers the social advantages of good day care without the disadvantage of *any* day care, the long hours away from home.

Keeping One Foot in the Work World

For women accustomed to holding a job in what is arguably called the real world, the elemental shock of motherhood is role loss. Once you worked definite hours — or longer hours by choice — and for definite rewards (money, status, a sense of accomplishment). Suddenly you are on 24-hour duty with no holidays, no weekends off. You are not paid for what sometimes feels like back-breaking, spirit-breaking work.

Your accomplishments are not honoured or even, perhaps, recognized. (If the baby's father takes over a night feeding, friends exclaim, "How wonderful!" Nobody thinks it wonderful that you handle all the other feedings and changings and comfortings.) Your time is fragmented, you're constantly pushed — and at the end of the day you may wonder, "What have I done except survive?"

For all these reasons, some sort of other-than-mother work is nice work if you can get it. What are the possibilities?

Flextime, Flexiplace

Flextime, often touted as the hope of the future, really holds no hope of rescue for mothers. As usually interpreted, flextime still involves eight hours on the job, its distinctive characteristic being that a worker has some choice as to *which* eight hours. What good is that to mothers of small children? Could they work a night shift, 11 P.M. to 7 A.M. and then rise blithely with the baby? It should come as no surprise that a major study, *Balancing Jobs and Family Life: Do Flexible Work Schedules Help?* came up with a resounding negative.[1] Enthusiastically acclaimed as a solution to family stress, flextime, it appears, is most helpful to those families with the fewest work-family conflicts — in other words, those without children. Shifts in scheduling alone don't significantly affect the sharing of family work or the pressure on women who hold jobs in addition to caring for children and home.

Flexiplace, moving the job to the home, looks a lot more promising. Some kinds of work normally done in an office can be performed in the kitchen or living-room, with a baby napping or playing near by. Editing, graphic design, typing, dress alterations, accounting and billing, telephone solicitation (and collecting) are all occupations which parents have successfully fitted into the rhythm of life at home with young children. The increasing use of home computer terminals has expanded work-at-home opportunities in word processing, insurance analysis, merchandising. Employers are finding that, in addition to serving valuable employees, the work at home option carries substantial benefits for them: reduced costs for heat, light and office space; continued activity of disabled employees who might otherwise be collecting workers' compensation; savings made possible by use of the company computer in off-peak hours; and, often, a boost in morale and productivity on the part of employees grateful for the chance to work at home. For just such reasons, Aetna Life and Casualty Company, Investors Diversified Services, Inc. and some Blue Cross-Blue Shield offices are introducing at-home work programs.

An alternative more radical but increasingly common is taking the baby to the job. Obviously this won't work in all settings, but a woman who runs her own business or occupies a senior position in the firm can make her own decision as to whether work and baby mix. Other women who have proven their value have bargained successfully for the right to have their babies with them on the job. This situation occurs typically in the entertainment world. Actress Lynn Redgrave sued CBS for the right to nurse her baby on the set. The co-host of "Good Morning America," Joan Lunden, negotiated a contract specifying that the network would not only furnish her office with necessary baby gear but also provide a nurse for any necessary job travel. During filming of *The Book of Daniel*, starring Lindsay Crouse, huge rolling cameras and dozens of cast and crew changed course to accommodate a nursing schedule. "In the middle of one rehearsal," the actress recalls, "an assistant director called out, 'Mr Lumet, Lindsay's baby is crying. Can we stop now so she can feed her?' "

A woman whose chief starring role is as wife and mother may win the same respectful consideration if she has ability and resolve. A therapist at a mental health centre takes baby and sitter to work, arranging nursing breaks between appointments. A fraternity house cook has taken both her little girls into the kitchen since infancy. (At eighteen months they became salad helpers, enthusiastically tearing lettuce.) A saleswoman at a children's boutique finds that her infant is a great attraction for shoppers and "fits the decor perfectly." A dancersize teacher often dances with her baby in her arms; other times she puts him on the floor and has the class dance around him. "Of course there are problems having a little one at work," a legal secretary says. "When Jenna was a baby, she had colic and cried a lot, so I held her in a baby carrier strapped to my chest while I typed or answered the phone. Occasionally I had to take her out for a walk. Now that she's older, she plays happily in my office or naps on a futon. When she's asleep, I work double-speed. That makes up for the interruptions when she needs a cookie or a hug." What would she do if her employer objected? "Get another job. I'm good at what I do, so good that I'll always find someone willing to accept slight inconvenience in return for superior work — and loyalty."

Working at Home
Home business is a tempting option for a mother with saleable skills and self-discipline. It takes a lot of discipline to work at home, in the midst of small-child demands, with the same regularity that one would bring to an outside job. The most obvious home work is child care. Many women who long to stay home with their own children find that a modest family day care undertaking kills two birds with one stone — guilt (I should be earning money) and dread (I don't want to leave my child). In many cases a new mother backs into her job. Home with her baby, she agrees to look after a working friend's child. Then, since she's already committed to the world of children, she thinks, Why not? and becomes, while her own family is young, a day care provider, informal or licensed. (Licensing requirements vary widely in different parts of the country. In some places, an applicant may simply be asked to describe the available play space, with information about exits and plans for evacuation in case of fire. In

others, an inspector visits to check safety and sanitation standards — loose wires, rusty nails, storage of medicines and cleaning supplies. Some licensing procedures include fingerprinting, a check for criminal records, a chest X-ray and a TB test.) A day care provider will certainly not get rich at the job; a usual fee is $12 per day per child, out of which she pays for lunches and snacks. But it's happy work for someone who loves children and it may well lead to a permanent, professional interest in early childhood education. One woman who took this route says, "I feel I have had the best of both worlds; I had the luxury of spending all day with my son and still contributed to the family finances. I feel too that I'm rendering a valuable service to working parents in my community. They wouldn't want to do what I'm doing, and I wouldn't trade places with any of them."

Services or products related to children are the foundation of many home enterprises. A woman knitting for her own baby at a drop-in centre found her imaginatively designed vests so much admired that she went into business. Now she uses a knitting machine to speed up production of her line — sweaters, hats, scarves and doll clothes made from leftover oddments of yarn. Another, mastering a camera to record her baby's growth, finds herself in great demand as a children's photographer specializing in natural action portraits. Women at home make and sell original tie-dyed baby T-shirts, quilted bibs and crib bumpers, terry cloth bath slings and no-button overalls. Many of the standard baby carriers were originally designed and produced by young mothers working at a kitchen table. Then there are child-related services like arranging day care and emergency sick care. In Washington, D.C. three women who were always being consulted about good nursery schools and pediatricians set up a locating service; for a modest fee, new families register their request for information — school, church, transportation, baby-sitters, recreation facilities, even hairdressers and caterers. They receive a custom-tailored package of names and addresses and can call on the relocation centre for special problems like finding a reliable auto repair shop or a chess partner.

Women working at home are not limited to child-connected enterprises. They do everything men do — teach music, operate a ceramics studio, repair small electric appliances, cater parties, design gardens and skyscrapers. A woman who left her job as a department store buyer to make silver jewellery in her basement says, "When my first child was born, I thought I'd sort of play with silver until the kids started school. What I've found isn't a small-change hobby; it's another life. I don't have to rush out mornings in high heels, with briefcase, and fight traffic. I have breakfast with the family. If one of the kids has been up all night, I can sleep in. Because I make my own schedules, a sick child or a Brownie meeting is no problem. My old job was well paid but stressful and not really creative. Lots of routine, lots of manoeuvring for position. With the silver, now, I've found the thing I do best, and I'm where I want to be, in charge of my own life." A woman who, with a friend, started a consulting service to assist companies in planning child care facilities says, at the end of a year's hard work and learning, "I feel very gutsy, very smart and very good about myself."

Part-Time Work

And then there's part-time work. Long viewed as an option indicating lack of serious commitment, part-time work is increasingly recognized as a temporary choice for individuals planning eventual return to fulltime work. In both the United States and Canada, the fastest growing segment of the labour force consists of people wanting to work less than forty hours a week.[2] Predictably, most of these are women. In Canada in 1983, 72% of all part-time employees were female. Or, to view the figures from a different perspective, almost one-quarter (23.8%) of Canadian women in the paid labour force worked part time.[3] The corresponding figure in the United States is 22%.[4] Predictions for both countries are that the present trend will continue and that part-time arrangements will be introduced gradually into areas traditionally dominated by fulltime workers.[5]

The most hopeful development in part-time work is the expansion of opportunities beyond the old familiars — the low skill, low paid jobs in sales, service and clerical work. At every level of private and public enterprise, employers are discovering the advantages of hiring part-time workers. Overtime and turnover are reduced; so is absenteeism. ("Part-time help has a special interest in reporting to work: *pay*," a business consultant observes.)[6] Lay-offs are cheaper and less damaging to morale. Fringe benefits are usually less generous — another saving. Part-timers are said to be the "least fatigued, least error-prone workers."[7] Since they provide not just extra hands but highly skilled and qualified hands, old prejudices are dissolving. The change is occurring most rapidly in the United States where, for instance, among women working part time by choice, almost one-fifth are in professional and managerial positions.[8] At the First National Bank of Boston, all fifteen part-time women hold high-level positions (loan officers, personnel officers or vice-presidents, with a fulltime salary range from $25,000 to $45,000). Part-time career-oriented work is opening up for social workers, probation officers, computer programmers, postal employees, mental health workers, etc. Even medicine, which once demanded a 24-hour commitment, is showing a new concern for "maintaining one's humanness"; The Harvard Reduced Schedule Residency is one of several projects allowing two physicians to share one house officer position. Government has played a major role in revolutionizing the workplace. In the United States, the Federal Employees Part-Time Career Employment Act (1978) and the Comprehensive Employment and Training Act (1979), CETA, both proposed an extension of part-time programs to meet the needs of "those with household obligations, including parents of young children." As of 1982, some twenty-five states had passed legislation increasing opportunities for part-time work. In Canada the Wallace Report (1983) concluded its investigation of part-time work with a strong recommendation that the federal government introduce legislation which would guarantee part-time workers the fringe benefits and pension plans (on a pro-rated basis) offered to fulltime employees.

How do mothers of young children handle part-time work? *With difficulty*. It is never easy to arrange superior care for pre-schoolers and seldom easy to leave them. But three, four or five hours a day is a manageable period for both parents and children. Some mothers prefer to work 2½ full days a week rather than five days with reduced hours; this gives them 4½ uninterrupted days. Whichever choice a woman makes, she'll probably find that she learns to move faster and do things more efficiently, both at work and at home. A social worker employed three hours daily, Monday to Friday, at a senior citizens' centre says, "When I was home all day with my two-year-old, I was busy all the time. I'm still busy — but no busier than I was. I just do more in less time. My job is an early afternoon thing. Noah naps while the sitter's here. When I get back, he's ready to play — and so am I. The rhythm of my centre life is oddly like what you get with a small child: slow, patient, gentle, steady. I don't experience any shock moving from home to work. At the same time, the work's a nice change. It gives me the feeling of being in touch with the outside world." A mother of an infant finds her job as a school bus driver, three hours a day, just right; she drops the baby off at a friend's house on her way to school, picks him up at route's end. ("I like getting out of the house — and I'm making close to $400 a month.") Women with any sort of medical training often have no trouble getting just the amount of work they want: a physical therapist makes her own schedule with a local hospital, a microbiologist goes to the lab two days a week, a family physician works one day a week for the school department. And of course, nurses are always in demand for whatever time they can give. The only common complaint arising from all these part-time working mothers is that some colleagues are unsympathetic (about breast-feeding schedules, for example) and that in general they work for lower pay with fewer benefits. A part-time utility clerk at a Canadian bank, on the other hand, not only earns the same hourly wage as fulltimers, but also qualifies for short-term disability insurance, a comprehensive medical plan, unpaid maternity leave and paid vacations (the last two adjusted according to length of service).

Such generous provisions may become more common as labour organizations, which once opposed part-timers as potential threats, put their weight behind part-time contractual agreements. One dramatic result — and perhaps a harbinger of things to come — has occurred in British Columbia, where part-time supermarket employees, almost all organized, get a wide range of benefits and $1.15 an hour *more* than fulltime co-workers.[9] Signs of change are evident from the briefest survey of business publications. Articles on parttimers carry titles such as "An Answer to the Computer Programmer Shortage," "Answer to Coffee Breaks," "Part-Time Workers Can Bring Higher Productivity" and, a model of brief wisdom, "Half a Librarian Is Better Than None." A positive view of part-time women employees in management poses a ringing rhetorical question: "If Madame Curie were alive, but could only work from 9:30 to 3:15, would you hire her?"[10]

Job Sharing

The newest and most promising way to combine mothering with a manageable work load is job sharing. In Britain "twinning" or "boxing and coxing" has been common since Barclay's Bank introduced its program during the late 1940s. (The term comes from a nineteenth century play about Box and Cox, two journeymen who unknowingly share an apartment and a fiancée.) British Rail, the Public Employees

Union, the Lotian Health Board and the National Union of Teachers all allow for job sharing. In the United States the concept caught on during the early 1970s, a notable instance being the hiring, by the Massachusetts Department of Public Welfare, of fifty women to fill twenty-five social work positions.[11] Today, between one and two percent of the 100 million working Americans share jobs.[12] The Canadian experience remains limited — trade unions and other employee organizations have been wary of anything other than fulltime contracts — but is likely to expand with the Wallace Commission's positive recommendations. A clear sign of the times appears in a brief from the Ontario Status of Women Council: "Job sharing is a positive, creative response which can offer an alternative to the low paid, low status and insecure nature of most part-time jobs."[13]

In job sharing, "two rectangular pegs fill one square hole." The job is fulltime but the holders are part-time, dividing a position according to tasks, responsibilities or time. Job-sharing teachers, for example, may split by subject — one taking English and history, the other math and science. They may split the day, changing guard at noon. They may split the week. Such arrangements give the employer insurance against no-shows (if Box is ill, Cox will come) and generally reduce lateness or time-off for medical appointments. With two workers on the job, there is a wider spectrum of available skills and, almost certainly, a higher energy level throughout the day. "Job sharing enables us to retain the services of highly trained people who, in most cases, would resign if not able to work reduced hours," an employer told the Wallace Commission. From the standpoint of job-sharing workers, in particular mothers of young children, the great advantage is a combination of shorter hours with assured back-up in case of emergency. For the average working mother, how to reconcile job and home obligations is a constant source of anxiety. The job-sharing librarian, on the other hand, knows that if she gets a distress call from her child's school or suspects that the toddler's rash is in fact measles, she can call on her partner. "I enjoy my job more and I no longer have guilt feelings about my children suffering because I work," a public health nurse says. Other voices, other themes: "We both have more energy and a fresh outlook to bring to the job." (Psychiatric social worker) "The four days a week that I'm away from work enables me to reflect and think about it, so the time I spend at work is more productive." (Town planner) "Sometimes two heads are better than one. I think we cover more cases and possibilities." (Social worker) On a practical level, a shared job (unlike some part-time work) generally carries fulltime fringe benefits — vacations, sick leave, dental plans — divisible by agreement between partners.

The range of jobs which lend themselves to sharing is very wide; the Wallace Report lists, among others, church minister, home economist, illustrator, medical technologist, radiographer, research technician, training and development officer. The professions are well represented. Physicians can share an office, an examining room, a nurse; in Toronto, for example, three young mothers of pre-schoolers share a neighbourhood family physician practice. "When *my* baby's due," says a pregnant team member, "I've got two back-ups to take care of patients who go into labour." The New York state attorney general's office employs nineteen staff lawyers, all women, on a job-sharing basis; each individual works nineteen hours a week, receives full medical benefits and half of a salary range which runs from $31,000 to $51,000. The lawyers are enthusiastic, and so is the department. "Productivity hasn't suffered," the attorney general says. "Now we have two energetic, hard-working lawyers where before we had one. It has increased *esprit de corps* in the department and has allowed us to retain lawyers who might otherwise have been forced to leave us. And it has enabled us to attract lawyers with superb credentials, who don't have this opportunity elsewhere."[14] Job sharing seems to work on all except the upper levels of management — "Part of being a manager is to be there" is a typical judgment — and even here the door is not absolutely closed.

A woman interested in job sharing should first consider whether the type of work she does lends itself to "twinning." Clerk-typist? Perfect. Counselling? Maybe. Stage manager? Probably not. Temperament is a factor. A job sharer needs to be flexible, co-operative, tolerant; dogmatism, intense competitiveness, even a highly individual style may work against successful sharing. The choice of partner is critical. A good choice requires someone with a comparable level of skills and talents; if the talents happen to be complementary, so much the better. Mutual respect and liking, honesty, ability to communicate are all things to look for; *responsibility* is the bottom line. The two parties to the agreement need to work out details of time schedules, provisions for keeping in touch, allocation of fringe benefits, conditions of ending or renegotiating the agreement. For help in this and all aspects of job splitting, consult *The Job Sharing Handbook* by Barney Olmsted and Suzanne Smith, published by Penguin Books.

Portrait: A Professional Mother Who Left Her Job To Be with Her Children

"As a mother who works outside the home in a professional field (or as a professional who became a mother as I thought of myself during my first pregnancy — how quickly the emphasis changed!) I have read all about the pros and cons of mother-child separation. I happen to be a psychologist, which gives me easy access to the literature on the subject. One theme that has always bothered me in particular is the famous 'quality versus quantity of time' argument. The advocates of combined working and mothering always ended their arguments by saying 'It's not how much time you spend with your child, but the quality of that time. It's better to spend two good hours a day than a whole day full of frustrations. Those mothers who stay home all day are not always interacting with their children, they spend most of their time on housework, on the telephone, watching television or chatting with their neighbour.'

"Initially I could not find a rational argument to counteract these statements, not one that had enough weight in any case. But my gut feelings told me that this philosophy was wrong so I took leaves of absence of about a year after each of my three children was born. Going back to work, even with a flexible schedule that allowed me to spend many hours at home, was always a heart-wrenching experience. Although I had excellent baby-sitters and seldom feared for my children's safety or general well-being, my anxiety reached very high levels. I found that the 'quality time' argument didn't work for me. I would come rushing in, happy to have two hours in mid-afternoon, full of plans: we'd go for a walk or we'd build paper boats and float them in the bathtub . . . I envisioned two happy hours filled with laughter and delight. But I would arrive to find the children involved in something else and, knowing I would have to leave again, they didn't seem to want to bother getting into something else with me. After all, how do you say to a two-year-old that you have two whole hours?

"When I came home for supper, all three children wanted individual attention and body contact. The youngest nursed, but the other two also wanted and needed exclusive time with me. All three fought for my tired body (two or three lectures a day do take a lot out of you) and it was impossible to call those hours 'quality time' by any stretch of the imagination. My husband and I cooked supper, interrupted many times to give attention, holding one or two kids in our arms at the same time. Supper was hectic, as is usual with very small children. Then it was bath time, story time and, of course, nursing time. By then all we really wanted was for the children to go to bed so we could flop on the couch for a few minutes to ourselves. We never rushed them, but they must have sensed how out of breath we were by the end of the day.

I felt unhappy; I am sure the children did too. I became obsessed with measuring the time I spent with them. No matter how much I increased it, I didn't feel any improvement. I seemed to have grown a 'punch clock' in my mind. Every evening I would add up my 'time in' at home and at work, as I felt an acute responsibility in the latter sphere too.

"My initial dislike of the 'quality time' notion grew even stronger. I think the turning point came one day when the baby-sitter told me how Christopher, then two and a half, had come to her all of a sudden and said 'Please hold me because I want my mummy to hold me but she's not here.' It suddenly hit me with its full force: what counts is not the number of hours spent with your children, nor the activities that you engage in during that time. What counts is being there when you're needed, not before, not after. Elementary. The technical term for it, in psychological lingo, is contingency. The latest psychological theories show the importance of contingency for learning of all sorts, intellectual, emotional, practical. It means that the consequences of a behaviour must follow that behaviour as soon as possible, immediately. The other side of the coin is that consequences that are non-contingent (i.e., picking up a child an hour after she needed to be picked up, stopped asking for it and got involved in something else) may be highly detrimental. Among other things, non-contingent consequences give us a feeling of helplessness and lack of control over our environment (feelings which have been suggested by some researchers as one of the roots of depression). Young children not only need a certain amount of cuddling, talking, eye-contact, etc., but they need it at specific times when the need arises. Human beings are highly flexible, and even as early as the second half of the first year of life babies are capable of coping with certain delays now and then. However, when long delays and non-contingent responses become the norm, something goes awry.

"Some of us, especially those with an academic orientation,

tend to think of quality time as those times we spend reading a story, playing a game, teaching our children how to work a puzzle or manipulate playdough, playing with paints or engaging in some other kind of creative, play-learn activity. Since so much of the time that children demand from us is taken up with wiping dirty faces or runny noses, giving a snack, mopping up a spill or changing a diaper, some people think that anybody can do these routine drudgery things — let's reserve the mother for the 'higher' moments. Children tend to disagree, though unfortunately they cannot explain it to their parents. And they have this habit of forming an intimate bond with the person who spends the most time with them, provided this person truly fulfils their needs. So we have basically two possibilities: 1) substitute caretaker responds to the child's needs for care, affection, attention, etc. and the child attaches very strongly to the caretaker, or 2) substitute caretaker fails to respond adequately to the child's basic needs and bonding doesn't occur, a situation which none of us willingly embraces but, unfortunately, one which is quite common. It seems that option (1) above is the ideal for a working mother. But then common sense makes me ask 'Why would anyone bring a child into this world if she then proceeds to "give the child away" to attach to someone else?' It is true that in the days of the extended family children had multiple attachments. But mother was there, she was around, she was visible, and she was usually available. This situation, in my opinion, is far different from the multiple attachment to baby-sitters who come and go (much less stable than relatives), and who interact with the child only in the mother's prolonged absence.

"The philosophy of quality rather than quantity time is just another of those modern myths, rationalizations to justify a guilty conscience. Much like saying that 'crying is good for the lungs.' A child, after the first two or three years, doesn't need mother so much for all the little everyday things nor for cuddling and physical comforting as often (although still much more than is commonly recognized). But he still needs to know that if the need should arise, mother is within easy reach. If mother is within reach, the need will arise with less and less frequency (often, ironically, with the result that she doesn't feel very needed), but should mother not be around, the needs will increase. There is another psychological principle that helps me explain this. It is the notion of cognitive control. It has been shown that when people believe that they have control over their situation, they can cope with much higher levels of pain, deprivation or other aversive events. If people are exposed to painful electric shock or loud aversive noise but are told they can terminate the shock or noise any time they want by pressing a certain button, they will withstand higher shock levels or longer periods of noise than individuals who do not have a button (i.e., do not have 'control'). This is true even if they never employ the button to terminate the aversive shock or noise and is true for other aversive situations such as hunger or sensory deprivation. For a child, the magic button of control is the knowledge that mother can be summoned or reached at will. Like the subjects in the experiments described above, children won't always use the button but it's important to know it is there. If the 'button' is there, children will acquire a sense of control over their environment and will be able to cope with aversive situations much more readily. Eventually the button will be needed less and less.

"A mother who stays home does not, in fact, spend hour upon hour interacting with her child. Of course, if she has three or four children, she will be interacting with a child much of the time, especially if the children are close in age (at least that is my experience). But the basic fact is that each child needs her a bit at a time throughout the day. These bits and pieces of mothering may add up to two or three hours of interaction, which is entirely different from two or three solid hours interacting with her. The latter is an artificial, emotionally charged type of interaction which does not satisfy a child's real needs. To make adults understand how a child might feel in such a situation I have two examples I like to use: 1) Imagine that you can eat only one meal every twenty-four hours; no matter how hungry you are, you just have to wait until the meal is brought to you in the evening. Then you gorge yourself, eating much more than you can comfortably digest; the last courses you hardly enjoy but you keep on eating to make up for the day's fast. 2) Imagine that your spouse's work takes him or her out of town for eleven months a year. The one month you are together, you are together all the time, day and night. You cling to each other and do everything together, trying to squeeze in every minute of togetherness that you can. You talk all the time, you go out a lot, you make love twice a day, to somehow accumulate enough interaction to last you the rest of the year. Do these situations sound like healthy life-styles? Of course not. And nine or ten hours a day is a long, long time for a little child to have to wait to 'make up' for lost time, especially when the 'make-up' is not really very satisfying. Of course, no analogy will truly reflect the situation of children who have to make do with a short daily period of massed interactions with mother. But I hope I've given a glimpse of what it must be like.

"To sum up, it is true that it is the quality and not necessarily the quantity of interaction that matters in the mother-child interaction. The catch is in the meaning of the word 'quality.' For a lot of adults it means a certain time slot in the day when they engage in various activities with their children: talking, touching, eating, etc. The fact that these interactions are massed within a short period of time rather than distributed throughout the day doesn't seem to give most adults any pause for thought. Children, however, need the interactions distributed throughout the day. Not every fifteen minutes, not every hour, not in any recognizable pattern but at random intervals depending on environmental circumstances (a stranger coming in, a storm blowing), incidental circumstances (a fall down the stairs, a finger caught in the door, a tooth starting to come loose), and all other types of events, both negative and positive (coming down with a cold, a fight with a best friend, falling in 'love' for the first time). Some days go very smoothly and others don't. So some days they will need mother five minutes once or twice a day, other days much more often. Of course, this is after weaning. While a child is still nursing, he or she will need mother very frequently.

"It is certainly painfully difficult for a mother to stop being active in a field she enjoys, or for a mother who needs it to do without the extra income. However, with widespread social support for mothering, it could be done. There are many possible solutions. Mothers could be granted part-time work with flexible timetables and without concomitant loss of status and benefits (as is now the case). Mini-nurseries could be installed within a short distance of their offices or places of work. There could be greater support for expansion of at-home work opportunities. Or, perhaps best of all, mothers could stay home with tangible compensation from society. Until some solution is found to the present situation, the mother-child relationship will continue to suffer and we will have entire populations with unmet childhood needs."

Elena Hannah
St John's, Newfoundland

Chapter IX

A Time to Grow

Two roads diverged in a yellow wood
And sorry I could not travel both
And be one traveller, long I stood
And looked down one as far as I could
To where it bent in the undergrowth . . .

— Robert Frost
"The Road Not Taken"

Anyone who says you can hold a fulltime job and give a small child fulltime mothering attention has got to be kidding. Anyone who says you can leave a satisfying job and be completely happy all day long with a small child hasn't tried it. The roads diverge, you cannot travel both and be one traveller. There is no free lunch. In the matter of kids, jobs and child care, as in every significant area of life, you make a choice. And any choice will involve loss as well as gain.

All mothers are working mothers; on that we can agree. Beyond this limited agreement rages an often acrimonious debate. Career mothers say their personal fulfilment enriches their children. Stay-at-home mothers say no stranger can give the devoted attention a small child needs. Stay-at-homes criticize working mothers as selfish, materialistic; working mothers accuse stay-at-homes of rejecting the hard-won advances of three decades for an archaic view of women's role (*Kinder, Kirche, Küche*). Beneath the rhetoric on both sides sounds a minor note: guilt. The magazine *Working Mother* devotes a whole department each month to working-mother anxieties: "It's 6 P.M. and All I Want Is a Hot Bath" (not quality time); "Darling, I'd Go on the Class Trip if I Could, but I

Can't." Women home with children carry their own guilts: they're too often cross or abstracted, their brains are turning to mush, they lack the glamour conferred by an attaché case and a tailored suit.

Searching for answers, women's magazines offer contrasted portraits: "I'm a Working Mother and I Don't Feel Guilty," "I'm a Stay-at-Home Mother and I Don't Apologize."[1] "I really do have it all," a typical working mother insists. When she stayed home with her child she "invented things to clean because [she] had so much undirected energy." Now she holds a challenging job; her earnings have made possible the family's first house. "We both wanted Robby to have a real backyard with a swing set. Every time I see him playing on it, I feel proud that I helped in making it possible." She'd work even if money were no object. "I'm a good mother because I'm a happy person." Across the page, a mother of seven says, "For me, being at home to help shape each little one's personality and help him realize his full potential is the richest, most joyful experience in life." No, she doesn't feel intellectually deprived; in the course of any day, she's psychologist, space planner, interior designer. Her children aren't deprived either. "People ask how we ever meet our family's needs without my working. It's that word *needs*. If you think about it, that mostly translates into *wants*. Our kids may not have every toy and gadget, but their needs are being well taken care of. They've learned not to demand a lot of material things and to share what they've got."

There's no one answer to the child care problem, no course that's right for every family. If a mother absolutely must work, then she owes her child the best care possible. If she does have a choice, then I think she owes it to *herself*, as well as to the child, to take two or three years for the most important work she may ever do, nurturing a new life. What about those women — and there are many — appalled by the prospect of a baby-centred existence? "I am bored stiff by infants and the whole domestic scene," a mother who is a college professor told me. "In the classroom, I come alive." Well, sure. But to earn her professional status, arrive at a life she loved, this young scholar ground away diligently at some things that bored her stiff. She studied Anglo-Saxon grammar in order that she might some day teach nineteenth-century poetry. Caring for an infant might similarly be viewed as investment in the future. It is surely no more boring than Anglo-Saxon verbs — and the boredom passes, the poetry comes. In fact — any experienced parent will confirm this — *childhood* passes more swiftly than the new parent can imagine. Remember that wistful folk song, "Where are you going, my little one, my pretty one, Where are you going, my baby, my own?" And the discovery: "Turn around and she's two, Turn around and she's four, Turn around and she's a young girl going out of the door . . . Turn around and she's a young wife with babes of her own." That's pretty much how it is — a period of what feels like endless tugging and pulling, the child's overwhelming neediness . . . and then sudden lift-off. I remember years when I longed to drive or walk, just once, without a child beside me. Then one day, heading for the car, I called to my eleven-year-old, "I'm going shopping, want to come?" and she looked up puzzled, almost astonished. "Why in the world would I want to do *that*?"

There are two ways of being a stay-at-home mother. One is grimly marking time or dutifully giving up one's own pursuits for the sake of children. I think that's sad, bad for both parent and child. The other is to take this brief period as a gift from life — a time to pause, reflect, play, a time for self-discovery. It will not be a rose garden. Children are often exasperating, exhausting, impossible. They keep you up nights. But ah, how they light your days — with their newness, their openness to experience, the wonder and joy of their growing. "Inside the world there are many things," my four-year-old began one day, announcing that she had a poem to tell me.

And crickets sing,
And bells do ring.
The flowers sing.
Ringing, ringing, bells are singing.
The world has many things I like.
I very much like animals.
The world is what I call
Some wonderful thing in my mind
Where birds are flying, babies are whining,
The world is worldly in many ways.

During those years at home, away from the academic concerns of my professional life, my children revealed to me a
world I had forgotten or perhaps never known.

When I was a young mother at home with children, I read
an essay by a psychologist whose warmth, compassion and
insight had always moved me. "We career mommas have
been horribly brainwashed," Eda Le Shan wrote. "It is my im-
pression that children get too little neglect. We hover over
them like anxious idiots, fearful that fulfilling ourselves must
somehow mean we are depriving them." This was nonsense,
she said. Working mothers who love their kids *and* their jobs
"bring something wonderful into their children's lives, the
message that people are happier and more loving when they
are allowed to discover their fullest potential."[2] That stung.
After all those years in graduate school, bent over *Paradise
Lost* and the *Divine Comedy*, here I sat reading *Winnie the
Pooh* to two little girls with sticky hands. Had I failed to
realize my full potential? The pang passed, my daughters
bloomed. Now, many years later — Eda Le Shan and I both
grandmothers now — I observe how her views have changed:

From my own experience, I would like to suggest that
sometimes the decision to work during the first year or

two of a child's life is made in too much haste. I had already worked for a number of years; I had an advanced degree. How could I possibly stop, midstream, and take a few years off? My brain would atrophy. I would lose my momentum; I was meant for better things. There are few decisions that I now regret more. Not for my child's sake, but for mine. She had much to teach me about wonder and curiosity, about joy and loving — and most of all about the refreshment of play. I wasn't mature enough to see that. What I could not comprehend was that when she left home at eighteen, I would be as vigorous as ever and have at least another twenty-five years of creative work ahead of me. I might have waited until she was three, or even two, and lost nothing and gained something I can't have now.

The childraising years are relatively short in our increased lifespan. It is hard for young women caught between diapers and formulas to believe, but there are years and years of freedom ahead. I regret my impatience to get on with my career. I wish I'd relaxed, allowed myself the luxury of watching the world through my little girl's eyes.[3]

By age three, the child is a social being, ready to profit from a good day care centre or a good nursery school. Secure in his parents' love and support, eager now to try his powers, to see and learn and do more, he goes forth into the worldly world, and bells do ring.

Appendix A

A Note on Sexual Abuse in Day Care

When the first widely publicized story broke — charges of at least one hundred children sexually molested over a period of years at a California centre — the response was horror and revulsion, accompanied by incredulity. A seventy-seven-year-old woman (the pre-school's founder) abusing children barely out of diapers? Seven teachers involved in unnatural sex acts with their helpless charges? A nightmare. Surely a mistake. In the months following that shocking 1984 disclosure, a succession of day care scandals has created a climate of anxiety and fear. It *can* happen anywhere. At New York City's Praca Day Care Center six employees were arrested in connection with the abuse of thirty-nine children (one, a four-year-old, raped by a teacher's aide). In Chicago charges were laid against a janitor and two teachers at a private child care centre; in Reno the owner of a pre-school was arrested, and in Alabama an entire day care staff was dismissed on charges of sexual abuse. In Florida the operator of an unlicensed baby-sitting service was charged with molesting some two dozen young children. Parents who at first asked, "How could obscene, criminal behaviour occur in a facility for children?" are being told that as a matter of fact, that's just where one should expect to find it. "There should be a presumption that child abusers will gravitate to work with children," observed Steven Matthews of the New York City controller's office. Scare headlines — "A Sordid Pre-school Game," "Sex Crimes in the Nursery" — cast a dark shadow over the already beleaguered day care world.

For parents of young children, two questions are paramount. Is sexual abuse as widespread as the headlines suggest? What can be done — by individuals, by regulatory agencies — to prevent its occurrence?

On the first question: there is no way to know, with certainty, just how often sexual molestation occurs in day care centres or anywhere else. The crime, by its very nature, is deeply hidden, particularly when the victims are so young. An abused three-year-old has too little life experience to place in perspective the strange or frightening thing that has happened. Maybe that's just how grown-ups behave, how life is. The very young child lacks the vocabulary to report and may have been terrorized into silence. Experts say (cold comfort) that sexual abuse is surely no more common in day care than at home. Probably true. An educated guess would be that it is less of a problem in day care than is infectious disease — or simple boredom, benign neglect.

The important issue is prevention. In the flurry of concern which followed the 1984 revelations, emphasis has focused chiefly on the need for screening of day care employees. The British example is instructive. Andrew Frey, of the National Society for the Prevention of Cruelty to Children, attributes the absence of day nursery sex scandals in Britain to "the rigorous checks of people who apply for jobs having anything to do with children." Private child-minders as well as nursery employees are thoroughly investigated. "Their background is checked, their health is checked, and their references are checked." The British Department of Health and Social Security maintains a consulting service that draws upon police information about people considered unfit to work with children. Such precautions would certainly have prevented the establishment, in Florida, of a baby-sitting service run by a man convicted of lewd and lascivious behaviour with a nine-year-old girl. The Praca teacher's aide with a history of narcotics convictions or the Texas worker who had served time in prison for murder and was charged with molesting three little girls would have been swiftly disqualified. Until now, in some parts of the United States privacy laws have prevented day care operators from checking job candidates for criminal records. That is changing. But regulations which permit such checks provide only partial protection. The pedophile is not always or even usually a person of known criminal habits. As recent events have demonstrated, he may be a person greatly respected in his community — a librarian, a devoted churchgoer . . . or a minister. Regular unannounced inspections of child care facilities would provide an important safeguard. (Current California regulations call for brief inspections once every *three* years; visits, by appointment only, have generally focused on details of the physical environment. The infamous McMartin Center, where the first major scandal broke, was licensed and had been regularly "inspected.") In the United States the National Association for the Education of Young Children is proposing a system of accreditation which would help parents identify quality child care programs. Licensing regulations, in the wake of the sex abuse cases, are sure to be strengthened and more strictly enforced.

All these measures will help. But the ultimate safeguard is parental vigilance. Granted that young children fantasize, exaggerate, invent, and that their attitude to day care may fluctuate for a hundred reasons, one must still wonder about the awareness level of the families of some abused children. The three-year-old who woke with nightmare screams of "Give me back my pants!" Was that his first distress signal? Or were his parents too distracted, too absorbed in their own concerns to observe his daily terrors when they dropped him off at nursery school? Unfortunately it is true that many working parents, pushed by job demands, need to believe that all's well with the children. Three days after the storm broke at the Praca Day Care Center — the air still thick with evidence of rape, sodomy and sexually transmitted disease — parents were bringing their children back. "Why stop the whole world?" one mother said. "We've still got to get to work."

Parents of a child going out to care should be on the alert

for signs of sudden change: loss of appetite, sleeplessness, intense new nervous mannerisms, more tears or fears than usual and, of course, resistance to leaving home. They should pay close attention to the personal qualities of caregivers and to the general atmosphere of the caregiving facility. A final caution comes from Bettye M. Caldwell, Professor of Education at the University of Arkansas at Little Rock and president of the National Association for the Education of Young Children: "No parent should ever enroll a child in a program with arbitrary rules about when parents can visit and whether unannounced visits may be made. And all parents should find the time and the opportunity to make unannounced visits to programs in which their children are enrolled."

Appendix B

Where to Get Information and Help

UNITED STATES

American Academy of Pediatrics
Box 1034
Evanston, Ill. 60204
Publishes brochures on many aspects of child development and care — including day care.

Child Welfare League of America
67 Irving Place
New York, N.Y. 10003
Devoted to improvement of services and care for children (particularly those deprived or neglected). Maintains reference library and information service, publishes regularly updated day care material.

Children's Defense Fund
122 C St., N.W.
Washington, D.C. 20001
Engages in research, public education, monitoring of federal agencies, legislative drafting and testimony and community organizing in areas of child care and development.

Coalition for Children and Youth
1910 K Street, N.W.
Washington, D.C. 20006
Information clearing-house for material on child development and child care.

Consultation for Community Development and Self-Reliance
Bank Street College of Education
610 West 112 St.
New York, N.Y. 10024
Provides materials and guidance for communities setting up child care programs.

Day Care and Child Development Council of America, Inc.
622 14th St., N.W.
Washington, D.C. 20005
Advocates day care legislation, serves as clearing-house for information on child care. Staff helps establish and improve day care centres.

Family Service Association of America
44 East 23 St.
New York, N.Y. 10010
National office provides referrals to local agencies for help with child care needs.

Get Set Day Care Program
Stevens Administrative Center
Spring Garden at 13th St.
Philadelphia, Pa. 19123
Day care program serving children of low income families, provides assistance in the areas of curriculum, health, parent involvement, food services. Publishes material related to these concerns.

National Association for Child
Care Management
1800 M St., N.W. #1030N
Washington, D.C. 20036
Represents commercial day care
organizations, both private and
franchised. Provides lists of
recommended centres in all
regions; also investigates parent
complaints about member centres.

National Black Child Development
Institute
1463 Rhode Island Ave., N.W.
Washington, D.C. 20005
Dedicated to helping black children
realize their fullest potential, the
Institute organizes and trains its
members for effective community assistance to black families.

FEDERAL AGENCIES CONCERNED WITH
DAY CARE ISSUES:

Office of Child Development
Department of Health, Education
and Welfare
400 6th St., S.W.
Washington, D.C. 20024

Women's Bureau
U.S. Department of Labor
200 Constitution Ave., N.W.
Room S-3315
Washington, D.C. 20210

CANADA

Alliance for Children
1240 Bay St.
Toronto, Ont. M5R 2A7
An alliance of provincial voluntary
agencies involved in services for
children.

Canadian Association for Young
Children/L'Association cana-
dienne pour les jeunes enfants
323 Chapel St.
Ottawa, Ont. K1N 7Z2
Concerned with all activities relating to the education and care
of young children.

The Canadian Association of Toy
Libraries
50 Quebec Ave., #1207
Toronto, Ont. M6P 4B4
Offers brochures on how to start a
toy lending library (with par-

ticular attention to toys for
handicapped children and toy
lending as an educational program).

Canadian Committee on Early
Childhood/Organisation cana-
dienne pour l'éducation
préscolaire
c/o Mrs M.E. Kee, Chairman
35 Delaware Ave.
Ottawa, Ont. K2P 0Z2

Canadian Mothercraft Society
983 Carling Ave.
Ottawa, Ont. K1Y 4B5

32 Heath St. West
Toronto, Ont. M4V 1T3
Provides guidance in the care of
infants and pre-schoolers, offers
child care courses, trains nannies
and provides day care services.

The Child in the City
455 Spadina Ave.
Toronto, Ont. M5S 2G8
A research unit of the University of
Toronto concerned with the effects of rapid societal changes on
children in urban environments.
Maintains an extensive collection of books and articles on day
care.

Family Services
Every major city has its own family
services association, as well as
(usually) both Jewish and
Catholic family service agencies.
Look in the yellow pages of the
telephone directory.

BRITAIN

The British Association for
Early Childhood Education
Montgomery Hall
Kennington Oval
London SE11 5SW
Distributes news sheets and books
to parents.

Meet-a-Mum Association (MAMA)
26a Cumnor Hill
Oxford OX2 9HA
A self-addressed envelope sent to
Mrs Mary Whitlock will bring
information about any local
mothers' groups in a particular
region. The organization aims to
provide practical and moral support for new mothers suffering
either from post-natal depression or simply cabin fever.

National Child-minding Association
13 London Road
Bromley, Kent
The association aims to improve the

National Day Care Information
Centre/Centre national de l'information sur la garde de jour
Social Service Program Branch
Health and Welfare
612 Brooke Claxton Bldg.
Tunney's Pasture
Ottawa, Ont. K1A 1B5
The centre provides, free of charge,
a wealth of information about
day care in Canada: provincial
standards, facilities and equipment, nutrition, staff training,
day care for children with
special needs, types of care
available, etc. Each province
maintains its own day care office
in charge of regional matters.

quality of child-minding by
establishing fruitful communication between day care providers,
disseminating helpful information and encouraging training
courses. It publishes a manual
(*Who Minds?*), offers free
leaflets to individuals interested
in becoming minders and
parents hoping to find a reliable
caretaker.

National Children's Bureau
8 Wakeley St.
Islington
London EC1V 7QE
An information service, supported
by a large library, on normal
child development and children
with special needs. As a research
organization, it publishes a
quarterly journal as well as
reviews of new findings and
ongoing activities in the world of
children.

National Playing Field Association
25 Ovington Square
London SW3 2LQ
This venerable organization produces material on every aspect of play, with special emphasis on adventure playgrounds and toy libraries.

Pre-school Playgroups Association
Alford House
Aveline St.
London SE11 5DH
Offers practical help and advice to parents wishing to organize groups in which tots and mothers can play and visit together.

Toy Libraries Association
Seabrook House
Wyllyotts Manor
Darkes Lane
Potters Bar, Herts EN6 2HL
Established to test and evaluate toys and play equipment, the association will direct parents to toy libraries in their area or advise on the setting up of a toy library.

Notes

CHAPTER I
THE WORKING PARENT'S DILEMMA

1. Genevieve Leslie, "Childrearing as a Social Responsibility," in *Good Day Care*, ed. Kathleen Gallagher Ross (Toronto: Women's Press, 1978), p. 35.

2. William E. Homan, *Child Sense* (New York: Basic Books, 1977), p. 202.

3. See, for example, Margaret O'Brien Steinfels, *Who's Minding the Children? The History and Politics of Day Care in America* (New York: Simon & Schuster, 1973).

4. Ibid., p. 36.

5. Patricia Vandebelt Schulz, "Day Care in Canada: 1850–1962," in Ross, *Good Day Care*, p. 141. Schultz is quoting from an article in *Saturday Night* (November 10, 1900), p.2.

6. Ibid., p. 143. Quoted from "Declaration of Incorporation of the Creche," Victoria Day Care Services, 1891.

7. Eli Ginzberg, quoted by Sheila B. Kamerman, *Parenting in an Unresponsive Society* (New York: Free Press, 1980), p. 8.

8. Kamerman, *Parenting*, p.9.

9. Ibid., and Howard Clifford, "Day Care in Times of Economic Uncertainty," Part 1. National Day Care Information Centre, Health and Welfare Canada (n.d.), p.2. Since 1977 in the United States, working mothers with babies (under one year) have increased by one-third, from 32% of the labour force to 41% — "a demographic reality of tremendous import." Edward F. Zigler, "Overview of Child Day Care" (Presentation at Infectious Diseases in Day Care Symposium, Minneapolis, June 21–23, 1984).

10. Bryna Siegel-Gorelick, *The Working Parents' Guide to Child Care* (Boston: Little, Brown, 1983), p.6.

11. Susan Edmiston, "The Psychology of Day Care," *New York Magazine*, April 6, 1971, p. 39.

12. Ruth Emery, "Women in the Labour Market: An Information Package," Employment and Immigration Canada, B.C./Yukon region, March 1981, p. 12.

13. Alison Clarke-Stewart, *Daycare* (Cambridge: Harvard University Press, 1982), p. 11.

14. Edward Shorter, *The Making of the Modern Family* (New York: Basic Books, 1976), *passim*.

15. Lisa Leghorn, "Child Care for the Child," *A Journal of Female Liberation*, April, 1970, p. 29.

16. Elizabeth Hagen, "Child Care and Women's Liberation" in *Child Care — Who Cares?* ed. Pamela Roby (New York: Basic Books, 1975), p. 117.

17. N.B. Graves, *City, Country and Childbearing in Three Cultures* (Denver: University of Colorado Institute of Behavioral Sciences, 1969).

18. Ontario Federation of Labour, *Parental Rights and Day Care: A Bargaining Guide for Unions* (Toronto: Ontario Federation of Labour, 1982), p. 17.

19. Jay Belsky et al., "The Ecology of Day Care," in *Nontraditional Families: Parenting and Child Development*, ed. Michael Lamb (Hillsdale, N.J.: Erlbaum, 1982), p. 76.

20. Caroline Bird, *The Two-Paycheck Marriage* (New York: Pocket Books, 1980), pp. 4-5.

21. National Council of Welfare, *Women and Poverty*, National Council of Welfare, October, 1979, Table 4.

22. Jerome Bruner, *Under Five in Britain* (Ypsilanti: High/Scope Press, 1980), p. 30.

23. See Dominique Demers, "Les garderies, jardins ou jungles?" *L'Actualité*, Sept. 1984 and "Reactions: La jungle des garderies, suite et fin," *L'Actualité*, November 1984.

24. Bridget Bryant, Miriam Harris, and Dee Newton, *Children and Minders* (Ypsilanti: High/Scope Press, 1980).

25. See Health and Welfare Canada, *Status of Day Care in Canada, 1977*, Health and Welfare Canada, 1977 and Bryna Siegel-Gorelick, *The Working Parents' Guide to Child Care* (Boston: Little, Brown, 1983), p.5.

26. Sally Provence, Audrey Naylor, and June Patterson, *The Challenge of Daycare* (New Haven: Yale University Press, 1977).

27. Jerome Kagan, Richard B. Kearsley, and Philip R. Zelazo, *Infancy: Its Place in Human Development* (Cambridge: Harvard University Press, 1980).

28. National Day Care Information Centre, *Provincial Day Care Requirements*, National Day Care Information Centre, September 1982.

29. Study of a nursery chosen as superior, conducted by the Tavistock Institute for the Department of Health and Social Security, *Times Educational Supplement*, July 24, 1981.

30. Clifford, "Day Care in Times of Economic Uncertainty," Part 1, p.4.

31. Canadian Press dispatch from Grande Prairie, reprinted in *Canadian Society for Prevention of Cruelty to Children Journal*, Winter 1980, p.5.

32. M.D. Keyserling, *Windows on Day Care* (New York: National Council of Jewish Women, 1972).

33. See John Bowlby, *Maternal Care and Mental Health*, World Health Organization, 1951; *Attachment and Loss* (London: Hogarth Press, 1969).

34. Rene Spitz, *The First Year of Life* (New York: International Universities Press, 1965).

35. James and Joyce Robertson, *A Two Year Old Goes to Hospital* (1952); *Young Children in Brief Separation*, I Kate (1967), II Jane (1968), III John (1968), IV Thomas (1971), V Lucy (1976). Tavistock Child Development Research Unit.

36. Harry F. Harlow and M.K. Harlow, "The Affectional Systems," in *Behavior of Nonhuman Primates*, Vol. 2, A.M. Schrier et al, eds., (London: Academic Press, 1965), pp. 293–298. For Harlow's journal publications, see extensive bibliography in Michael Rutter, *Maternal Deprivation Reassessed* (Harmondsworth: Penguin, 1981), p. 236.

37. Rutter, *Maternal Deprivation Reassessed*, p. 130.

38. Quoted in David Cayley, *The World of the Child*, CBC Ideas transcript, 1983, p. 11.

39. Donna S. Lero, *Factors Influencing Parents' Preferences for, and Use of Alternative Child Care Arrangements for Pre-School-Age Children*, Health and Welfare Canada, 1981, p. 140.

40. Sheila B. Kamerman, *Parenting in an Unresponsive Society* (New York: Free Press, 1980), pp. 52–53. Some Canadian studies — a Saskatchewan survey in 1980 and one in metro Toronto in 1973 — reported more than 50% of parents as dissatisfied with day care arrangements. See Canadian Advisory Council on the Status of Women, *Better Day Care for Canadians*, Canadian Advisory Council on the Status of Women, 1982, p. 10.

41. Quoted in Ross, *Good Day Care*, p. 58.

42. T. Moore, "Exclusive Early Mothering and Its Alternatives: The Outcome at Adolescence," *Scandinavian Journal of Psychology*, 1975, pp. 255-272.

43. See M.D. Ainsworth, "Patterns of Attachment Behavior Shown by the Infant in Interaction with His Mother," *Merrill-Palmer Quarterly*, 1964, pp. 51-58 and Ainsworth and B.A. Wittig, "Attachment and Exploratory Behavior of One-Year-Olds in a Strange Situation" in *Determinants of Infant Behaviour*, ed. B.M. Foss (New York: Methuen, 1969).

44. Quoted by Jay Belsky and Laurence D. Steinberg, "The Effects of Day Care: A Critical Review," *Child Development* 49 (1978), pp. 929-949.

45. Siegel-Gorelick, *The Working Parents' Guide*, p. 82.

46. Quoted in Cayley, "The World of the Child," p.11.

47. Provence et al., *The Challenge of Daycare*, p. 221.

48. Greta G. Fein and Elaine R. Moorin, "Group Care Can Have Good Effects," *Day Care and Early Education*, Spring 1980, p. 17. Apart from radical feminist papers, it is difficult to find any expert willing to take a strong positive stand on day care as a contribution to the average child's life. (Disadvantaged children are a special case.) What one finds, rather, is reluctant concession to necessity. Here is Edward F. Zigler, Yale Professor of Psychology, former Chief of the U.S. Children's Bureau and first director of the Office of Child Development, a self-described "veteran of the day care wars": "Having said that day care need not be detrimental and can even be beneficial, I in no way mean to give most of the existing day care in this country a clean bill of health. Poor quality day care exists and it is clearly harmful, destructive." From "Overview of Child Day Care," address to Infectious Diseases in Day Care Symposium.

CHAPTER II

DO YOU REALLY WANT A CHILD?

1. Charles Novogrodsky, "A Father in Day Care," in *Good Day Care*, ed. Kathleen Gallagher Ross (Toronto: Women's Press, 1978), p.20.

2. Julie Mathien, "Legislation and Funding," in Ross, *Good Day Care*, p. 181.

3. Chris Judge, "Day Care Workers," in Ross, *Good Day Care*, p. 135.

4. Penelope Leach, quoted in "The World of the Child," CBC Ideas transcript, ed. David Cayley, 1983, p. 13.

5. Mia Kellmer-Pringle, quoted by Michael Raven, "Review: The Effects of Childminding, How Much Do We Know?" *Child Care Health and Development* 7 (1981), p. 106.

6. Patricia Morrisroe, "Mommy Only," *New York*, June 6, 1983, p. 22.

7. See, for example, "And Baby Makes Two," *Homemaker's*, May 1983, pp. 48-58; "Man, Woman and Child," *The Globe and Mail*, April 9, 1983, p. E16, and "Beating the Clock," *The Globe and Mail*, Sept. 20, 1984, p. E4.

8. Quoted in Morrisroe, "Mommy Only," p.25.

9. Penelope Leach, *Who Cares?* (Harmondsworth: Penguin, 1979), p. 40. See also "Having children should be only for those who want children and will actively enjoy children" (Rudolph Schaffer, *Mothering*, Cambridge: Harvard University Press, 1977, p. 93); "What is the point of choosing to have a baby and then handing it over to a caretaker for its most vulnerable years?" (Joyce Roberston quoted in "Taking the Side of the Under-Threes," *Australian Women's Weekly*, July 20, 1977, p.4); "People who choose to create new life [should] mutually discuss how that baby's needs are going to be met" (Burton White, *The World of the Child*, p. 20); "Working is not incompatible with motherhood, but the two roles conflict enough to oblige you to consider whether, if fact, you wouldn't rather choose between them . . . If you just want to put your child in a storage bin, then you decided wrong about having a child." (Joseph Church, *Understanding Your Child from Birth to Three*, New York: Pocket Books, 1976, pp. 215, 218).

10. Mary Howell, *Helping Ourselves: Families and the Human Network* (Boston: Beacon Press, 1975), p. 139.

11. John Lennon quoted in *Canadian Society for Prevention of Cruelty to Children Journal*, March 1982, centrefold.

CHAPTER IV
CHILD DEVELOPMENT AND CHILD CARE

1.For an overview of recent research on infant capacities, see Rudolph Schaffer, *Mothering* (Cambridge: Harvard University Press, 1977), pp. 27-58; Robert B. McCall, *Infants* (New York: Vintage, 1980), pp.

29–100; Alice S. Honig, "Current Research in Infant Development," *Bulletin for the Montessori Society* 8 (December 1979), pp. 1–38.

2. Alice S. Honig, "The Gifts of Families: Caring, Courage and Competence" (Paper presented at the Family Strengths Conference, Lincoln, Nebraska, May 1981), p. 16.

3. Sally Provence et al., *The Challenge of Daycare* (New Haven: Yale University Press, 1977), p. 228.

4. D.M. Levy, *Behavioral Analysis* (Springfield: Thomas, 1958).

5. A typical instance of such insensitivity is reported in Caroline Garland and Stephanie White, *Children and Day Nurseries* (Ypsilanti: High/Scope, 1980), p. 77. "The idea that a child might appreciate a cuddle seemed never to have occurred . . . Twice, faced with an infant working itself up into an hysterical state, two separate members of staff bent over the respective playpens clucking and waggling a soft toy within a few inches of the infant's face, making it cry even harder. Both these babies were under one year old."

6. Sheila Kitzinger, *Women as Mothers* (London: Fontana, 1978), pp. 163–164.

7. Margaret Mead, *Blackberry Winter: My Earlier Years* (New York: William Morrow, 1972).

8. James Lynch, *The Broken Heart* (New York: Basic Books, 1977), p. 219.

9. Linda Wolfe, "The New York Mother," *New York*, Sept. 10, 1984, pp. 32–39.

10. Penelope Leach, *Who Cares?* (Harmondsworth: Penguin, 1979), p. 66.

11. Margaret Mead, *Family* (New York: Macmillan, 1965), p. 18.

12. William and Wendy Dreskin, *The Day Care Decision* (New York: Evans, 1983), p. 92.

13. Provence et al., *The Challenge of Daycare*, p. 63.

14. Selma Fraiberg, *Every Child's Birthright: In Defense of Mothering* (New York: Basic Books, 1977), pp. 68–69.

15. Humberto Nagera, "Day Care Centres: Red Light, Green Light or Amber Light," *Child and Family* 14(2), (1975), p. 125.

16. Philippe Muller, *The Tasks of Childhood* (New York: McGraw-Hill, 1969), pp. 181–183.

17. Linda Hamilton Clinton, "Who's In Charge?", *Working Mother*, February, 1985, pp. 59–62.

18. Abraham Maslow, *Toward a Psychology of Being* (New York: Van Nostrand, 1968), p. 46.

19. Garland and White, *Children and Day Nurseries*, p. 87.

20. Provence et al., *The Challenge of Daycare*, p. 105.

21. Leach, *Who Cares?*, p. 76.

22. Quoted in *The New York Times*, November 25, 1984.

23. Lois Hoffman, "Maternal Employment: 1979," *American Psychologist*, Oct. 1979, pp. 859–865.

24. Merle Puertas, quoted in Harry Stein, "The Case for Staying Home," *Esquire*, June, 1984, pp. 147–148.

CHAPTER V
THE KINDS OF CARE

1. University of Regina, Sample Survey and Data Bank Unit, 1980.
2. Jane Whitbread, "Who's Taking Care of the Children?" *Family Circle*, Feb. 20, 1979, pp. 88–103.

3. The "freedom to explore" argument really deserves an essay in itself. What kind of exploration? To explore what? Jane Price, an eminently reasonable spokeswoman for the combination of child-raising with a fulltime job, says centres "are designed so that children can experiment without inhibitions. No one worries when a child spills milk or paint on the floor; toys and equipment are meant to be banged around. Some of the enriching experiences of these child care programs — such as sloshing around at the water-table — would be hard to replicate at home." (*How to Have a Child and Keep Your Job*, Penguin, 1980, p. 142.) By the time a toddler gets to the banging and sloshing age, most mothers are pretty skilled at finding satisfying outlets for these impulses. The enriching experiences no centre can wholly replicate are the daily routines of any household — sorting clothes for laundry, walking to the store and choosing dinner supplies, emptying wastebaskets, going next door for a cup of sugar, making a jelled dessert and above all, meeting people. Small encounters — with the postman, the meter-reader, the delivery truck driver, the friend who stops by for tea — enrich the child's world.

4. See Action Day Care, *For Universally Accessible Publicly Funded Non-Compulsory Day Care in Canada*, Toronto, 1982, p. 9 and Action Day Care and Social Planning Council of Metro Toronto, *Effects of Government Restraints on Day Care Services in Metro Toronto*, 1980.

5. Patricia Gerald Bourne, "What Day Care Ought to Be," *The New Republic*, Feb. 12, 1972, p. 22.

6. See C. Coeler et al., *Day Care Ethics in the U.S.* (Cambridge: Abt Books, 1979). Compare, in Lillian Rubin's *Worlds of Pain* (New York: Basic Books, 1976), p. 87, the mother explaining why she prefers care by relatives. "I don't want my children brought up by strangers. [This way] we do not have to worry what kind of stuff some stranger is teaching them."

7. Quoted in *Action Day Care Newsletter*, Toronto, January 1984.

8. Ellen Roseman, "Mini-Skool: Where Day Care Spells Big Business," *The Globe and Mail*, March 17, 1983.

9. Vance Packard, *Our Endangered Children* (Boston: Little, Brown, 1983), p. 157.

10. See Ontario Federation of Labour, *Parental Rights and Day Care*, p. 81.

11. The problem of inadequate supervision is, of course, not limited to centres. In August 1984, a home care facility in Dorchester, Massachusetts was suspended after one of its charges, a toddler, was hospitalized with bite marks, welts and bruises inflicted by an older child during unsupervised play (*Newsweek*, Sept. 10, 1984).

12. *The Boston Globe*, Sept. 16, 1983 and days following.

13. Quoted in *Action Day Care Newsletter*, January 1984.

14. Ellen Galinsky and William H. Hooks, *The New Extended Family* (Boston: Houghton Mifflin, 1977), pp. 127–141.

15. Donna S. Lero, *Factors Influencing Parents' Preferences for, and Use of Alternative Child Care Arrangements for Pre-School-Age Children*, Health and Welfare Canada, 1981.

16. Bryna Siegel-Gorelick, *The Working Parents' Guide to Child Care* (Boston: Little, Brown, 1983), p. 38. Dr Siegel-Gorelick is a child psychologist at the Stanford University Medical Center and the Children's Hospital at Stanford.

17. Charles Novogrodsky, "A Father in Day Care," in *Good Day Care*, ed. Kathleen Gallagher Ross (Toronto: Women's Press, 1978), p. 20.

18. See Galinsky and Hooks, *The New Extended Family*, pp. 35–49.

19. The following report of church-sponsored day care is based on Eileen W. Lindner, Mary C. Mattis and June R. Rogers *When Churches Mind the Children* (Ypsilanti: High/Scope Press, 1983).

20. *Families at Work: The General Mills American Family Report, 1980–81*, survey conducted by Louis Harris and Associates, 1981.

21. James Hymes, Jr., quoted by Caroline Zinsser, "The Best Day Care There Ever Was," *Working Mother*, October 1984, p. 80.

22. Donald Ogilvie, *Employer-Subsidized Child Care* (Inner City Fund, 1972), p. 139.

23. This encouraging figure perhaps needs to be seen in light of the fact that during the period of the Intermedics survey, year-end monthly rates for absenteeism and turnover as cited in the *Bureau of National Affairs Quarterly Report*, 1982, were the lowest in the report's nine-year history.

24. Sandra L. Burud, Pamela R. Aschbacher, and Jacquelyn McCroskey, *Employer-Supported Child Care* (Boston: Auburn House, 1984), p. 25.

25. U.S. Department of Labor,*Employers and Child Care: Development of a New Employee Benefit*, Pamphlet 23, August 1982, p.5.

26. Social Planning Council of Metro Toronto, *Report of the Task Force on Work-related Day Care* (Toronto: Social Planning Council of Metro Toronto, 1982), p.5.

27. Bureau of National Affairs, *Employers and Child Care: Development of a New Employee Benefit*, 1984, p.3.

28. Ibid., p. 4.

29. Barbara Joan Freedman, "Workplace Day Care," in Ross, *Good Day Care*, pp. 100, 101.

30. Quoted in Department of Labor, *Employers and Child Care*, p. 12. More information about specific workplace day care programs may be found in: Kathryn S. Perry, *Child Care Centers Sponsored by Employers and Labor Unions in the United States* (U.S. Department of Labor, Women's Bureau, 1980); Women's Bureau, Ontario Ministry of Labour, *Workplace Child Care*, 1981; Linda Grant, Patricia Sai-Chew, and Fausto Natarelli, *Children at Work: An Inventory of Work-related Day Care in Canada* (Social Planning Council of Metro Toronto, 1985).

31. Pamela Thayer, Principal Social Work Service Officer at the U.K. Department of Health and Social Security (1976), quoted in Bridget Bryant, Miriam Harris, and Dee Newton, *Children and Minders*, (Ypsilanti: High/Scope Press, 1980), p. 12.

32. Ibid., p. 1.

33. Laura Climenko Johnson, *Who Cares?* (Project Child Care, Toronto Social Planning Council, 1977), p. 32.

34. Penelope Leach, *Who Cares?* (Harmondsworth: Penguin, 1979), p. 165.

35. Bryna Siegel-Gorelick, *The Working Parents' Guide to Child Care* (Boston: Little, Brown, 1983), p. 35.

36. Greta Fein and Alison Clarke-Stewart, *Day Care in Context* (New York: Wiley, 1973).

37. A Vanderbilt University study comparing family day care homes with group centres found the homes "more flexible in terms of overall schedule and social-emotional climate." Researchers concluded that freedom from regimentation — lining up, doing specified things at specified times — produced an atmosphere more favourable to child development. (Robert B. Innes et al., "A Comparision of the Environments of Day Care Centers and Group Day Care Homes for 3 Year Olds," *Journal of Applied Developmental Psychology* 3 (1982), pp. 41–56.

38. Leach, *Who Cares?*, p. 164.

39. For governments too. At a U.K. conference on low cost provision for under-fives held at the Civil Service College, Sunningdale (1976), Brian Jackson observed that "with childminders, no basic buildings are required. They operate from their own home. No expensive professional training is needed . . . We do not want three-year courses at a Royal College of Childminding. With childminders no expensive kitting-out is needed. It is a matter of modest help — toys, books, play equipment."

40. Siegel-Gorelick, *The Working Parents' Guide*, p. 56.

41. Day nursery — £1,000 per child, annually; minding — £280. From Jerome Bruner, *Under Five in Britain* (Ypsilanti: High/Scope, 1980), p. 37.

42. Laura C. Johnson and Janice Dineen, *The Kin Trade* (Toronto: McGraw-Hill Ryerson, 1981), pp. 34–35.

43. Ibid., p. 71.

44. Ibid., p. 18.

45. Ibid., p. 3.

46. "What Price Day Care?", *Newsweek*, September 10, 1984, p. 19.

47. *Project Child Care*, a survey of parents using private-home day care and of the women providing that care (Social Planning Council of Metropolitan Toronto, 1977); *Children and Minders* (Oxford Preschool Research Project, 1975-1978). Material which follows is based on published reports of these studies.

48. Quoted in *Daycare Deadline 1990*. Brief to the Government of the Province of Ontario on the Future of Daycare Service in Ontario by the Ontario Coalition for Better Daycare, 1981, p. 9.

49. Bryant et al., *Children and Minders*, p. 201.

50. Ibid., p. 177.

51. Johnson and Dineen, *The Kin Trade*, p. 81.

52. Jack Tizard, quoted in Bryant et al., *Children and Minders*, p. 17.

53. B. Mayall and P. Petrie, *Minder, Mother and Child* (London: University of London Institute of Education, 1977).

54. Penelope Leach says, "Day minders are not professional child-care workers, so the care which they offer to children does not exclude the natural parents nor lower their self-esteem. Of course any individual minder may have strong views on particular aspects of child-rearing, but where these are at variance with the parents', they can be discussed between equals rather than between 'expert' and 'client'." (*Who Cares?*, pp. 164–165.) Hmm.

55. Laura C. Johnson, "Child Care as a Cottage Industry" in Ross, *Good Day Care*, p. 121.

56. This kind of exchange doesn't occur in most day care centres either. In "Parents and Day Care Workers: A Failed Partnership?" Edward F. Zigler and Pauline Turner report that the average amount of time parents spend in even a very hospitable centre is 7.4 minutes per day. Approximately ten percent of the parents didn't even enter the building with their children mornings — and another ten percent of the children were typically brought by someone other than a family member. Is there something in the formal day care arrangement which leads parents to abdicate responsibility? See Edward F. Zigler

and Edmund W. Gordon, eds., *Day Care, Scientific and Social Policy Issues* (Boston: Auburn House, 1982), pp. 174–183.

57. Jonathan Gathorne-Hardy, *The Unnatural History of the Nanny* (New York: Dial, 1973), p.7.

58. In Pamela Roby, *Child Care — Who Cares?* (New York: Basic Books, 1975), pp. 5, 13, 124.

59. Georgia Dullea, "Ranks of American Nannies Are Growing," *New York Times*, January 18, 1985, p. 18.

60. This and the preceding anecdote are reported in S. Arnold, "The British Nanny Carries On, Though She's Being Updated," *The Smithsonian*, Jan. 1984, pp. 97–104.

CHAPTER VI
THE EFFECTS OF DAY CARE

1. *The General Mills American Family Report*, conducted by Yankelovich, Skelly and White, Inc., 575 Madison Ave., New York.

2. Quoted in "Bringing Up Superbaby," *Newsweek*, March 28, 1983, p. 62.

3. See, for example, Alison Clarke-Stewart, *Daycare* (Cambridge: Harvard University Press, 1982), pp. 66–70 and Jerome Kagan, *Infancy: Its Place in Human Development* (Cambridge: Harvard University Press, 1980), pp. 155–160. "The experiences associated with social class, rather than the form of supplementary rearing, seem to have the greatest influence on cognitive development."

4. Humberto Nagera, "Day-Care Centres; Red Light, Green Light or Amber Light," *Child and Family* 14(2), (1975), pp. 110–136.

5. Urie Bronfenbrenner, *The Ecology of Human Development* (New York: Cambridge, 1979), pp. 166–167.

6. "The Effects of Day Care: A Critical Review," *Child Development* 49 (1978), p. 934.

7. Kagan, *Infancy*, p. 156.

8. J. Conrad Schwarz, Robert G. Strickland, and George Krolick, "Infant Day Care: Behavioral Effects at Preschool Age," *Developmental Psychology* 10(4), (1974), p. 505.

9. Mary Ann Pulaski, "The Rich Rewards of Make Believe," *Psychology Today*, January 1974, pp. 68–74.

10. Alice S. Honig, "The Developmental Needs of Infants," *Dimensions* 2(2), (1974), p. 31.

11. Robert B. Innes et al., "A Comparison of the Environments of Day Care Centres and Group Day Care Homes for 3 Year Olds," *Journal of Applied Developmental Psychology* 3 (1982), p. 55.

12. Sally Ledesma, Hiram Fitzgerald, and Cathleen McGreal, "Parents' Perceptions of Their Infant's Day Care Experience," *Infant Mental Health Journal* 1(1), (Spring 1980), pp. 42–55.

13. See Judith L. Rubenstein et al., "A Two-Year Follow-up of Infants in Community-based Day Care," *Journal of Child Psychology and Psychiatry* 22(3), (1981), p. 216 and Michael Rutter, *Maternal Deprivation Reassessed* (Harmondsworth: Penguin, 1981), p. 164.

14. Jay Belsky, Laurence D. Steinberg, and Ann Walker, "The Ecology of Day Care," in *Nontraditional Families, Parenting and Child Development*, ed. Michael E. Lamb (Hillsdale: Erlbaum, 1982), p. 94.

15. "With a Little Help from Our Friends," in *Good Day Care*, ed. Kathleen Gallagher Ross (Toronto: Women's Press, 1978), pp. 21–24.

16. Bryna Siegel-Gorelick, *The Working Parents' Guide to Child Care* (Boston: Little, Brown, 1983), p. 189.

17. Address to a Harvard University conference, spring 1983. Quoted in *Working Mother*, November 1984, p. 23.

18. Otto Weininger, "The Daycare Dilemma: Some Reflections on the Current Scenario," unpublished article (1984), p. 21.

19. Ibid., p. 22.

20. T. Moore, "Children of Full-Time and Part-Time Mothers," *International Journal of Social Psychiatry*, Special Congress Issue 2 (1964), pp. 1–10.

21. Ledesma, *Parents' Perceptions*, pp. 50–51.

22. J. Conrad Schwarz et al., "Infant Day Care: Behavioral Effects at Preschool Age," *Developmental Psychology* 10(4), (1974), p. 505.

23. Neal W. Finkelstein, "Aggression: Is It Stimulated by Day Care?", *Young Children* (Sept. 1982), pp. 3–9.

24. J. B. Raph et al., "The Influence of Nursery School on Social Interactions," *Journal of Orthopsychiatry* 38 (1964), pp. 144–152.

25. "Day Nurseries Damage Children," *Times Educational Supplement*, July 24, 1981.

26. See James Q. Wilson, "Raising Kids," *The Atlantic Monthly*, October, 1983, p. 46.

27. Greta G. Fein and Elaine R. Moorin, "Group Care Can Have Good Effects," *Day Care and Early Education* (Spring, 1980), p. 17.

28. Anne Robertson, "Day Care and Children's Responsiveness to Adults" in *Day Care: Scientific and Social Policy Issues*, eds. Edward F. Zigler and Edmund W. Gordon (Boston: Auburn House, 1982), p. 169.

29. Kagan, *Infancy*, p. 171.

30. Selma Fraiberg, *Every Child's Birthright: In Defense of Mothering* (New York: Basic Books, 1977), pp. 33–62.

31. Anthony Storr et al., *Churchill: Four Faces and the Man* (London: Allen Lane, 1969).

32. Weininger, *Daycare Dilemma*.

33. See Michael Rutter, *Maternal Deprivation Reassessed* (Harmondsworth: Penguin, 1981), p. 15.

34. H.R. Schaeffer and P.E. Emerson, "The Development of Social Attachments in Infancy," Monographs of the Society for Research in Child Development 152 (1973).

35. D. Farran and C. Ramey, "Infant Day Care and Attachment Behaviors toward Mothers and Teachers," *Child Development* 48 (1977), pp. 1112–1116.

36. Rutter, *Maternal Deprivation*, p. 127.

37. Sally Provence et al., *The Challenge of Daycare* (New Haven: Yale University Press, 1977), p. 65. Attachment is of course not the only measure of emotional health. The "Bermuda Day Care Study" — Bermuda having been chosen because of its well-developed, stable day care programs which involve ninety percent of Bermudians by their second year of life — concluded that "the age at which the children entered group care affected their emotional adjustment, even when the quality of that care was controlled. Children who began group care in infancy were rated as more maladjusted than those who were cared for by sitters or in day care homes for the early years and who began center care at later ages." Kathleen McCartney et al., "Environmental Differences among Day Care Centers and Their Effects on Children's Development" in Zigler and Gordon, *Day Care*, p. 148.

38. Ellen A. Farber and Byron Egeland, "Developmental Consequences of Out-of-Home Care for Infants in a Low-Income Population," in Zigler and Gordon, *Day Care*.

39. Kagan, *Infancy*, p. 236.

40. Rutter, *Maternal Deprivation*, p. 161.

41. A 1981 report on American colleges and universities found students dominated by *me*-ism — a combination of individualism, cynicism and materialism. See Arthur Levin, *When Dreams and Heroes Died: A Portrait of Today's College Student*, A Report for the Carnegie Council on Policy Studies in Higher Education, Jossey-Bass, 1981.

42. Talk given to the Women's Educational and Industrial Union, Boston, April 2, 1969.

43. Jerome Kagan and Philip Whitten, "Day Care Can Be Dangerous," *Psychology Today* (April 1970), pp. 36-37.

44. Caroline Garland and Stephanie White, *Children and Day Nurseries*, (Ypsilanti: High/Scope, 1980), p. 53.

45. Rita Kramer, *In Defense of the Family* (New York: Basic Books, 1983), p.39.

46. H. Ricciuti, "Fear and Development of Social Attachments in the First Year of Life," in *The Origins of Human Behavior: Fear*, eds. M. Lewis and L.A. Rosenblum (New York: Wiley, 1974).

47. Judith L. Rubenstein, Carollee Howes, and Patricia Boyle, "A Two-Year Follow-up of Infants in Community-based Day Care," *Journal of Child Psychology and Psychiatry* 22(3), (1981), pp. 209-218.

48. The phrase is Urie Bronfenbrenner's.

49. J. Conrad Schwarz, Robert G. Strickland, and George Krolick, "Infant Day Care: Behavioral Effects at Preschool Age," *Developmental Psychology* 10(4), (1974), pp. 502-506.

50. M.A. Lippman and B.H. Grote, "Socio-emotional Effects of Day Care: A Final Report," Western Washington State College, 1974.

51. T. Moore, "Children of Full-Time and Part-Time Mothers," *International Journal of Social Psychiatry*, Special Congress Issue 2 (1964), pp. 1-10 and "Exclusive Early Mothering and Its Alternatives: The Outcome to Adolescence," *Scandinavian Journal of Psychology* 16 (1975), pp. 255-272.

52. Schwarz et al., "Infant Day Care," p. 502.

53. M.M. Cochran, "A Comparison of Group Day Care and Family-Rearing Patterns in Sweden," *Child Development* 48 (1977), pp. 702–707.

54. Urie Bronfenbrenner, *Two Worlds of Childhood* (New York: Russell Sage, 1970), p. 102.

55. Ibid.

56. In one of the rare attempts to measure imponderables, Elizabeth Prescott of Pacific Oaks College offered a comparison of "creative exploring" as found in centres, family day care and home situations. She reported that in highly structured centres, this kind of activity constituted 16.2% of a child's day. In family day care settings, the proportion rose to 23.4%. In a home plus nursery school combination, 28.4% of the children's time was judged to be spent creatively.

57. The classic study of kibbutz life and mentality is Bruno Bettelheim's *Children of the Dream* (New York: Macmillan, 1969); of Chinese child care, Ruth Sidel's *Women and Child Care in China* (Harmondsworth: Penguin, 1982). For the Russian scene, I rely largely on my own visits to Soviet *yaslis*.

58. Bennetta B. Washington, quoted in June Bingham, "Child Care," *Glamour*, May 1971, p. 275.

59. Sidel, *Women and Child Care in China*, p. 185.

60. Margaret Mead, "A Cultural Anthropologist's Approach" in *Deprivation of Maternal Care: A Reassessment of Its Effects*, ed. Mary D. Ainsworth (New York: Schocken, 1966), p. 249.

61. Donald F. MacKinnon, *The Creative Person*, University of California Press, 1962.

62. Weininger, "*The Daycare Dilemma*." This speculation is supported — or answered — by research which indicates that children who stay home play longer with a familiar toy than do day care children. (M.A. Provost, "The Effects of Day Care on Child Development," *Canada's Mental Health* 28(1), pp. 17–20.)

63. Fred Rogers, *Mister Rogers Talks with Parents* (New York: Berkley, 1983), p. 132.

64. Jerome L. Singer, *The Child's World of Make-Believe* (New York: Academic Press, 1973) and "The Importance of Dreaming," *Psychology Today* (April 1968).

65. See M.A.S. Pulaski, "The Rich Rewards of Make-Believe," *Psychology Today* (January 1974), pp. 68–74.

66. Valerie Suransky, *The Erosion of Childhood* (Chicago: University of Chicago Press, 1983), pp. 63–64.

67. Jerome Bruner, *Under Five in Britain* (Ypsilanti: High/Scope Press, 1980), pp. 151–154.

68. Theodore Sizer, *Places for Learning, Places for Joy* (Cambridge: Harvard University Press, 1973), p. 35.

69. Kornei Chukovsky, tran. Miriam Morton, *From Two to Five* (Berkeley: University of California Press, 1965).

70. Families low on the socio-economic scale may produce bright, articulate offspring. A study of low-income black families found that when parents read frequently to children (and discussed the stories), talked a lot with them and engaged in animated mealtime conversations, the children's speech tended to be fluent, colourful and humorous. (R.W. Swan and H. Stavros, "Child-rearing Practices Associated with the Development of Cognitive Skills of Children in Low Socio-economic Areas," *Early Child Development and Care* 2 (1973), pp. 23–38.)

71. B. Tizard, "Language at Home and at School," in *Language in Early Childhood Education*, ed. Courtney B. Cazden (National Association for the Education of Young Children, 1981). Even the presence of a stranger appears to affect the range of a young child's speech. British psychologist Ruth Clark, comparing tape transcriptions of her 2½-year-old's talk at home with just family and at home with a (familiar) visitor present, found striking differences. With the stranger present, Ivan's speech contracted — many one-word answers, many repetitions and direct imitations. With just parents he produced quite complex original sentences. ("I'm trying to get all the things in. I'm tidying *all up* in." "You're eating an egg, that egg would make me sick." To father undressing him: "Now I can swim cos I haven't any other on my pants on.") Ruth Clark, "Assessing Language in the Home," in *Language and Learning in Home and School*, ed. Alan Davies (London: Heinemann, 1982), pp. 143–148.

72. W. Condon has shown that infants move synchronously with adult speech as early as the first day of life. "Speech Makes Babies Move," in *Child Alive*, ed. R. Lewin (New York: Doubleday, 1975).

73. D.N. Stern, "Mother and Infant at Play: The Dyadic Interaction In-

volving Facial, Vocal and Gaze Behaviours," in *The Effects of the Infant on Its Caregiver*, eds. M. Lewis and L.A. Rosenblum (New York: Wiley, 1974).

74. Rudolph Schaffer, *Mothering* (Cambridge: Harvard University Press, 1977), p. 68.

75. J.S. Watson has labelled "the Game" the playful interactions in which the baby first realizes that he can make things happen. He gurgles, mother laughs; he jumps up and down on her knee and she continues bouncing; he sings and she provides a chorus, imitating and elaborating. ("Smiling, Cooing and 'The Game,'" *Merrill-Palmer Quarterly* 18 (1972), pp. 323–339.

76. Schaffer, *Mothering*, p. 75.

77. See Peter A. and Jill G. de Villiers, *Early Language* (Cambridge: Harvard University Press, 1982), pp. 98–109.

78. Siegel-Gorelick, *The Working Parents' Guide*, p. 18.

79. P.M. Pickard, *The Activity of Children*, (New York: Humanities Press, 1968), p. 54.

80. Clark, "Assessing Language in the Home," p. 134.

81. Ibid.

82. An entire chapter of Catherine Garvey's *Play* (Cambridge: Harvard University Press, 1977) is devoted to play with language: jokes, incantations, games with alliteration and rhyme. Sometimes a child appropriates a snatch of familiar verse; seeing that a doll lacks one shoe, she sings, "One shoe off and one shoe on, Diddle, diddle dumpkin my son John." And sometimes he just plays with sound, like the 2½-year-old chanting *"Let Bobo bink. Bink ben bink. Blue kink."* (*Play*, pp. 59–76.)

83. E. Bates, "Peer Relations and the Acquisition of Language" in *Friendship and Peer Relations*, eds. M. Lewis and L. Rosenblum (New York: Wiley, 1975).

84. M.M. Lewis, *How Children Learn to Speak* (London: Harrap, 1957).

85. William Steig, *Tiffky Doofky* (New York: Farrar, Straus & Giroux, 1978).

86. See, for example, B. Tizard, H. Carmichael, M. Hughes, and G. Pinkerton, "Four Year Olds Talking to Mothers and Teachers" in *Language and Language Disorders in Childhood*, ed. L.A. Her-

soveval, *Journal of Child Psychology and Psychiatry*, Supp. No. 2 (Pergamon, 1980).

87. B. Tizard, O. Cooperman, A. Joseph, and J. Tizard, "Environmental Effects on Language Development," *Child Development* 43 (1972), pp. 337–358.

88. Bruner, *Under Five in Britain*, p. 62.

89. Ibid., pp. 62–63.

90. Provence et al., *The Challenge of Daycare*, pp. 115–116.

91. Courtney C. Cazden, "Language Development in Day-Care Programs" in *Language in Early Childhood Education* (Washington: National Association for the Education of Young Children, 1972), p. 93.

92. Rutter, *Maternal Deprivation*, p. 94.

93. Kathleen McCartney et al., "Environmental Differences among Day Care Centers," pp. 126–151.

94. Ellen Goodman, "Who Cares?" reprinted from the *Boston Globe* in *Young Children*, March 1983, pp. 9–10.

95. Mary Howell, "Is Day Care Hazardous to Health?", *Working Mother*, July 1983, pp. 37–38.

96. Ibid.

97. Stanley H. Schuman, "Day-Care-Associated Infection: More Than Meets the Eye," *Journal of the American Medical Association* 249, No. 1 (Jan. 7, 1983), p. 76.

98. Dan M. Granoff, "Meningitis and Other Invasive Bacterial Diseases" (Presentation at Infectious Diseases in Day Care Symposium, Minneapolis, June 21–23, 1984).

99. Stephen C. Hadler et al., "Hepatitis A in Day-Care Centers," *New England Journal of Medicine* (May 29, 1980), pp. 1222–1227.

100. Ibid., p. 1226. See also G. Storch et al., "Viral Hepatitis Associated with Day-Care Centers," *JAMA* 242 (1979), pp. 1514–1518; S.U. Williams et al., "Hepatitis A and Facilities for Preschool Children," *Journal of Infectious Diseases*, 131 (1975), pp. 491–494; S.H. Gehlbach et al., "Spread of Disease by Fecal-Oral Route in Day Nurseries," *Health Services Report* 88 (1973), pp. 320–322.

101. Mark L. Rosenberg et al., "Shigellosis in the United States: Ten-Year Review of Nationwide Surveillance, 1964-1973," *American Journal of Epidemiology* 104, No. 5 (1976), pp. 543–550.

102. Jack B. Weissman et al., "The Role of Preschool Children and Day-Care Centers in the Spread of Shigellosis in Urban Communities," *The Journal of Pediatrics* (June 1974), p. 801. The precise risk is hard to quantify. In another study, Weissman and his colleagues traced 87% of shigellosis cases in a Portsmouth, New Hampshire outbreak to two day care centres; in a Wood County, Ohio outbreak, the attack rate for children attending day care centres was twelve times as high as that for home care children. ("Shigellosis in Day-Care Centres," *Lancet*, January 11, 1975, pp. 88–90.)

103. Larry K. Pickering et al., "Occurrence of Giardia Lamblia in Children in Day Care Centers," *Journal of Pediatrics* (April, 1984), pp. 522–526.

104. R.E. Black et al., "Handwashing to Prevent Diarrhea in Day-Care Centers," *American Journal of Epidemiology* 113 (1981), pp. 445–451.

105. Granoff, "Meningitis and Other Bacterial Diseases."

106. See Charles M. Ginsburg et al., "Haemophilus influenzae Type B Disease: Incidence in a Day-Care Center," *JAMA* (Aug. 15, 1977), pp. 604–607.

107. K. Strangert, "Respiratory Illness in Preschool Children with Different Forms of Day Care," *Pediatrics* 57 (1976), pp. 191–196.

108. "Acute Respiratory Infectious and *Otitis Media*," Infectious Diseases in Day Care Symposium.

109. Robert F. Pass et al., "Cytomegalovirus Infection in a Day-Care Center," *New England Journal of Medicine* (Aug. 19, 1982), pp. 447–479.

110. Schuman, "Day-Care-Associated Infection," p. 79.

111. Contrast this situation with that of an Israeli kibbutz children's house, with a stable child population and a more-or-less permanent caretaker. One hears nothing of epidemics in these houses.

112. Jerome O. Klein, "The Infectious Disease Model and Day Care," Infectious Diseases in Day Care Symposium.

113. Hadler et al., "Hepatitis A in Day-Care Centers," p. 1226.

114. Klein, "Infectious Disease Model."

115. Reports from the University of Washington and the Washington Association for Children with Learning Disabilities. See *Journal of Family Practice* Vol. 17, p. 219.

116. Ruth Highberger and Mary Boynton, "Preventing Illness in Infant/Toddler Day Care," *Young Children*, March 1983, p.3.

117. Commenting on such cases, a CDC report from the Viral Diseases Division, Bureau of Epidemiology, says that "institution of sanitary measures cannot be expected to prevent all transmission of infection." Williams, "Hepatitis A."

118. Granoff, "Meningitis."

119. Vladas Kaupas, "Tuberculosis in a Family Day-Care Home," *JAMA* (May 13, 1974), p. 851.

120. Zigler, "Overview of Child Day Care."

121. These suggestions are based on a concept paper "Health and Safety Issues in Day Care" by Peggy Pizzo and Susan S. Aronson prepared for U.S. Department of Health, Education and Welfare, September 1976), and the Sanitary Food Code of the State of New Hampshire (HEW, 1976).

CHAPTER VII
CHOOSING DAY CARE

1. Study at the Educational Testing Service Infant Laboratory of Princeton, N.J., reported by Jane Price, *How to Have a Child and Keep Your Job* (Harmondsworth: Penguin, 1979), p. 140.

2. T. Berry Brazelton, *On Becoming a Family* (New York: Delta, 1981), p. 189.

3. Ibid., p. 191.

4. Quoted in "Taking the Side of the Under Threes," *Australian Women's Weekly*, July 20, 1977, p. 5.

5. Elizabeth Prescott, "Is Day Care as Good as a Good Home?" *Education Digest*, April 1978, p. 60.

6. Stella Chess, Alexander Thomas, and Herbert Birch, "The Origin of Personality," *Scientific American* 223 (1970).

7. U.S. Department of Labor Statistics, 1983.

8. Georgia Dullea, "When Parents Work on Different Shifts," *The New York Times*, Oct. 31, 1983, p. 17.

9. Ibid.

CHAPTER VIII
STAYING AT HOME: HOW TO KEEP FROM CLIMBING THE WALLS

1. Halcyone H. Bohen and Anamaria Viveros-Long, *Balancing Jobs and Family Life: Do Flexible Work Schedules Help?* (Philadelphia: Temple University Press, 1981).

2. See Labour Canada, *Part-Time Work in Canada*, The Wallace Report, 1983.

3. Wendy Weeks, "Part-Time Work: The Business View on Second-Class Jobs for Housewives and Mothers," Women's Bureau, Ministry of Labour, 1983, p. 69.

4. Kaye Lowman, *Of Cradles and Careers* (Franklin Park: La Leche League International, 1984), p. 12.

5. See, for example, Marianne Bossen, *Part-Time Work in the Canadian Economy* (1975) and William P. Werther, "Part-Timers: Overlooked and Undervalued," *Business Horizons*, Feb. 1975. ("The trend for the next two decades will be toward more part-time work, with part-timers becoming a much more significant part of the work force.")

6. William P. Werther, "Mini-Shifts: An Alternative to Overtime," *Personnel Journal*, March 1976, p. 131.

7. Ibid.

8. Lowman, *Of Cradles and Careers*, p. 16.

9. John Partridge, "The Problem with Part-Timers," *Canadian Business*, October 1982, p. 68.

10. F.J. Rehman, "Part-Timers in the Managerial Ranks?" *Industry Week*, October 14, 1974, p. 44.

11. Labour Canada, *Part-Time Work in Canada*, p. 174.

12. Nancy C. Baker, "Divide and Conquer," *Working Mother*, January 1982, p. 16.

13. Quoted in Labour Canada, *Part-Time Work in Canada*, p. 176.

14. Glenn Collins, "Take This Job and Share It," *The Toronto Star*, July 20, 1984.

CHAPTER IX
A TIME TO GROW

1. *Family Circle*, May 29, 1984, pp. 126ff.

2. Eda J. Le Shan, *Natural Parenthood* (New York: Signet, 1970), p. 121.

3. Eda J. Le Shan, "The Working Mother and Her Children" in *Childhood* (Blue Cross Association, 1976).

Selected Bibliography

Auerbach, Stevanne. *Confronting the Child Care Crisis*. Boston: Beacon Press, 1979.

Bowlby, John. *Attachment and Loss*. New York: Basic Books, 1969.

_____. *Maternal Care and Mental Health*. New York: Schocken Books, 1966.

_____. *Separation: Anxiety and Anger*. Harmondsworth: Penguin Books, 1978.

Brazelton, T. Berry. *On Becoming a Family*. New York: Delta, 1981.

Bronfenbrenner, Urie. *The Ecology of Human Development*. New York: Cambridge, 1979.

Bruner, Jerome. *Under Five in Britain*. Ypsilanti: High/Scope, 1980.

Bryant, Bridget, Miriam Harris, and Dee Newton. *Children and Minders*. Ypsilanti: High/Scope, 1980.

Clarke-Stewart, Alison. *Daycare*. Cambridge: Harvard University Press, 1982.

Collins, Alice H., and Eunice L. Watson. *Family Day Care*. Boston: Beacon Press, 1976.

Dreskin, William and Wendy. *The Day Care Decision*. New York: M. Evans, 1983.

Fraiberg, Selma. *Every Child's Birthright: In Defense of Mothering*. New York: Basic Books, 1977.

Galinsky, Ellen, and William H. Hooks. *The New Extended Family*. Boston: Houghton Mifflin, 1977.

Garland, Caroline, and Stephanie White. *Children and Day Nurseries*. Ypsilanti: High/Scope, 1980.

Glickman, Beatrice M., and Nesha B. Springer. *Who Cares for the Baby?* New York: Schocken Books, 1978.

Johnson, Laura C., and Janice Dineen. *The Kin Trade*. Toronto: McGraw-Hill Ryerson, 1981.

Kagan, Jerome, Richard B. Kearsley, and Philip R. Zelazo. *Infancy: Its Place in Human Development*. Cambridge: Harvard University Press, 1980.

Kamerman, Sheila B. *Parenting in an Unresponsive Society*. New York: Free Press, 1980.

Kramer, Rita. *In Defense of the Family*. New York: Basic Books, 1983.

Lamb, Michael E., ed. *Nontraditional Families: Parenting and Child Development*. Hillsdale, N.J.: Erlbaum, 1982.

Leach, Penelope. *Who Cares?* Harmondsworth: Penguin Books, 1979.

Lindner, Eileen, Mary C. Mattis, and June R. Rogers. *When Churches Mind the Children*. Ypsilanti: High/Scope, 1983.

Packard, Vance. *Our Endangered Children*. Boston: Little, Brown, 1983.

Price, Jane. *How to Have a Child and Keep Your Job*. Harmondsworth: Penguin Books, 1979.

Provence, Sally, Audrey Naylor, and June Patterson. *The Challenge of Daycare*. New Haven: Yale University Press, 1977.

Roby, Pamela. *Child Care — Who Cares?* New York: Basic Books, 1975.

Ross, Kathleen Gallagher. *A Parents' Guide to Day Care*. Vancouver: Self-Counsel Press, 1984.

_____. *Good Day Care*. Toronto: The Women's Press, 1978.

Rutter, Michael. *Maternal Deprivation Reassessed*. Harmondsworth: Penguin Books, 1981.

Scarr, Sandra. *Mother Care/Other Care*. New York: Basic Books, 1984.

Schaffer, Rudolph. *Mothering*. Cambridge: Harvard University Press, 1977.

Siegel-Gorelick, Bryna. *The Working Parents' Guide to Child Care*. Boston: Little, Brown, 1983.

Suransky, Valerie Polakow. *The Erosion of Childhood*. Chicago: University of Chicago Press, 1982.

White, Burton L. *A Parent's Guide to the First Three Years*. Englewood Cliffs, N.J.: Prentice-Hall, 1980.

Zigler, Edward F., and Edmund W. Gordon. *Day Care, Scientific and Social Policy Issues*. Boston: Auburn House, 1982.